BASEBALL
Memories
1930-1939

A COMPLETE PICTORIAL HISTORY
OF THE "HALL OF FAME" DECADE

MARC OKKONEN

Sterling Publishing Co., Inc. New York

FOREWORD

As with previous books in this series, the encyclopedic volumes pioneered by TURKIN & THOMPSON and NEFT & COHEN were indispensable in gathering and organizing the lists of players, their teams, and the years they played between 1930 and 1939. Another vital source of information and pictures was the National Baseball Library in Cooperstown, which provided a wealth of rare materials, particularly from their collection of scrapbooks, guide books, and vintage team publications. I am also indebted to numerous individual SABR (Society for American Baseball Research) members for providing much information from their personal possessions and local sources.

A very special thanks goes to Bill McAlister, a recognized expert on the 1930s, and to the Chicago area's great baseball photographer, George Brace, and his seemingly inexhaustible supply of player photos. Among McAlister's unique reservoir of expertise is his skilled and accurate colorizations of black-and-white photos, many of which appear throughout this volume.

Sources & Contributors:

AAF Library—Los Angeles	Bob Davids	Ed Luteran
Muskegon County Library, MI	Joe Dittmar	Bill McAlister
Library of Congress	Elias Dudash	Sally O'Leary
National Baseball Library	Allen Feinberg	Paul Pogharian
Bill Anderson	Tom Guerne	Brad Sullivan
Ray Billbrough	Eliot Knispel	Jeff Suntala
Lefty Blasco	Ed Koller	Rich Tourangeau
Bud Boccone	Terry Konkle	Hank Utley
George Brace	Bob Littlejohn	

Photos xerographed from files of the National Baseball Library, microfilm copies of period newspapers, club yearbooks, scrapbooks, and various miscellaneous sources.

Original line art (uniform illustrations) copyrighted by the author.

Published by Sterling Publishing Company, Inc.
387 Park Avenue South, New York, N.Y. 10016
© 1994 by Marc Okkonen
Distributed in Canada by Sterling Publishing
℅ Canadian Manda Group, P.O. Box 920, Station U
Toronto, Ontario, Canada M8Z 5P9
Distributed in Great Britain and Europe by Cassell PLC
Villiers House, 41/47 Strand, London WC2N 5JE, England
Distributed in Australia by Capricorn Link (Australia) Pty Ltd.
P.O. Box 6651, Baulkham Hills, Business Centre, NSW 2153, Australia

Printed and Bound in Hong Kong

Sterling ISBN 0-8069-0574-3

Design & paste-up assembly:
  Marc Okkonen

Typesetting:
  Sharon Tingley

Photocopy work:
  PROFESSIONAL COLOR SERVICE, Muskegon, MI
  BRIDGES NETWORK, Muskegon, MI

10 9 8 7 6 5 4 3 2 1

Library of Congress Cataloging-in-Publication Data

Okkonen, Marc.
    Baseball memories, 1930–1939 : a complete pictorial history of the "Hall of Fame" decade / by Marc Okkonen.
        p.   cm.
    Includes index.
    ISBN 0-8069-0574-3
    1. Baseball—United States—History—20th century—Pictorial works.   I. Title.
GV863.A10384   1994   94-20698
796.357′0973—dc20   CIP

TABLE OF CONTENTS

Official Score Card
1930
Price 25¢

for the
Championship
of the
World

St. Louis
vs
Philadelphia

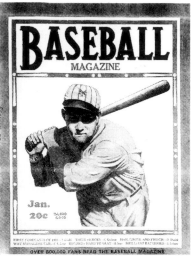

BASEBALL
MAGAZINE

Jan.
20¢

OVER 500,000 FANS READ THE BASEBALL MAGAZINE

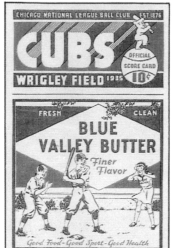

CHICAGO NATIONAL LEAGUE BALL CLUB EST.1876
CUBS
WRIGLEY FIELD 1935
OFFICIAL SCORE CARD 10¢

FRESH   CLEAN
BLUE VALLEY BUTTER
Finer Flavor

Good Food - Good Sport - Good Health

JOE DI MAGGIO, Yankees

Ask for the
BATS
They use!

LOUISVILLE SLUGGER
HILLERICH & BRADSBY C°
LOUISVILLE KY

LOUISVILLE SLUGGER BATS

OFFICIAL
WORLD'S CHAMPIONSHIP

SOUVENIR PROGRAM
25 CENTS   1931

Detroit Tigers
IN PICTURE

1934

15 cents

Souvenir Program
ALL STAR GAME

Twenty-five cents

CLEVELAND STADIUM ★ JULY 8, 1935

Who's Who
in the
MAJOR LEAGUES
4TH EDITION
1936

PHOTOS, STORIES AND RECORDS
OF EVERY PLAYER IN THE
AMERICAN and
NATIONAL LEAGUES

25¢

by Harold (Speed) Johnson

The
Sporting News
RECORD BOOK for 1932

Published by
CHARLES C. SPINK & SON
ST. LOUIS, MO.
Price: Ten Cents the Copy

THE
REACH
OFFICIAL
AMERICAN LEAGUE
BASE BALL GUIDE
1933

PRICE   CENTS

A. J. REACH COMPANY
PHILADELPHIA

MEMBER OF
JIMMIE FOXX
SPENCER SHOE
BASEBALL CLUB

PENNANT WINNERS
JOE CRONIN
WASHINGTON
WORLD SERIES
1933

"GEE" WALKER
Supercharger
CLUB
MEMBER 1937

THE CINCINNATI ENQUIRER
VOL. XCV. NO. 46—DAILY   SATURDAY MORNING, MAY 25, 1935   34 PAGES THREE CENTS

REDLEGS DEFEAT PHILS IN NIGHT GAME

AIR WAVES
To Carry Music

MERGING
Of Boards Waits.

Scenes At First Night Game

BIG PAUL
Shoots 'Em Over.

PREMIERES
At May Festival!

BASEBALL CENTENNIAL
SOUVENIR - 1839-1939
DETROIT
IN BASEBALL

Copyright 1939 by Detroit Baseball Company

BASEBALL'S AMERICA
OF 1930-39

A DECADE OF DRAMA AND DESPAIR

Despite the many positive developments and fascinating personalities that emerged in America during the 1930s, the one phrase that best characterizes that decade would have to be HARD TIMES. The stock market crash of late 1929 triggered a monumental economic stagnation that affected everyone and persisted stubbornly well into 1939. As one wag put it, it was the "golden age of poverty." For America, it was a crucial decade of self-analysis and an endless struggle to reestablish and redefine the "American Dream." Our cherished political system was suddenly placed under a world microscope and the validity of alternative societies, particularly the ultra-nationalist and Marxist systems in other parts of the world, was temporarily fortified. But fortunately, an element of perennial optimism, fueled by the hope that new prosperity was always just "around the corner," prevailed despite the ongoing hardships. The majority of Americans remained convinced that the system would rebound and threats of any real major upheaval or revolt were minimal. Depression or no, it was "business as usual" for most facets of American life and few if any U.S. institutions became extinct—including major league baseball.

President Herbert Hoover and his Republican administration, perhaps unfairly, were held responsible for the ongoing economic malaise as the decade began. The public clamored for a wholesale "housecleaning" in the presidential election of 1932, and New York's Governor Franklin D. Roosevelt was swept into power in a Democratic landslide. FDR responded to this mandate with a frenzy of immediate measures to combat the sluggish economy and create a new spirit of optimism. Banks were temporarily closed to ward off a potentially disastrous wave of panic withdrawals by investors. A myriad of new programs was created overnight to provide jobs and offer incentives for industry. The traditional conservative approach to government intervention in the private sector of the economy was discarded as Roosevelt's "New Deal" swept the country. The results of the New Deal programs were less than spectacular in FDR's first two terms, but he unquestionably awakened the public and helped downplay the national mood of despair that prevailed when he took office.

Newspaper headlines heralded the "changing of the guard" at the White House in early 1933.

Shanty towns, or "Hoovervilles" as they were cynically titled, sprang up across the U.S.A. as a by-product of the economic collapse of the early thirties.

Selling apples on the sidewalks of Manhattan symbolized the desperate plight of many Americans trying to survive the ravages of unemployment.

Deposed Chief Executive Hoover and President-elect Roosevelt on their way to the inauguration

Roosevelt's dynamic persona dominated the balance of the decade and even well into the 1940s. He had many critics and indeed notable political arch-enemies, but his popularity with the general public was phenomenal and his reelection in 1936 was the most lopsided in U.S. history. The widespread appeal of his now famous "fireside chats" with the American public via radio was a testament to the force of his personality. In an era when the muckraking and vindictive journalism of today's media was unheard of, FDR's physical paralysis (from polio) was carefully shielded from public view and many Americans were completely unaware of his crippling condition. Despite this, he presented a vigorous image and energetically supported baseball throughout his presidential years. He enthusiastically participated in the season's opener at Griffith Stadium every April.

FDR was an enthusiastic supporter of the national game. Here he tosses out the ceremonial first ball at the 1937 opener at Griffith Stadium.

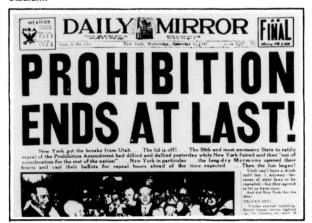

Breweries and distilleries were once again legalized with the arrival of the New Deal in 1933. The repeal of this unpopular law was widely welcomed by the general public and the baseball world.

Mobster Al Capone's bootlegging dynasty was finally over with the end of Prohibition. He entered federal prison on a charge of income tax evasion.

Bonnie Parker and Clyde Barrow went on a rampage of bank robberies and killings before they were finally gunned down in May 1934.

One of the significant events that followed the 1932 election was the repeal of Prohibition. Distilleries and breweries were legally back in business for 1933 and baseball fans were once again permitted to partake of cold beer at most ballparks. The bootleggers and their networks of mobsters were now out of business and the most infamous of these gangsters, Al Capone, was finally behind bars on a charge of income tax evasion. But the continuing climate of mass unemployment and poverty encouraged a wave of criminal acts, most notably a series of bank robberies by daring desperadoes like John Dillinger and the duo of Clyde Barrow and Bonnie Parker. The relentless pursuit of these "public enemies" by the newly formed FBI and other so-called "G-men" led by J. Edgar Hoover made headlines daily in the thirties. The exploits of such anti-heroes captured the imagination of the Depression-weary public and provided profitable fodder for the movies and radio dramas like "Gangbusters." One by one they all came to a spectacular demise—Bonnie and Clyde ambushed by Texas Rangers in 1934 and Dillinger gunned down by Federal agents outside a movie house in Chicago in the same year. The most famous criminal case of the decade was the abduction of the Lindbergh baby for ransom in 1932. The infant son of the famed aviator was later found dead and in a sensational trial one Bruno Hauptman was convicted and executed—a tainted verdict that elicits controversy to this day.

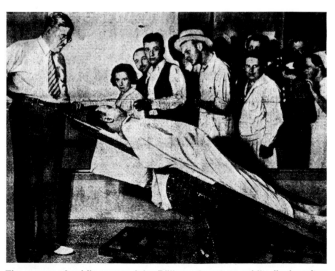

The corpse of public enemy John Dillinger is put on public display after being ambushed by Federal agents outside a Chicago movie house in 1934.

Many unforgettable celebrities emerged in the 1930s from all walks of life. Perhaps the strangest was a man the American public never really knew—New York State Supreme Court Justice Joseph Crater. Judge Crater simply vanished from the face of the earth in 1930 and to this day no one has a clue to explain his disappearance. Disappearance and/or tragic death were the calling cards for many of the familiar names of the decade. Fabled Notre Dame football coach Knute Rockne died in a plane crash in 1931. The same fate overtook famed aviator Wiley Post and humorist Will Rogers in 1935. Another famous aviator, Amelia Earhart, vanished somewhere in the South Pacific in 1937 and the details of her disappearance are still unknown. Louisiana's Senator Huey Long, the political "gadfly" of the decade, was assassinated in Baton Rouge in 1935. Another "rabble-rouser" who gained national fame by promoting radical ideas and schemes was the Detroit priest Father Coughlin, who used the new medium of radio to create an enormous following. On a lighter note, the American public was captivated by some younger celebrities—namely, the delightful charm of little Shirley Temple of the movies and the fascination over the Canadian-born Dionne quintuplets.

The emergence of the New Deal made the nation ripe for significant social as well as political change. New economic theories encouraged government spending on a scale never imagined before. In an effort to offset economic stagnation and present the alienated public with a more benevolent leadership, costly programs and novel legislation were a regular diet, especially in the middle years of the decade. The so-called "alphabet agencies" like the WPA, PWA, and TVA were created to restore confidence in the system and put millions back to work. The Agricultural Adjustment Act (AAA) was one of the more successful experimental programs in the New Deal package, rescuing thousands of farm families from the brink of bankruptcy. The FDIC was created to protect banks from overnight failure and to restore public faith in the banking system itself. The Social Security Act gave U.S. citizens a mechanism to escape total poverty in their post-retirement years. Organized labor made huge gains in the thirties—the Wagner Act of 1935 gave unions the right to collective bargaining, among other concessions. But recognition by the auto manufacturers and other industrial giants was accompanied by a prolonged and sometimes violent struggle. The formation of the CIO by John L. Lewis and subsequent "sit-down" strikes finally gave recognition to the demands of millions of unskilled industrial workers. Organized labor became a political force to be reckoned with by the end of the decade.

The National Recovery Act (NRA) tried to reenergize the sluggish economy in the early years of FDR's New Deal.

Aviatrix Amelia Earhart was idolized by the public up to her disappearance over the South Pacific in 1937.

Louisiana's Huey Long was already a political legend at the time of his assassination in Baton Rouge in 1935.

Detroit's Father Coughlin enjoyed a meteoric following with his controversial political pronouncements to a national radio audience in the mid-thirties.

Organized Labor found a new tactic, the "sit-down" strike, to win concessions from management. Auto workers in a GM plant in Flint, Michigan, are pictured here biding their time on car seats.

The transportation industry, despite the sluggish economy, made significant technological progress in the 1930s. The railroads struggled with losses in revenue but maintained their dominance of long-distance travel and continued to invest heavily in more modern and powerful equipment. By the end of the decade, diesel and diesel/electric power had arrived on a limited basis but would not replace steam power on any large scale until the following decade. Steadily improving networks of surface highways fueled the growth of the trucking industry, which began to lure some freight business from the railroads. And the growth of passenger airplane service lured away many of the wealthier and more adventurous cross-country travelers. The arrival of the Douglas DC-3 in the late thirties gave the airline industry its biggest boost and firmly established air travel as a swifter and more reliable way to cover long distances. The Cincinnati Reds experimented with occasional airplane travel in the mid-thirties, but trains remained the most practical method of traveling from town to town and continued to be the principal means of conveying major league baseball clubs to their scheduled destinations.

Passenger train service, using traditional steam locomotives as in the above scene, was still the principal means of cross-country travel in the 1930s.

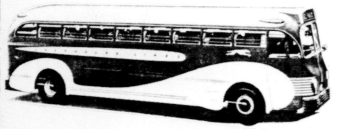

With improved highway systems, bus travel increased in popularity in the '30s. Styling of buses also changed dramatically, mirroring the streamlined changes in passenger cars.

Passenger airplane service, despite hard times, came of age in the thirties. No longer a novelty, it began to attract more everyday travelers. The workhorse in the early years of the decade was the famous Ford Tri-motor, shown on the right at a passenger terminal in Columbus, Ohio.

New streamlined versions of steam engines symbolized the confidence of the railroad industry in the future of both passenger and freight service, even in hard times.

The Douglas DC-3 (on the left) proved to be a capable replacement for the Ford Tri-motor and a catalyst in the rapid growth of air travel in the late thirties.

The Cincinnati Reds were the first baseball club to utilize air travel in the mid-thirties. Team members pose before boarding a flight to Chicago in 1934.

The automobile industry struggled with stagnant sales of its products and many of the smaller independent manufacturers went out of existence in the 1930s. By the end of the decade, the industry was reduced to a handful of familiar model names, mostly under the umbrella of the three giants—GM, Ford, and Chrysler—plus some more popular independents like Studebaker, Packard, and Nash. Automobile styling changed dramatically from 1930 to 1939. The "boxy" and mostly black sedans of 1930 evolved into the more streamlined and colorful vehicles of the late '30s. The grandiose New York World's Fair of 1939-40 gave visitors a glimpse of more startling transportation ideas as well as other technologic wonders, such as television, planned for the coming generations.

A CAR FOR HER, TOO

Women everywhere helped design the NEW CHEVROLET SIX

1931

THE UNIVERSAL CAR BROADENS ITS FIELD *Ford V-8* FOR 1937

1937

1939

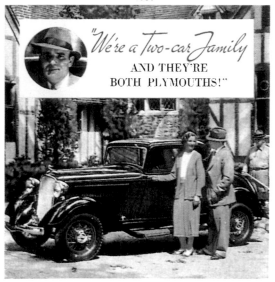

"We're a Two-car Family AND THEY'RE BOTH PLYMOUTHS!"

An Interview with JOHN ALDEN THAYER, Editor and Publisher, Ridgefield Press

$445 AND UP F.O.B. FACTORY, DETROIT

PLYMOUTH SIX WITH PATENTED FLOATING POWER

1934

LINCOLN-ZEPHYR V·12

1939

The automobile industry in the 1930s spared no expense in trying to seize their share of a sluggish market. These colorful ads illustrate the point and also reveal the dramatic styling evolution from the boxy sedans of 1930 to the more aerodynamic streamlined bodies of the late thirties. The mostly black or muted paint colors of the 1920s also gave way to a virtual "rainbow" of color choices by 1939. A brand-new auto could be purchased for the equivalent amount of a monthly payment in today's market.

Calamities and disasters seemed all too common in the 1930s and only added to the prevailing misery of economic hard times. As if the farmers of the lower Great Plains didn't have enough hardship in surviving, mother nature joined in their persecution by producing the disastrous "dust bowl" wind storms that permanently ripped away the vital topsoil of the farm belt. Floods and killer tornadoes, particularly severe in 1936 and 1937, raised havoc in America's heartland. A devastating earthquake in Long Beach, California, in 1933 rattled the nerves of West Coast residents, recalling the frightening destruction of San Francisco in 1906. A tragic fire in the Columbus, Ohio, penitentiary in early 1930 killed 320 inmates. A school explosion in New London, Texas, in 1937 took 413 lives. Six hundred perished as a result of a monster hurricane that battered the Northeast coast in 1938. In 1934, 134 lives were lost when the cruise ship MORRO CASTLE caught fire off the New Jersey shoreline. The German dirigible HINDENBERG came to a spectacular end, bursting into flames while attempting to dock at Lakehurst, New Jersey, after a trans-Atlantic crossing in 1937. No wonder a nervous public reacted with alarm to a convincing radio dramatization of a fictional Martian invasion, as presented by Orson Welles on his Mercury Theatre broadcast in 1938. The real horror arrived in late 1939 when Hitler's Germany invaded Poland and set the world on a collision course with World War II.

Cincinnati's Crosley Field is inundated by a disastrous Ohio River flood in early 1937.

A killer hurricane ravaged New York and New England in the fall of 1938.

The American public also was distracted by some important world events that made headlines in the 1930s. Japanese troops invaded Manchuria in 1931 to begin their campaign to dominate Asia. Mussolini's army marched into helpless Ethiopia in 1935 to flex their fascist muscles before the world. In Germany, Adolf Hitler's Nazi Party assumed full control of the nation's destiny and was rapidly building up its military machine to avenge the humiliating defeat of the Great War. A brutal civil war in Spain in the late thirties brought yet another European dictator into power. Soviet Premier Stalin conducted his infamous "purge" of Red Army generals that solidified his ruthless control of events in that country. In Great Britain, Winston Churchill's warning cries failed to fully alert the country to its imminent danger. The entire world was captivated by the abdication of the crown in 1936 by Edward VIII for the sake of the woman he loved.

Young Orson Welles sent much of the nation into panic with a realistic radio broadcast of a mythical Martian invasion on his Mercury Theatre presentation of Halloween 1938.

A monstrous dust cloud envelops a small Texas town in 1935—a common occurrence in the mid-thirties.

In Europe, the emergence of Adolf Hitler's Nazi movement set the stage for an eventual global war by the decade's end.

The entertainment industry fared better than most other facets of the slump-ridden economy of the thirties. More affordable Victrolas gave more families access to recorded music, a pleasant diversion from the sordid reality of everyday life. A handful of talented composers and artists produced a plethora of popular melodies that sold by the millions. George Gershwin, Irving Berlin, Jerome Kern, Cole Porter, and Duke Ellington were among the creative musical geniuses of the era, composing an endless repertoire of hit songs. Less conventional music also made inroads in the thirties, notably "swing" and the "big band" sound. Benny Goodman's famed concert at previously "stuffy" Carnegie Hall in 1938 was a milestone in the evolution of popular music. Composer/folk singer Woodie Guthrie and some of the movies' cowboy troubadours like Gene Autry were the musical spokesmen for the grass-roots American tastes. The motion picture industry, buoyed by landmark technological breakthroughs like "talkies" and technicolor, thrived

through the entire decade. Movies were one of the affordable "escapes" for the Depression-weary public and films of all levels of quality were cranked out by the Hollywood Studios in record numbers. Many memorable films of the thirties have become classics—notably ALL QUIET ON THE WESTERN FRONT, CIMARRON, IT HAPPENED ONE NIGHT, THE INFORMER, and the 1939 epic GONE WITH THE WIND. Perennial stars like Fredric March, Jean Harlow, Carole Lombard, Bette Davis, Spencer Tracy, Wallace Beery, Katharine Hepburn, Clark Gable, and the Inimitable Shirley Temple were part of the Folklore. Movie audiences were spellbound by the dancing duet of Fred Astaire & Ginger Rogers and the singing duet of Nelson Eddy & Jeanette Mcdonald. Baseball was a rare theme for movie scripts, but comedian Joe E. Brown, himself a devoted fan, appeared in several mindless but entertaining films that gave us a feel for what the game was like in the 1930s.

Theatre audiences in 1933 were spellbound by the spectacle of an oversized gorilla named King Kong.

The musical genius of George Gershwin gave the American public some unforgettable melodies to brighten the dreary years of the Great Depression.

SHIRLEY TEMPLE
JUST AROUND THE CORNER
WITH CHARLES FARRELL · JOAN DAVIS · AMANDA DUFF · BERT LAHR
BILL ROBINSON · PANGBORN AND WITHERSPOON · BARTLETT

Little Shirley Temple entertained millions with her unique charm. She was arguably the top movie star of the decade.

Disney's SNOW WHITE AND THE SEVEN DWARFS was a big hit in the late thirties. It was the first full-length feature using hand-drawn animation.

WILL ROGERS

The motion picture industry survived the Depression remarkably well. Its success spawned new movie houses all over the U.S.A., like Chicago's Will Rogers Theatre pictured above. The architecture was distinctly art deco style, the latest trend of the period.

Radio broadcasting was the entertainment medium that truly came of age in the decade of the thirties, and its development had a significant impact on baseball. By 1930, radio receivers were a common item in American households and tuning in on the airwaves had become a national preoccupation. Major networks, based out of New York City, offered a daily menu of news, music, comedy, and drama to listeners across the country. Among the most popular shows and personalities were RUDY VALLEE, KATE SMITH, FRED WARING, AMOS 'N ANDY, LUM 'N ABNER, BURNS & ALLEN, FRED ALLEN, LOWELL THOMAS, THE LONE RANGER, EASY ACES, and ONE MAN'S FAMILY. Sports coverage of national import was usually provided by the networks (NBC, CBS, MUTUAL) with a stable of well-known voices like NYC-based GRAHAM McNAMEE, TED HUSING, and DON WILSON plus established sportscasters from other affiliate cities like FRANCE LAUX (KMOX-St. Louis) and BOB ELSON (WGN-Chicago). Major prizefights, top college football matchups, and baseball's World Series and All-Star games were covered by network broadcasts for national audiences. The new medium of television made its modest debut in sports broadcasting by covering a Brooklyn game in 1939—but its impact was delayed by the coming of global war.

In 1930, Pasadena's Rose Bowl was the only major post-season matchup in collegiate football. Pictured above is Southern Cal's rout of Pitt, 47-14. By the end of the decade, the Sugar, Orange, and Cotton Bowls were born.

Colorado's Byron "Whizzer" White was a unanimous All-American.

Sammy Baugh was a stand-out collegian (TCU) and a star quarterback for the NFL's Washington Redskins.

Spending the evenings listening to the radio became a national habit in households across the U.S.A. in the 1930s. Music, news, comedy, and sports were the menu offered by both local stations and national networks.

A quartet of top collegiate football coaches together in 1932—L to R: Tad Jones, Glenn "Pop" Warner, Bernie Bierman, and Howard Jones

Major league baseball and collegiate football were the two team sports that monopolized national sports news in the 1930s. Howard Jones' USC Trojans of the early thirties and Bernie Bierman's Minnesota Golden Gophers of the mid-thirties were two of the winningest college gridders of the period. Three new post-season bowl games joined the Rose Bowl as national attractions in the thirties—the Orange in '33, Sugar in '35, and Cotton in '37. Some of the legendary collegiate gridders of the decade were Yale's Albie Booth, Tennessee's Beattie Feathers, Alabama's Don Hutson, and the quarterback tandem from TCU—Sammy Baugh and Davey O'Brien. The Downtown Athletic Club of New York City initiated an annual football tradition in 1935 with the first Heisman Trophy Award for the top collegiate star of the year—Jay Berwanger of the University of Chicago. A pair of Duke Blue Devils, Clarence "Ace" Parker and Eric Tipton, went from gridiron glory to major league baseball with Connie Mack's Athletics in the late '30s. Another pair of collegiate footballers from that era, Gerald R. Ford of Michigan and Byron "Whizzer" White of Colorado, went on to greater fame in public service. Professional football's NFL began the decade of the '30s as a struggling "bus league" operation with franchises in mostly small Midwest towns like Green Bay, Wisconsin; Decatur, Illinois; and Portsmouth, Ohio. Founder George Halas was able to recruit some "marquee" collegiate stars like Red Grange and Bronco Nagurski, and one by one, the franchises would ultimately transfer to major market cities like New York and Detroit during the early mid-thirties (only Green Bay has survived from the NFL's embryonic formation of the 1920s). By 1939, pro football had begun to attract respectable space on the sports pages of the major dailies. Although no team seemed to lay claim to a football dynasty, the New York Giants won five Eastern Division championships and two outright NFL championships from 1933 to 1939. Pro football would come of age as a major sport in the following decade of the forties. Collegiate basketball (there was no professional circuit) also grew in popularity during the thirties and gave birth to the first NCAA national championship tournament in 1939 (won by the University of Oregon).

Boxing was the most publicized individual sport of the 1930s and the reigning heavyweight in the closing years of the decade, Detroit's Joe Louis, was the sport's big name. The "Brown Bomber" took the title from Jimmy Braddock in 1937, then avenged his only professional defeat with a sensational first-round knockout of Nazi Germany's Max Schmeling in 1938. He clearly outclassed the field and reduced the corps of challengers to a so-called "bum of the month" series of title defenses in the ensuing years. Other outstanding fighters in lower weight categories included lightweight/welterweight Barney Ross and Henry Armstrong, who actually won three separate championships (featherweight, lightweight, and welterweight). In golf, amateur Bobby Jones was already a living legend in 1930 with a rare "grand slam" of major tournament wins. Gene Sarazen, Horton Smith, Ralph Guldahl, and Byron Nelson were the big winners in the top golf tournaments of the 1930s. In tennis, Ellsworth Vines, Fred Perry, and Don Budge were the superstars of the men's ranks while Alice Marble and Helen Jacobs dominated in women's tennis. Track and field produced a host of sports heroes in the 1930s and the Olympic Games of 1932 (Los Angeles) and 1936 (Berlin) added further glory to their achievements. Mildred "Babe" Didrickson captured the gold medal in the 80-meter hurdles at LA in '32 and went on to a fine golfing career—arguably the U.S.'s greatest woman athlete ever. Glenn Cunningham was the world's fastest miler (4:06.8) in the mid-thirties and Earle Meadows captured the gold medal in pole vaulting in the '36 Games. The world's fastest sprinters in the '30s were Americans— Eddie Tolan at the 1932 Games and Jesse Owens at Berlin in 1936. Owens also won the long jump and came home with three gold medals, generating a much-publicized U.S. propaganda coup by deflating the myth of Hitler's "master race" theories. Clarence "Buster" Crabbe followed in Johnny Weismuller's footsteps by pursuing a career in the movies after winning gold medals in swimming at the 1932 Games.

The Brown Bomber, Detroit's Joe Louis, won the heavyweight title from Jim Braddock in 1937. He completely dominated the boxing scene in the late '30s and became an international sports hero.

Bobby Jones, an amateur, won golf's coveted "grand slam" in 1930 and became one of the game's great legends.

The U.S. Post Office issued commemorative stamps to publicize the 1932 Olympic games. Los Angeles hosted the summer games while the winter games were held in Lake Placid, New York.

Jesse Owens brought fame and glory to the U.S. Olympic team with gold medals in track and field at the '36 games in Berlin.

Glenn Cunningham was America's premier distance runner, holding world records for the mile run.

Don Budge (in the far court) was a tennis superstar in the late thirties. He is shown in the process of capturing the U.S. Open title at Forest Hills, New York, in 1938.

STATUS OF BASEBALL IN THE THIRTIES

Like nearly every profit-oriented enterprise in the 1930s, major league baseball struggled with dwindling patronage once the Great Depression took hold in the early years of the decade. The total attendance for both leagues dropped to barely 6 million in 1933 from 10 million in 1930—a decline of 40%. The predicament was so calamitous for baseball that Commissioner Landis took a voluntary 40% reduction in salary. Even the pennant-winning clubs were hurting at the gate and Connie Mack's championship aggregation of 1929-30-31 was shamefully broken up by selling off most of the superstars for cash by the mid-thirties. Many Philadelphia fans never forgave Mack for saddling the city with a sorry collection of cellar-dwellers for the balance of the decade and beyond. But even the desperate purchases of Connie's stars by other clubs failed to produce the expected results with the possible exception of Detroit, where the arrival of catcher/manager Mickey Cochrane gave the Motor City consecutive pennants in 1934-35 and their first World Series victory in '35. Millionaire Red Sox owner Tom Yawkey was the unfortunate epitome of extravagant spending that failed to elevate the Boston club into contention. In addition to a massive renovation of Fenway Park in 1934, Yawkey dipped into his bank account to procure superstars Grove, Cronin, Foxx, and the Ferrell brothers from less affluent AL clubs. For most big league clubs, the poor gate receipts created an acute "catch-22" situation—they could not hope to improve attendance with losing clubs, but the funds to purchase first-rate players were simply not available. Thus, they were forced to take the opposite approach and sell off their own best players to minimize their financial losses. The only salvation for some clubs would be the personal wealth of owners like Yawkey, Crosley of Cincinnati, and Briggs of Detroit with available cash from other enterprises. Owners who depended primarily on the revenue of their baseball operations were the ones who suffered the most. But, excepting the four-year run of Yankee championships at the close of the decade, the thirties provided fairly balanced competition and some interesting pennant races. The decade produced and showcased as many talented players as any other ten-year period and fan interest seemed high despite the disappointing attendance figures.

Club owners and league executives in the thirties were on the lookout for new ideas and formulas that might stimulate sagging patronage. Even new and more colorful uniform schemes were introduced after a decade of basically standardized plain looks. The numbering of players' shirts, begun in 1929 by the New York Yankees, slowly won acceptance by club owners and became standard for all ML teams by 1934. Loud speaker systems for the fans' benefit became standard in big league parks in the thirties. Even more adventurous paint colors in the ballparks and dressier ushers were introduced. Very likely it was no coincidence that many more clubs hired player/managers in the thirties—an economical move that basically covered two salaries for the price of one. In Philadelphia and Pittsburgh, the financial plight of the three Pennsylvania franchises finally convinced the state legislature in 1934 to throw out the antiquated "blue laws" that prohibited Sunday baseball. Curiously, the scheduling of doubleheaders on Sundays and holidays was never challenged. Present-day owners have somehow squeezed this time-honored "giveaway" out of the schedule with little fan protestation, but apparently the baseball owners of the thirties were convinced that the added attraction for the traditional doubleheaders more than offset the losses of additional playing dates for single games.

Two AL legends passed on in 1931. Ban Johnson (left) was founder/president and Charles Comiskey (right) was White Sox owner from the league's beginning in 1900.

The New York Giants' great leader, John McGraw (shown with Mrs. McGraw), finally retired from managing in 1932 after 30 years. Two years later he was dead.

THE PASSING OF GIANTS

The first six years of the 1930s witnessed the passing of numerous prominent figures in the annals of twentieth-century major league baseball—indeed a "roll call" of many of the game's legendary "giants." Longtime Phillies owner William F. Baker, for whom the home park was named, died unexpectedly in December 1930 to begin the grim reaper's march through the ranks of baseball's elite. The American League's legendary founder, Ban Johnson, and his successor, AL President Ernest Barnard, expired within hours of each other in early 1931. A month later, Garry Herrmann, former president of the Cincinnati club and onetime chairman of baseball's National Commission (the three-man ruling body that preceded Judge Landis's appointment in 1920), was gone. Then in October of '31 came the news of the death of Chicago's "Old Roman," Charles Comiskey, one of the principals in the formation of the American League. Other notables who passed on in 1931 were former Cubs President Charles Murphy and famed baseball writer Charles Dryden. In February 1932, Pirates' longtime owner Col. Barney Dreyfus's death followed that of his son, Samuel Dreyfus (club treasurer), by a matter of months. Onetime St. Louis Browns owner Robert Hedges succumbed in 1932 and the following year the club's current owner, Phil Ball, was also gone. The Cubs' front office also took a "double hit" with Chairman William Wrigley's death in 1932 followed by the same fate for club president William Veeck in 1933. In 1934, a pair of National League legends who were once teammates on the famed Baltimore Orioles of the 1890s, John McGraw of NY Giants fame and "Uncle Wilbert" Robinson of Brooklyn fame, drew their last breath. Two more club presidents passed on in 1935: Tom Shibe of the Philadelphia Athletics and Frank Navin of Detroit. For Navin, who guided the Tigers' fortunes since their earliest years, there was at least some poetic justice to his final days. After three decades of frustration, his beloved Tigers finally captured their first world championship over the Chicago Cubs, a team that had embarrassed the Detroits in Navin's first two years as president (the World Series of 1907-08). Navin collapsed from a heart attack two weeks after the championship was finally his. Ned Hanlon, a legendary player and manager dating far back into the last century, died at age 79 in 1937. Before the decade was over, two more club owners were gone—Giants owner Charles Stoneham in 1936 and in 1939 brewery magnate Col. Jacob Ruppert, who gave New York Yankee fans some awesome dynasties and larger-than-life heroes, not to mention a grandiose stadium, during his tenure as club owner.

RADIO COVERAGE OF THE GAME

Another technology that had an historic impact on major league baseball in the thirties was radio—more specifically, radio's role in reporting the game. While financially strapped owners were eagerly open to new ideas to stimulate attendance, they were equally wary of radio's potential to discourage fans from paying money to visit the parks when they could follow the play-by-play action for free by listening in on their radios. After all, most fans followed the game primarily in the newspapers and even the most rabid did not attend the games in person on a daily basis. It was an enigmatic dilemma that proved near impossible to resolve one way or the other, and a wide range of policies with respect to radio coverage existed in the major league cities. For some cities (particularly Chicago), the field was wide open and as many as six different radio stations gave their own live accounts of Cubs and White Sox home games. For others (specifically New York City), it was a total radio blackout for most of the decade. All three New York clubs not only prohibited local play-by-play accounts, but even forbade visiting teams from relaying play-by-play reports of New York (and Brooklyn) games back to their home cities. In other ML cities, the radio coverage was not wide open as in Chicago but subject to various types of restrictions. For some, only road games were allowed play-by-play reporting via teletype reports. Direct live reports from the road parks were unthinkable, so this unique art form in sports broadcasting was perfected by many skilled radio announcers. Some made no pretext about the fact they were simply reading and interpreting the skeleton prose that came off the wires and in fact made no effort to disguise or muffle the "tickety-tick" sound of the teletype machine. But to other announcers it was a challenge to create the illusion that they were actually witnessing the game itself, and artificial studio sound effects were set up to augment the deception. Indeed, many listeners were often convinced that they were listening to an eyewitness account of game action by clever announcers with vivid imaginations. Some of the more powerful radio stations in remote areas used their own announcer to describe the games of their favorite major league club via the wire reports. One notable example was WHO in Des Moines, with Ronald "Dutch" Reagan at the mike reporting Chicago Cubs games in the mid-thirties.

Most clubs that permitted local stations to cover their games prohibited reports of holiday and Sunday home dates (and even Saturdays in some cases). The stations and announcers were not contracted to the clubs as they are today, but of course they had to obtain legal consent to carry the games. As the decade came to a close, sponsorship by advertisers became more of an integral ingredient of the broadcasts and announcers freely injected slogans and other product plugs into their verbal reports. General Mills (more specifically their cereal product WHEATIES, the so-called "Breakfast of Champions") was the most active advertiser in several major league cities, but other firms who used baseball broadcasts to promote their wares were Socony Vacuum (Mobilgas) Oil Co , the Ford Motor Company, and various national cigarette brands. In the New York City area, the only concessions made to the broadcasting of major league games consisted of season openers, the World Series games, and beginning in 1933, the annual All-Star game. These broadcasts were produced by the New York-based national networks (NBC, CBS, MUTUAL) and they used a mixed team of home-based network announcers and selected announcers who worked for their affiliate stations in other major league cities. For listeners it was a rare treat to experience the unique skills and styles of local broadcasters from another area that they would otherwise never hear. In retrospect, it is tempting to conclude that a policy of unlimited broadcast rights would have been the wisest course for major league clubs, using Chicago as the model. Home attendance at Cubs and Sox games, while not leading the leagues, was no worse than in other cities with better winning clubs. More likely, legions of new fans were drawn in from the width and breadth of the station's signal strength and were encouraged to find their way to Wrigley Field and Comiskey Park to see their heroes perform.

The White Sox' Lew Fonseca tunes in to hear a ball game on one of the more bizarre radio sets of the early thirties.

The national radio networks were already transmitting radio accounts of World Series and All-Star games through their affiliate stations across the U.S.A. in the 1930s.

Some typical radio receivers of the 1930s

Red Barber (left) and Bob Elson (right) were top-flight local announcers who also participated in national network broadcasts of important games.

THE INTRODUCTION OF NIGHT BASEBALL

Another novelty that drew the attention of profit-starved major league owners was the sudden emergence of night baseball in the minor leagues in 1930. Portable lighting systems had been tried by some barnstorming teams in the twenties with mixed success, but the Des Moines club of the Western League installed a permanent lighting system at their park in early 1930 and the idea spread like wildfire throughout the minors. Once the initial exposure satisfied the "curious," it was apparent that the idea of playing under the lights, especially in the hot heartland in midsummer, attracted significantly larger crowds and drew minimal criticism on how it affected play. Minor league executives from all over the country flocked to Des Moines to see for themselves and within a month 11 minor league cities decided to install their own lighting systems. By 1931, the number of floodlit minor league parks increased to 56, including most of the AAA Pacific Coast League cities as well as four in the AAA International League and Indianapolis of the American Association. And of course, the owners of big league clubs followed this phenomenon with more than casual interest. Night baseball was an inevitable eventuality, but the overall financial plight of most major league franchises in the mid-thirties paved the way for its speedier acceptance by a generally conservative corps of club owners. The Cincinnati Reds were the first to take the plunge with this radical new concept. Baseball history was made on May 24, 1935, when 20,422 fans at Crosley Field watched the Reds' Paul Derringer outduel the Phils' Joe Bowman for a 2-1 Cincinnati victory. FDR himself, by remote control from Washington, turned the lights on to usher in a new era in baseball. The reception was surprisingly favorable with few negative reactions. The Reds would continue to schedule only seven dates at night for each year (roughly one game with each visiting club) for the balance of the decade, a concession to die-hard proponents of day baseball. Night game attendance, while not always spectacular, proved to be profitable in the Cincinnati experiment, and in 1938, Brooklyn's Ebbets Field introduced its version of night baseball for Dodger fans. The night game attendance in Brooklyn was more bountiful than in Cincinnati as they averaged 27,000 for seven dates—all this despite a second-division team. The Brooklyn experience paved the way conclusively for more night baseball in both leagues in the following seasons. Three more parks installed lights for 1939—Philadelphia's Shibe Park, Cleveland's Municipal Stadium, and Chicago's Comiskey Park. Night baseball at the major league level was here to stay, no longer an experiment. And credit (or blame, for those who still protest it) is due to its pioneering executive Larry MacPhail, the general manager at Cincinnati in 1935 and Brooklyn in 1938.

THE BIRTH OF THE ALL-STAR GAME

The city of Chicago orchestrated one of the most elaborate fairs of the twentieth century in 1933 to celebrate its 100th birthday as a city. The fair was titled "A Century of Progress" and major league baseball was invited to the party by staging a novel "dream game." CHICAGO TRIBUNE Sports Editor Arch Ward was the architect of the affair and it was to be called the All-Star game. The best players at each position were chosen for each league and would play for baseball's "bragging rights" at Chicago's Comiskey Park. The American Leaguers, led by Connie Mack, prevailed 4-2 over John McGraw's National Leaguers. Everybody's hero, Babe Ruth, led the assault with, what else (?)—a home run. A capacity crowd netted $42,000 for the benefit of the Association of Professional Ball Players. This enthusiastic reception encouraged an encore for 1934 and it has become an annual tradition ever since. The American Leaguers dominated the first seven contests, winning five times. Some unforgettable moments were produced in these games in the thirties. Carl Hubbell's consecutive strikeouts of Ruth, Gehrig, Foxx, Simmons, and Cronin in the 1934 game at the Polo Grounds is the stuff of legends. In the 1937 game at Washington, Dizzy Dean's injured toe began his demise as an over-powering pitcher. The rosters, including pitchers, were selected in the first five contests by fan vote in newspaper polls conducted across the U.S.A. The first two finishers at each position were automatically named to the team and each manager was permitted to select five additional players. In 1938, the entire squads were named by the respective managers in hopes of silencing complaints about the starting selections, but the criticisms were, if anything, more numerous using this formula. As time would tell, no formula has been yet devised that would satisfy everyone. But, complaints or no, the All-Star game has remained a popular feature of midsummer to this day.

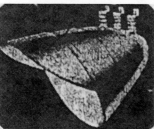

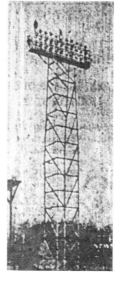

Baseball under the lights was an overnight success in the minor leagues in the early '30s. Seattle, Washington, is the scene of the above game action photo. The tower on the right is from the very first permanent lighting system installed at Des Moines, Iowa, in 1930. The banks of lights were composed of individual incandescent lamps as depicted on the left. Five years later, the idea was finally introduced in the big leagues at Cincinnati's Crosley Field.

A ticket to the first All-Star contest at Chicago's Comiskey Park in 1933

THE HALL OF FAME AND BASEBALL'S CENTENNIAL

Before 1936, a variety of unofficial versions of a baseball Hall of Fame surfaced from time to time, notably the ones put forth by the Spalding company. Commissioner Landis, with the support of the Baseball Writers Association of America (BBWAA), decided in 1935 that the time was ripe, especially in view of the upcoming so-called "centennial" of the game, to establish an official roll call of diamond greats and select a home for the new Hall, which would also include an elaborate museum to put the game's history on display. Since efforts to pinpoint a specific time and place when baseball might have been invented proved factually fruitless, the historically flawed conclusions of the Mills Commission of 1907 were grudgingly used to settle the issue. The Mills Commission credited "invention" of the game to one Abner Doubleday in the village of Cooperstown, New York, in 1839. Cooperstown, an idyllic setting in central New York State that seemed quaintly locked into a 19th century "time warp," was instantly receptive and plans were laid for construction of a new brick facility on the town's Main Street. Completion and dedication were timed for the summer of 1939, the 100th anniversary of the Doubleday "myth." Selection of candidates began in 1936 with the following five "charter members" of baseball's new Valhalla—Babe Ruth, Ty Cobb, Honus Wagner, Walter Johnson, and Christy Mathewson. By 1939, when the Hall of Fame and Museum officially opened its doors, 25 names of both players and founding fathers of the game were honored with plaques in their names. Eleven of the fourteen former players inducted were still alive and participated in the ceremonies. Ty Cobb was inexplicably delayed in his arrival and unfortunately failed to appear in the historic group photo of the game's living immortals. As part of the scheduled events, an exhibition game featuring selected major league stars and managed by Eddie Collins and Honus Wagner was played at historic Doubleday Field. The following year, this game was replaced by a contest between two AL and NL clubs, a feature that became an annual tradition for induction ceremonies. The Post Office observed the occasion with a special stamp that depicted the game in its infancy. A special red, white, and blue sleeve patch was developed for the 1939 centennial year and was worn on every uniform in organized baseball that summer.

The charter members (less Ty Cobb) of the new Hall of Fame sit for a portrait at the inaugural ceremonies in Cooperstown.

A sleeve patch was worn by every team in organized baseball that summer.

Crowds congregate in front of baseball's new shrine on the day of dedication.

Baseball's centennial year was observed with a special postage stamp in 1939.

Cooperstown's historic Doubleday Field, the so-called birthplace of our National Pastime, as it appeared in 1933. A new grandstand was erected for the 1939 opening of the Hall.

PUBLICIZING AND PROMOTING THE GAME

In addition to the aforementioned historic role that radio played in keeping the public informed on baseball's daily doings, other forms of public media and promotions kept the national game in the spotlight in the 1930s. The daily newspapers were without question the most prolific source of baseball dope for the average fan. Like every enterprise in the thirties, the newspapers struggled to survive but their lifeblood, the advertisers, had no choice but to sink or swim with expenditures to attract a dwindling number of consumers. Fortunately, even hard-pressed readers could somehow afford to purchase their favorite dailies either at dirt-cheap subscription rates or at the two or three cents they cost on the newsstands. Covering baseball doings was a vital ingredient of the daily news, perhaps even amplified by the pleasant "escape" baseball provided from grimmer happenings of the period. Sports pages provided an abundance of game accounts, box scores, statistics, photographs, and cartoons dealing with the pennant races in the summer months. Informative and often entertaining columns and commentaries by celebrated sports writers had become a daily reading habit in the big city newspapers. An ample number of legendary baseball scribes like Shirley Povich of the WASHINGTON POST, Fred Lieb of the NY POST, H. G. Salsinger of the DETROIT NEWS, John Carmichael of the CHICAGO DAILY NEWS, and J. Roy Stockton of the ST. LOUIS POST-DISPATCH graced the sports sections of their respective dailies in the 1930s. Detroit fans, caught up in the frenzy of pennant-winning clubs in 1934-35, religiously devoured the musings of "Iffy the Dopester" (by Malcolm Bingay) in the pages of the DETROIT FREE PRESS.

Photo action by on-the-field photographers was a vital ingredient of baseball coverage in the media.

The Reach/Spalding annual guide books were required reading for serious baseball fans.

On a national basis, the weekly SPORTING NEWS was still "the bible" for serious baseball fans. The full-sized journal (it was reduced to tabloid size during WWII) was packed with articles, box scores, and photos of every facet of the game and at every level. The monthly BASEBALL MAGAZINE continued to be the other prime source of baseball news for a national audience. The SPALDING and REACH annual guide books provided complete summaries of the past season, including final statistics for both major and minor leagues. THE SPORTING NEWS also printed up more abbreviated pocket-sized annual record books in the thirties—a forerunner to their expanded booklets that would replace the Spalding/Reach guides in the early forties. In the latter years of the decade, some other popular annual guide books appeared, notably the Whitman series and "WHO'S WHO IN THE MAJOR LEAGUES," first edited by Harold "Speed" Johnson and later by John Carmichael. These annual guides are now valuable collector's items and are also treasured by baseball researchers and historians. Other popular printed items for fans of the thirties, especially youngsters, were the baseball cards that were offered with a sheet of bubble gum at grocery stores and candy counters nationwide. These cards often portrayed brightly hand-colored portraits of all the familiar major league favorites of the decade.

St. Louis' SPORTING NEWS was the fans' weekly window to all the happenings in the baseball world.

One of the annual record books published by THE SPORTING NEWS in the thirties

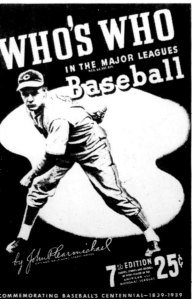

Another popular annual in the 1930s

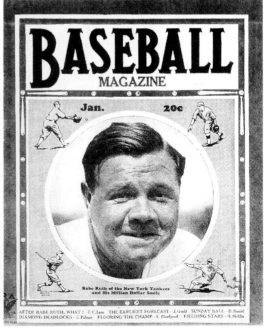

The most popular monthly publication on baseball, BASEBALL MAGAZINE

By the end of the thirties, legions of advertisers were using baseball's popularity to plug their brand names. Besides their sponsorship of more and more radio play-by-play, they used and compensated the baseball heroes of the day to promote their products in newspapers and magazines. For the younger audiences, breakfast cereals (particularly WHEATIES) hired big-name stars to extol the benefits of their particular brands. For adult readers, baseball's biggest names were enlisted to testify as to the benefits of a particular brand of cigarettes in an age when the health risks of smoking were virtually unknown and certainly not considered. And of course, the makers of more directly related items like bats and gloves used the popularity of name players to endorse their equipment. Hillerich & Bradsby held a historical monopoly of bat manufacture, especially for the big leagues, and got lots of profitable mileage from the signatures of star players that were burned into the barrels of their bat models. Glove manufacturers used the same method to convince buyers that they could emulate the equipment preferences of their favorite players.

Major league baseball also saw the wisdom of spending money to promote its own product, the national game itself, in the early thirties. Ex-American League player and manager Lew Fonseca was hired to produce motion pictures that portrayed the virtues of big league baseball. Well-known baseball names Roger Peckinpaugh and George Moriarty also participated in the production of these films. The film titled TAKE ME OUT TO THE BALLGAME was widely distributed to schools, churches, lodges, and associations in the mid-thirties. In substance, the film was more "hype" than historically informative, but in a non-television age where the motion picture had a unique hold on the public it seemed like a positive way to sustain interest in the game. Similar films were produced by both leagues later in the decade and are now valued for their rare historic glimpses at baseball as it looked some six decades ago. Unfortunately, this motion picture venture made no attempt to preserve the great moments in baseball of the thirties for future generations, particularly World Series highlights. Not until the following decade did Fonseca's venture include packaging the more meaningful visual records of the time and, in retrospect, a commendable project was virtually wasted on trivial propaganda. We are forced to rely on rare tidbits of newsreel footage and some scattered pieces of amateur film to find any worthwhile images of baseball heroes and highlights of the decade.

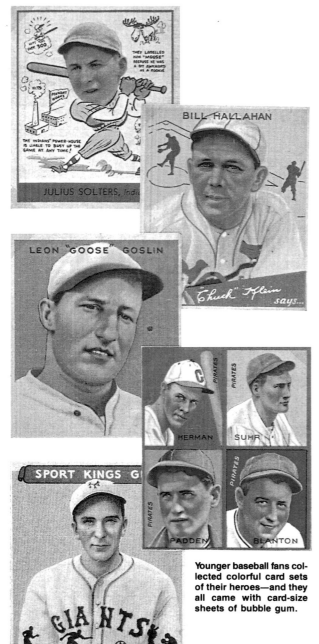

Younger baseball fans collected colorful card sets of their heroes—and they all came with card-size sheets of bubble gum.

Breakfast cereals used sponsorships and endorsements from baseball names to sell their product to American families.

Tobacco companies used baseball stars like Joe DiMaggio (left) and Bucky Walters (right) to plug their cigarette brands.

Some well-known smokes in the '30s

WHEATIES, the "breakfast of champions," linked its fictional radio hero, Jack Armstrong, with big-name baseball stars in a series of simulated color comic strip tales in the Sunday papers of the late thirties. WHEATIES was also highly visible in various baseball-related promotions such as rewarding home run hitters with a free case of the popular cereal. They also sponsored the radio broadcasts of ball games in many major and minor league cities.

UNIFORMS AND TOOLS OF THE TRADE

The costumes worn and equipment used by baseball's big leaguers through the decade of the thirties changed little from 1930 to 1939 but some subtleties and minor trends are worth noting. One important feature of the uniform that every fan noticed was the gradual appearance of player numbers on the shirt backs from 1930 to 1934, when it finally became unanimous. Now taken for granted, it seems hard to believe that it took so long to be adopted. The fabric remained constant—the heavy-grade flannel that must have been insufferable in the midsummer heat. Lighter grades and blended fibers were still another decade away. But a couple of features that dealt with player comfort gradually faded out of existence by 1940. The abbreviated collar extension known as the "sun collar" was still standard in 1930, but as more and more players surgically removed these useless features with scissors in the early thirties, uniform manufacturers finally took the hint and began to eliminate them altogether. Full and 3/4 sleeve lengths were also fairly common as the decade began, but the standard 1/2 length was a regular feature by 1939. A few traditionalists managed to retain the longer sleeves by special order—most notably Yankee Manager Joe McCarthy, who preferred the full sleeve length variety of jersey. But perhaps because financially plagued owners overlooked nothing that might make the games more attractive, more adventurous color schemes were the hallmark of 1930s major league uniforms. After a decade of bland, monotone, austere uniforms, many clubs introduced sartorial fireworks on the clothing of their hirelings. White and gray cap crowns, colorful new stocking stripes, multi-colored piping features, and new monograms were some of the newer trim features of the new decade. Alternate versions of both home and road suits were introduced almost annually by the Chicago Cubs in the mid-thirties. Many clubs simply improved their packaging by adding a secondary trim color, as the Browns did with orange to dress up the traditional brown. The Detroit club broke with a long tradition by displaying a novel script "Detroit" on both home and road shirts in 1930, and added some orange trimmings to complement the new designs. The most radical color experiments were in Cincinnati and Brooklyn. The Reds wore all-red trousers on one version of their alternate uniform in 1936 and the Dodgers shocked the baseball world with all-green trimmings in 1937. Another new tailoring feature that began to appear on some big league jerseys in 1937 was the zippered front. Unfortunately, almost all of the surviving photography of the thirties was glorious black and white, so it is difficult to appreciate the exciting color revolution that took place with respect to the baseball uniforms of the day.

The Boston Braves/Bees were strictly second division for most of the decade, but they were among the league leaders in colorful uniform designs.

In 1939, Commissioner Landis banned the use of strap-type webbing in all gloves. Tiger first baseman Hank Greenberg displays the approved (left) and disallowed (right) versions.

Gloves changed very little during the ten-year period. A bit more padding on fielder's gloves and first baseman's gloves grew a little longer with somewhat deeper pockets. Wider, composite leather webbing appeared at the end of the decade, but was temporarily banned by Commissioner Landis, who for unknown reasons insisted that webbing must be single strands of leather as before. Bats changed not at all, but the composition of the baseball was tinkered with often, especially after seasons of excessive batting averages and an over-abundance of home runs. 1930 was such a season and the inner windings of the baseball were altered for 1931 in an attempt to restore a more normal balance between pitchers and hitters by "deadening" the ball. Up to 1934, the official baseballs of the National League (SPALDING) and the American League (REACH) were manufactured independently and were not necessarily internally identical. Whatever differences might have affected performance were very likely insignificant, but nevertheless both leagues agreed to finally standardize the fabrication of the ball (except for the outside stampings) to downplay any debates about the differences. Prior to that year, the stitching on both balls was two-colored thread (RED and either BLUE or BLACK). The new standard ball was now entirely stitched with red thread, a standard feature still in effect today.

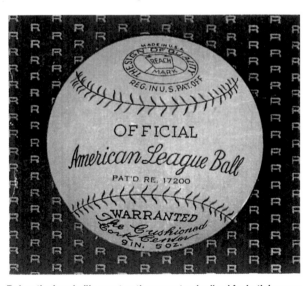

Before the baseball's construction was standardized for both leagues in 1934, the seam stitching was a combination of red and blue (or black) thread as shown in this illustration of the AL ball on the back cover of the 1933 Reach Guide. Of course, the stamping on each ball differed in identifying the AL (Reach brand) and the NL (Spalding brand) versions.

THE BALLPARKS OF THE THIRTIES

Although several major league parks in the thirties underwent extensive reconstruction or expansion, only one brand-new park was built in the entire decade. Cleveland's Municipal Stadium, a giant oval that would seat over 70,000, opened for business in June 1932. The contrast in size with the traditional band-box, League Park, was staggering—over 50,000 additional seats for baseball. Throughout the balance of the decade, this proved to be a dilemma for the Cleveland ball club. One park was far too expansive for the average meager crowds that the perennially fourth-place Indians drew on a normal day, and the other park was far too small to accommodate the rare "windfall" crowd that might occasionally be attracted to a Tribe contest. Their policy vacillated from divided usage in 1932 to full use of the Stadium in 1933, back to exclusive use of cozy League Park from 1934 to 1937, and then back again to divided use of both parks in 1938-39. This pattern continued through 1946 when old League Park was abandoned for good. The controversial new "horseshoe" enjoyed its greatest "day in the sun" in 1935 when it hosted the annual All-Star contest before 70,000 paying customers.

Besides the on-again, off-again existence of

Cleveland's League Park, only one other major league facility became extinct in the 1930s. The home of the Philadelphia Phillies, Baker Bowl, was finally abandoned in 1938 as the National Leaguers moved into more spacious Shibe Park, the home of the Athletics. Shibe Park joined St. Louis's Sportsman's Park as the only two ballparks that hosted teams from both leagues. All of the parks in use in the 1930s, including the new Cleveland Stadium, were of the classic concrete and steel design with upper decks and full roofs supported by numerous steel girders. Scoreboards were still basically manually operated—that is, the numbers were inserted by hand—but remotely controlled electric lights were used to indicate the number of outs, hits vs. errors, and the count on the batter. Huge batteries of loudspeakers, usually mounted above the scoreboard, were employed to blare out announcements to the crowd. A few auxiliary scoreboards, like those in Detroit's Briggs Stadium, displayed score numbers electronically, much like the character configurations in modern-day electronic devices. Toward the end of the decade, the foul poles in some parks incorporated the parallel screening eventually adopted universally to facilitate umpires' calls of drives that entered the stands along the foul lines.

Batteries of loudspeakers for PA systems became standard in ballparks of the 1930s. Fans appreciated being immediately informed about line-up changes, explanations of umpiring and scoring decisions, as well as other informative announcements. The horn-type speakers can be seen along the top of Cleveland Stadium's new scoreboard shown above.

Cleveland's magnificent new Municipal Stadium nearing completion in 1931. The facility's enormous seating capacity (80,000) was both a blessing for important games and a curse for routine games, where even decent crowds made the place seem nearly empty. Throughout the decade, Cleveland management continued to use the more intimate League Park on a part-time basis, even abandoning the big stadium entirely from 1934 to 1937.

Anticipating a World Series appearance for the pennant-bound Reds, Cincinnati owner Powell Crosley added a second deck to the left and right field pavilions of Crosley Field in late summer 1939.

Foul pole screens, which often relieved umpires of difficult and controversial decisions, made their appearance late in the decade and were quickly adopted as standard in all ML parks.

Despite the less-than-capacity attendance figures throughout the major league parks, some of the more affluent owners were willing to fund massive reconstruction programs to better accommodate their patrons. Tom Yawkey of Boston and Walter O. Briggs of Detroit made the most significant park improvements. After the massive rework of Fenway Park in 1934, the seating capacity was increased from 28,000 to 40,000. After consecutive pennants in 1934 and 1935, new Detroit owner Briggs was confident that his Tigers would continue to be in the thick of pennant races in subsequent seasons and wanted to be sure the expected crowds would be accommodated. The double-decking of the Navin Field stands took two years to complete and doubled the seating capacity to 58,000 in 1938. It was rechristened Briggs Stadium, only the second park to be renamed during the decade— the other being Cincinnati's Redland Field, renamed

Crosley Field in 1935. Following a convincing World Series triumph in 1929, the Philadelphia Athletics restructured the main grandstand behind home plate—mainly to incorporate a new press box row on the facing of the upper deck for improved coverage of more anticipated Fall Classics. The upper grandstand was also enlarged to provide an additional 2000 seats. Lesser modifications were made at Chicago's Wrigley Field in the late thirties—a total rebuild of the outfield wall and centerfield bleachers. Yankee Stadium's grandstand was extended around the right field foul pole and new concrete bleachers were built in center field in the late '30s. One feature of all the major league diamonds of the thirties that gradually disappeared in the following decade was the dirt pathway from the mound to home plate. The reasons for its being in the first place and the reasons for its disappearance have never been fully explained.

THE DECADE'S OUTSTANDING PLAYERS AND HEROIC MOMENTS

A glance at the accompanying chart of Major League All-Stars of 1930-39 would suggest that a mythical team of the finest talent of this decade could match up as arguably superior to a similar roster of any other decade past or present. In addition to those listed (based mainly on their number of productive seasons throughout the 10-year period), one might include Hall of Famers like Babe Ruth, Joe DiMaggio, Ted Williams, Johnny Mize, Bob Feller, Dazzy Vance, Burleigh Grimes, etc.—players whose careers ended or began in the 1930s. The exploits of these legendary stars helped to stave off even more calamitous gate receipts, a life-threatening fact of life for major league baseball through the decade. With a fairly well distributed spread of winning teams from 1930 to 1939, almost every city enjoyed its share of heroes and heroic moments. St. Louis fans were treated to the reckless antics of their "Gas House Gang," led by the daring baserunning of Pepper Martin and the delightful braggadocio of Dizzy Dean. The Cardinals failed to win any more flags after 1934, but were consistently an entertaining club with an ongoing stable of talented stars. Philadelphia followers were entertained by one of the most star-studded dynasties in the history of the game with their pennant-winning Athletics teams of 1930-31. But by the mid-thirties, Mack had peddled away his star players and the Athletics went "south" for the balance of the decade. The New York Yankees still had the game's biggest attraction in Babe Ruth and Lou Gehrig in the early years of the decade and the 1932 team is rated as one of the most awesome one-year juggernauts the game has ever seen. Their frightening destruction of the Chicago Cubs in the World Series of that year is deeply engraved in baseball lore, highlighted by the controversial "called shot" by the Bambino in the third game at Wrigley Field. And their four-year run of world championships at the close of the decade resurrected their reputation as baseball's ruling elite. Young Joe DiMaggio's arrival in 1936 gave the New Yorkers a new hero to atone for the Babe's departure in 1934. The touching human drama of Lou Gehrig's amazing longevity coming to a heartbreaking end in 1939 is one of baseball's most unforgettable moments. New York's other team, the Giants, also gave their fans some great seasons and great performers—Bill Terry's .401 season in 1930, a World Series victory in 1933 plus two more NL flags in 1936-37, the slugging of young Mel Ott, and the pitching wizardry of Carl Hubbell.

Workmen toiled through the winter of 1933-34 in the extensive reconstruction of Boston's Fenway Park. New owner Tom Yawkey was determined to rescue his floundering franchise by modernizing and expanding the home field—then shelling out big bucks for star players in the ensuing years.

Detroit's Briggs Stadium (Navin Field) is shown in early 1938 with its new left field and center field upper deck nearing completion. It was the most massive park expansion of the decade and took over two seasons to complete.

Connie Mack's Athletics were the "cream" of the baseball world in 1930-31. Their crack infield of (L to R) Foxx, Bishop, Boley, and Dykes was the envy of other clubs in the AL.

The most awesome 1-2 punch in the game still belonged to the Yankees in the early '30s... Babe Ruth and Lou Gehrig.

New York Giants' superstar player/manager Bill Terry crosses the plate after homering in a 1932 contest at Philadelphia's Baker Bowl.

The St. Louis Cardinals, victors over the mighty Mackmen in the 1931 World Series, boasted a star-studded line up including (from L to R): center fielder Pepper Martin, shortstop Charley Gelbert, second baseman Frankie Frisch, and first baseman Jim Bottomley.

The Yankees' new outfield star, Joe DiMaggio, the heir apparent to the departed Babe, confers with another popular New Yorker of the late thirties, Mayor Fiorello La Guardia, at the 1938 World Series.

A poignant moment in May 1939—the "Iron Horse," Lou Gehrig, has just benched himself in Detroit after playing in 2,130 consecutive games.

The 1933 Washington Senators, led by player/manager Joe Cronin, captured a rare AL pennant but lost the big prize to the New York Giants in the post-season classic.

Lynwood "Schoolboy" Rowe, the young pitching sensation of the 1934 pennant-winning Tigers

Two key ingredients in the new-found success of the 1934-35 Detroit clubs—ace hurler Tommy Bridges (L) and catcher/manager Mike Cochrane

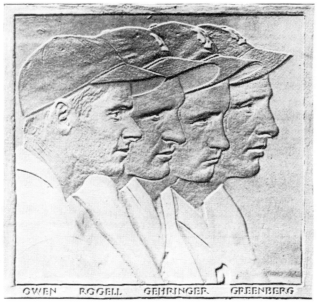

OWEN   ROGELL   GEHRINGER   GREENBERG

Detroit papers christened them the "Battalion of Death"—the AL's premier infield of the mid '30s: Marv Owen, Billy Rogell, Charley Gehringer, and Hank Greenberg.

Clark Griffith's loyal followers had their "moment in the sun" in 1933 when their talented shortstop and field manager Joe Cronin led the Washington Nationals to a rare AL championship. Alvin Crowder and Earl Whitehill gave Manager Cronin quality pitching to keep the Senators in the hunt. But the most excited American League city in the thirties was Detroit, where newly acquired catcher/manager Mickey Cochrane gave the Motor City consecutive pennants in 1934-35 and finally their first world championship in the latter season. After some disappointing years under Bucky Harris (1930-33), Tigers' owner Frank Navin, with the financial backing of partner Walter O. Briggs, sought to wake up the franchise with the acquisition of Hall of Famers Cochrane and Goose Goslin. The timing proved brilliant as many of the established regulars had career years and some emerging youngsters finally matured into genuine major leaguers. Dependable Charlie Gehringer had his usual sparkling season on the field and at the plate. And, along with the slugging of first baseman Hank Greenberg and outfielder Goslin, they formed the fabled corps called "G-men." To complement the reliable pitching of ace Tommy Bridges, young hurling prospect Lynwood "Schoolboy" Rowe literally set the league on fire with 16 consecutive victories and a final tally of 24-8. The Bengals lost a seven-game World Series to the Cardinals' Dean brothers but returned to the post-season classic the following year (1935) to face the Chicago Cubs. In the sixth and final game at Navin Field, the ninth-inning heroics of Bridges, who retired the side after Stan Hack opened the inning with a triple, and Goose Goslin, who singled in Cochrane with the winning run, sent the city of Detroit into a frenzied celebration seldom seen in baseball—"Happy Days were Here Again" (to paraphrase a popular song of the time). Unfortunately, the magic was gone after 1935 as the popular Cochrane's career nosedived after a mysterious illness in 1936 and a near-fatal beaning by Yankee pitcher Bump Hadley in 1937. The other new hero, the "Schoolboy," also developed arm trouble after 1936 and was never the same overpowering pitcher again.

The Chicago Cubs, modern-day baseball's perennial losers, gave Northside fans three pennant-winning clubs in 1932, 1935, and 1938 and featured an array of established stars in their lineup. Catcher Gabby Hartnett was easily the premier NL backstop of the decade and virtually delivered the 1938 pennant personally with a dramatic home run in the twilight at Wrigley Field in a crucial September contest with second-place Pittsburgh. Second baseman Billy Herman and third baseman Stan Hack had few peers at their respective positions. Pitchers like Lon Warneke, Charlie Root, Guy Bush, Larry French, Big Bill Lee, and even Dizzy Dean gave the Cubs consistent first-rate pitching through the decade. The cross-town White Sox were mostly second-division during the thirties but they showcased a couple of future Hall of Famers in shortstop Luke Appling and pitcher Ted Lyons. The Cleveland club proved to be the most consistent of the decade but, unfortunately, their consistency usually guaranteed them a distant third, fourth, or fifth place with their annual 80 to 85 victories. Their heroes in that period were outfielders Earl Averill and Joe Vosmick, first baseman Hal Trosky, and a corps of brilliant moundsmen the likes of Wes Ferrell, Mel Harder, Willis Hudlin, Johnny Allen, and youngster Bobby Feller. Rapid Robert, the 17-year-old Iowa farm boy, electrified Cleveland fans with his blazing speed and record toll of strikeouts in his debut season in 1936. And he proved to be no "flash in the pan" as he continued with spectacular pitching feats that eventually made him the most revered baseball name in Cleveland history (with apologies to Nap Lajoie and Tris Speaker).

The Cincinnati Reds buried themselves in or near the NL cellar for most of the thirties, but suddenly surged to the top of the mountain by the end of the decade, thanks to some excellent pitching by Paul Derringer, Bucky Walters, and Johnny Vander Meer and some productive offense by Frank McCormick, Ernie Lombardi, and Ival Goodman. Under new ownership (Powell Crosley) and creative general managers Larry MacPhail and Warren Giles, the Reds organization took the first gamble on baseball under the lights in 1935 and then shrewdly assembled a winning combination that gave the Queen City consecutive pennants in 1939-40 and its first world championship since the tainted "Black Sox" series of 1919. In the early thirties, they presented faded veterans like Harry Heilmann, Babe Herman, and even Edd Roush as hometown heroes. But the most spectacular individual achievement came in 1938 when Johnny Vander Meer became the first and only pitcher to hurl consecutive no-hit games.

The outfield of the 1935 NL champion Cubs (L to R): Augie Galan, Kiki Cuyler, and Chuck Klein

First baseman Hal Trosky was a Cleveland favorite in the thirties.

The Reds of 1939 gave Cincinnati their first pennant in 20 years.

A dramatic moment in September 1938—catcher/manager Gabby Hartnett has just homered in the "twilight" to defeat the runner-up Pirates and virtually clinch the NL flag. He was understandably mobbed by players and fans after crossing the plate.

AL fans in the late '30s were awed by the fire-balling teenager Bobby Feller of the Cleveland Indians.

The Reds' Johnny Vander Meer did the inconceivable in 1938—two consecutive no-hitters.

The Pittsburgh Pirates had the curious misfortune of presenting the most stable lineup of quality stars throughout the decade of the thirties to go along with a consistently mediocre, if not downright dreadful, pitching staff. The only 20-game winner for the Pirates in the period 1930-39 was veteran Ray Kremer in 1930, but his ERA was 5.02. Even in the infamous "year of the slugger," Kremer had to be very lucky to enter the charmed circle with that kind of earned run performance. Even the Bucs' team BA of .303 in 1930 was below five other NL clubs, but it must have provided enough run production at the right times to win games for the 37-year-old hurler who, along with the Cubs' Pat Malone, topped the NL in pitching wins. After 1930, Pittsburgh's lineup of solid stars and future Hall of Famers continued to uphold an impressive team BA in the .285 range, but were able to make only two serious threats for the championship—those being in 1933 and 1938 when the Giants and Cubs edged them out. Their infield featured first sacker Gus Suhr, shortstop Arky Vaughan, and third baseman Pie Traynor to go along with the fabled Waner brothers in the outfield. These players were all steady hitters but failed to provide the other missing ingredient, the long ball, that would have made the Pirates a pennant threat throughout the 1930s. Pittsburgh favorites Paul Waner and Gus Suhr established endurance records in the late thirties—Suhr playing in an NL record 822 consecutive games, and Waner collecting 200 or more hits for the eighth time, another league record.

Braves slugging star Wally Berger welcomes another over-the-hill slugger named Babe Ruth to the 1935 roster.

The formidable brother battery of catcher Rick Ferrell (left) and pitcher Wes were Red Sox teammates in 1934-37. From there they were reunited in Washington for two more seasons together.

For Boston fans, the 1930s were mostly forgettable years—not as dreadful as the 1920s when neither club even escaped the second division and more often than not finished dead last—but almost as bad. Only a couple of fourth-place finishes for the Braves in 1933-34 and a surge up to second place by the 1938-39 Red Sox finally gave Hub fans at least an occasional glimmer of hope. The only bright spots for Braves followers in the first half of the decade were the slugging of outfielder Wally Berger and some pretty good pitching from Ed Brandt, plus the brief presence of aging Babe Ruth in 1935. Desperate to discard their losing image, the Braves rechristened themselves the Bees in 1936. New uniforms of royal blue and gold and an unlikely tandem of over-30 rookie pitching sensations, 20-game winners Lou Fette and "Milkman" Jim Turner, rekindled some fan interest in '37 but the depth of talent simply wasn't there to provide a bona fide resurgence in the standings. Red Sox fans had more reason to hope as free-spending owner Tom Yawkey added some high-priced and attractive superstars to the payroll in the mid-thirties—namely, pitchers Wes Ferrell and Lefty Grove, catcher Rick Ferrell, shortstop Joe Cronin, first baseman Jimmy Foxx, and third baseman Pinky Higgins. To their credit, all of these costly acquisitions lived up to their credentials and had individually productive seasons for their new club. For a few more seasons, the new "ringers" failed to even lift the Sox out of the second division, but team fortunes began to change for the better when some home-grown stars like Bobby Doerr and Ted Williams arrived in 1938-39. Unfortunately, the New York Yankees, in the midst of one of their great dynasties, proved too formidable to overtake in the final years of the decade.

The Waner brothers, Paul (left) and Lloyd (right), paced some good hitting Pirate clubs in the 1930s.

The Boston Bees experienced a rare tandem of 20-game winners in Lou Fette (left) and Jim Turner in 1937.

The Brooklyn Robins (as they were more often called in the early thirties when "Uncle Robby" was at the helm) were an interesting collection of characters that were entertaining to watch but unable to seriously challenge the NL's top clubs. Their greatest success was their ability to torment their hated rivals, the Giants, by handing them numerous defeats that often thwarted the pennant hopes of the Polo Grounders. They began the decade with colorful slugging outfielder Babe Herman and aging Brooklyn favorite Dazzy Vance. Durable Al Lopez was among the league's top catchers. Muscular outfielder Hack Wilson added some home run power and some "adventurous" outfielding from 1932 to 1934. After Wilbert Robinson's departure, they reidentified themselves as "Dodgers" and hired another colorful Flatbush favorite, Casey Stengel, as field boss. Fire-balling hurler Van Lingle Mungo was another crowd pleaser who gave the club some decent pitching in the mid-thirties. The acquisition of Leo Durocher and

executive Larry MacPhail in 1938 signaled the beginning of a new, more promising era in club fortunes. The two most abysmal clubs throughout the decade were the Philadelphia Phillies and the St. Louis Browns. For the Phils, the slugging of their only real hero, Chuck Klein, helped them finish a distant fourth in 1932 but for the balance of the decade they remained hopelessly mired in 7th or 8th place. They finally abandoned their antiquated home park, Baker Bowl, in 1938 and moved in to share Shibe Park with the Athletics, but it did nothing to change their status as genuine losers. The Browns proved equally pathetic and set record lows in attendance during the 1930s. Not even hard-driving manager Rogers Hornsby could ignite the hapless Brownies from their doldrums. Harlond Clift gave them some consistency at third base and Buck Newsom somehow won 20 games for them in 1937, but it is fair to say that they gave a handful of St. Louis fans a steady diet of minor league baseball in the thirties.

The 1930s had its share of colorful and fascinating personalities who helped to keep the game interesting and entertaining for the fans. The incomparable and outspoken Dizzy Dean, whose lack of modesty only enhanced his popularity, was undoubtedly the most newsworthy player of the decade. The reckless baserunning and constant clowning of teammate

Pepper Martin was the other main ingredient in the mid-thirties saga of what was called the "Gas House Gang." The legendary home run feats and equally horrendous fielding feats of the powerful Hack Wilson caught the fancy of fans throughout the league in the early thirties. But there was also a tragic side to the popular Wilson and it undoubtedly shortened his brilliant career—the "bottle." Leo Durocher, the fiery shortstop during the "Gas House Gang" years, was always an NL fan favorite (or a favorite player to hate by the opposition) with his combative yapping and bench-jockeying antics. Dick Bartell was from the same mold and was always in the eye of the storm when things got out of hand in the field. The gregarious Buck Newsom, baseball's most traveled pitcher, was always a crowd favorite wherever he happened to hang his hat. Babe Ruth was, of course, far and away the biggest gate attraction in the game, even in his "bumbling" twilight years. The Brooklyn Dodgers paid him a handsome salary in 1938 in a meaningless coaching capacity—his real role was to participate in batting practice and entertain the fans with his patented drives into the far reaches of Ebbets Field. Catcher Moe Berg was baseball's resident intellectual, fluent in seven or more languages. His personal life outside the game was equally unique—among other things, he participated in some genuine high-level espionage for the U.S. government during the ominous pre-war international climate of the thirties. Among the lesser knowns, Detroit newspapers had a delightful time covering the antics of the eccentric Baron "Boots" Poffenberger, a pitcher with some promise but with an excess of colorful personal "baggage" in his makeup.

Dodgers pilot Casey Stengel (left) and his hard-throwing ace, Van Lingle Mungo

Chuck Klein (left) and Dolph Camilli gave forlorn Phillie fans some quality performances in the thirties.

The hapless St. Louis Browns did showcase an occasional star player, such as third baseman Harlond Clift.

The Dean brothers, Dizzy (left) and Paul, were first-rate characters as well as top-flight hurlers in the mid-thirties.

"Boots" Poffenberger was a delight for Detroit scribes and their readers in the late '30s.

POSITION PLAYERS AND PITCHERS OF THE DECADE

The decade of the thirties, perhaps only because of the "accident" of its chronology, proved to be a meeting point, or common ground, of the career years of many of baseball's greatest players—more so than any other ten-year period. Legendary names like Ruth, Sisler, Hornsby, Dazzy Vance, and even briefly Eddie Collins and Grover Alexander made player appearances into 1930 and beyond. Later era stars like Feller, DiMaggio, and Ted Williams appeared on the major league scene as the decade ended. To single out the outstanding position player and pitcher of the decade for each league is a ticklish and inevitably debatable task. But, using the most prolific performance years during the full ten-year span as the principal criterion, the choices have to narrow down to the following players. In the Senior Circuit, Giants outfielder Mel Ott barely edges Joe Medwick, only because Ott played out the full

decade while Medwick's career began in 1932. The NL pitcher selection easily goes to Carl Hubbell, who won 190 games for the Giants from 1930 to 1939, over Dizzy Dean, whose dazzling career was only dazzling for six seasons. The American League's premier position player selection goes to Jimmy Foxx, three-time MVP with triple crown offensive numbers throughout the decade—comparable to the great Babe Ruth's output in the 1920s. Detroit's Charlie Gehringer has to be considered for the honor with his consistent stickwork and superior defensive skills, a commodity that might give him a clear edge over Foxx. The AL's pitcher of the decade selection has to be Lefty Grove, who won 199 games—often without the offensive support that his Yankee rivals Ruffing and Gomez enjoyed.

CARL HUBBELL

LEFTY GROVE

CHARLEY GEHRINGER   JOE MEDWICK   LOU GEHRIG

MEL OTT

JIMMY FOXX

MAJOR LEAGUE ALL-STARS OF 1930-39

NATIONAL LEAGUE

Outfielders:

		Utility Players:
Wally Berger	Jo-Jo Moore	Tony Cuccinello
Chuck Klein	Mel Ott	Joe Stripp
Pepper Martin	Lloyd Waner	Pep Young
Joe Medwick	Paul Waner	

Third Basemen:	Shortstops:	Second Baseman:	First Basemen:
Stan Hack	Dick Bartell	Lonnie Frey	Rip Collins
Pie Traynor	Leo Durocher	Frank Frisch	Gus Suhr
Pinky Whitney	Arky Vaughan	Billy Herman	Bill Terry

Catchers:	Pitchers:	
Spud Davis	Dizzy Dean	Carl Hubbell
Gabby Hartnett	Paul Derringer	Charlie Root
Ernie Lombardi	Fred Fitzsimmons	Hal Schumacher
	Larry French	Lon Warneke

AMERICAN LEAGUE

Outfielders:

		Utility Players:
Earl Averill	Al Simmons	Ossie Bluege
Ben Chapman	Johnny Stone	Red Kress
Doc Cramer	Joe Vosmik	Cecil Travis
Goose Goslin	Sam West	
Heinie Manush		

Third Basemen:	Shortstops:	Second Basemen:	First Basemen:
Pinky Higgins	Luke Appling	Charley Gehringer	Jimmy Foxx
Marv Owen	Joe Cronin	Buddy Myer	Lou Gehrig
Red Rolfe	Billy Rogell	Tony Lazzeri	Hank Greenberg

Catchers:	Pitchers:	
Mickey Cochrane	Tommy Bridges	Mel Harder
Bill Dickey	Wes Ferrell	Ted Lyons
Rick Ferrell	Lefty Gomez	Buck Newsom
Luke Sewell	Lefty Grove	Red Ruffing
	Bump Hadley	Earl Whitehill

FIELD MANAGERS

Three of the legendary figures in baseball, their joint careers dating back to the 19th century, were still managing big league clubs when the decade began. John McGraw was finishing his third decade as New York Giants field boss, but had mellowed considerably by 1930. Age and poor health had subdued his fiery spirit and by this time he was more of an idolized father figure for Giants baseball, appearing more often in street clothes in the image of his AL contemporary, Connie Mack. McGraw finally called it quits in early 1932 after a poor start and turned over the reins to first baseman Bill Terry. Over in Brooklyn, rotund Wilbert Robinson, the revered figurehead of the Ebbets franchise, stepped aside after the 1931 season and was replaced by Pirate legend Max Carey. Both McGraw and Robinson died only months apart in 1934. For the other legendary pilot, ageless Connie Mack of the Athletics, it was a different scenario as his team was in the midst of a three-year dominance of the American League as the decade began. For Mack it was business as usual, his familiar angular presence waving the habitual scorecard from the shade of the dugout. By the midyears of the decade, he had alienated many Philadelphia fans by selling off his star players and abruptly ending another glorious period in Athletics history. But his storied credentials as a big league manager plus the fact that he basically controlled the entire franchise made him immune to any prolonged backlash and his position was never seriously threatened.

The legendary John McGraw stepped down in 1932.

Wilbert Robinson, Brooklyn's veteran boss, called it quits after the 1931 season.

Joe McCarthy replaced Bob Shawkey at the Yankees helm in 1931 and became one of the team's many legendary figures.

The most successful and arguably the shrewdest manager in the 1930s was Yankee pilot Joe McCarthy. "Marse Joe" had led the Chicago Cubs to a pennant in 1929, and Yankee owner Jake Ruppert recruited McCarthy to succeed the late Miller Huggins after an interim tenure by Bob Shawkey in 1930. McCarthy's 1931 Yankee squad won 94 games, but was unable to overtake the still mighty Athletics. But 1932 was a different story as the potent Bronx Bombers duplicated Mack's 107 victories of '31 and crushed the Cubs in four straight for the world championship. Then in 1936, McCarthy's new legions ushered in another typical Yankee championship monopoly with the first of four consecutive and relatively effortless World Series victories. In the National League, another veteran manager with Hall of Fame credentials, Bill McKechnie, held the reins at Boston for most of the decade without much success, but then transferred to Cincinnati and delivered pennants in 1939-40. Bucky Harris, one-time "boy wonder" as player/manager in the nation's capital, began the decade as Detroit manager. From there he went to the Red Sox for one year (1934). Then after Yawkey signed Joe Cronin as player/manager, he returned to Washington to finish out the decade with the hapless Senators. Bucky, despite his mediocre results throughout the 1930s, was always highly regarded by baseball brass and continued on to a long career as a big league field boss. Casey Stengel, who would also go on to an illustrious career as a Hall of Fame manager, had a couple of disappointing tours in the mid-thirties as boss of the Brooklyn Dodgers and Boston Bees.

The venerable A's pilot Connie Mack (in suit) confers with his coaches in 1930 (L to R): Earle Mack, Eddie Collins, and Kid Gleason.

Bucky Harris managed three AL clubs throughout the 1930-39 period.

Casey Stengel had two disappointing stints as boss of the Dodgers and Bees in the mid-thirties.

Bill McKechnie (right), shown with Bees' boss Bob Quinn in 1936, was one of the most respected field managers in the game.

The decade of the 1930s was the golden age of player/managers as no less than six pennants were won with active players in charge. And to this list may be added eight more names of managers who did not win pennants but were on the active player roster during their stewardships. First baseman Charlie Grimm led the Cubs to flags in '32 and '35, then was replaced by catcher Gabby Hartnett in the successful 1938 pennant chase. Shortstop Joe Cronin emulated his Washington predecessor of the mid-twenties, Bucky Harris, by playing and managing the Nats to a pennant win in 1933. His victorious counterpart in the 1933 Fall Classic was NY Giant first baseman/manager Bill Terry, who also captured NL flags in 1936-37. The most dynamic player/manager of the decade was Detroit's fiery catcher Mickey Cochrane, who led his Tigers to winning seasons in 1934-35. Frankie Frisch played second base and managed the "Gas House" Cardinals to victory in 1934. The other player/managers of that era were Rogers Hornsby, Lew Fonseca, Marty McManus, Jimmy Dykes, Jim Bottomley, Pie Traynor, Jimmy Wilson and last, but not least, Leo Durocher. Durocher's credentials as a first-rate field manager would soon follow his final year as a full-time player (1939) with contending clubs in subsequent decades.

CLUB OWNERS AND EXECUTIVES

As previously mentioned, a number of major league club owners passed on in the 1930s. In many such instances the torch was passed to a surviving relative or business partner without too much disruption or change in year-to-year operation of the franchise. However, even members of the same family can differ greatly in personality. Sometimes the heirs lacked the administrative skills or forceful personality of the departed and sometimes the opposite was true. Charles Comiskey was an executive of legendary charisma, but his surviving son, J. Louis Comiskey, never exhibited the genuine commitment to baseball nor the leadership qualities of his father and as a result the White Sox operation floundered under its new ownership. For the Northside Cubs, it was a different story. When death ended the Wm. Wrigley/Veeck era, the club fell into the hands of the younger Wrigley (P.K.), an active owner who was determined to make the operation self-supporting and field more winning teams. Phil Wrigley was his own man and was willing to spend money on park beautification and fan comfort as well as making controversial player acquisitions to seek a winning formula. He gave Cub fans two more pennants in 1935 and 1938. But his conservatism on some issues would retard the future development of the franchise—specifically, his reluctance to develop a full-fledged farm system and his refusal to install lights at Wrigley Field.

By 1930, the most successful front office in baseball resided in Yankee Stadium where the tandem of owner Jacob Ruppert and General Manager Ed Barrow had already assembled winning Yankee dynasties of mythical proportions. Blessed with baseball's biggest drawing card (win or lose) in Ruth and Gehrig plus the game's largest and grandest cathedral (Yankee Stadium), the New York American League franchise was the envy of all of baseball's front offices. Ruppert, with his brewery fortune in hand, pulled the purse strings with consummate business skill and Barrow, with a keen mind and eye for talent, orchestrated the ongoing assembly of winning combinations. The Yankees, quicker than many other clubs to notice the benefits of the Cardinals' empire of minor league operations, followed the new trend, beginning with the outright purchase of the AAA Newark club in 1931. Before the decade ended, the Yankee farm chain rivaled that of Rickey's, and the effort had almost immediate success. The Newark club of the mid-thirties was the class of the minor leagues and many of its players became key members of the great Yankee teams in the late thirties and early forties. The guiding genius of this vast enterprise was George Weiss, who would later help write more Yankee history from a desk at Yankee Stadium.

JOE CRONIN

MICKEY COCHRANE

The 1930s saw an abnormal number of player/managers in the big leagues. About half of them were players with future Hall of Fame credentials like the above three.

BILL TERRY

J. Louis Comiskey succeeded his legendary father as White Sox president, but was unable to resurrect the dormant franchise.

Philip K. Wrigley was able to continue the Cubs' three-year winning cycle, but his team continued to disappoint their fans in World Series play.

Col. Jacob Ruppert, the wealthy brewing magnate, forged his Yankee enterprise into a mighty dynasty.

Ed Barrow gave the Yankees a lifetime of baseball expertise during his tenure as business manager and later president.

Among the more revolutionary developments in the 1930s that affected the structure of baseball at the big league level, the growth of the farm systems is arguably the most monumental. Its creation was the brainchild of Wesley Branch Rickey, vice president and business manager of the St. Louis Cardinals club under owner Sam Breadon. Rickey was a uniquely gifted and qualified individual, combining a brilliant mind for creative administration of the business with a keen knowledge of the game rooted in a long career as player, coach, and field manager. His wisdom and oratorical talents outgrew his limited role as team boss and he was elevated to the front office in the mid-twenties. He immediately convinced club owners that the surest way for the perennially hapless Cardinal club to produce winning teams was not only to sign a huge reservoir of players but to negotiate exclusive working agreements with and even purchase outright a chain of minor league operations to corral all this potential talent. His visionary program brought almost immediate results with NL pennants in 1926, 1928, and 1930-31, and the so-called "farm system" was here to stay. Despite its success, the formula had many critics, including Judge Landis himself, who saw it as a devious scheme by which wealthier clubs could manipulate the distribution of baseball talent to serve their own ends and thereby undermine the competitive balance of major league baseball. But before the decade was out, most clubs followed suit and developed at least modest if not comparable minor league networks of their own.

Another club owner who surfaced in the mid-thirties and made a significant impact on major league baseball was Powell Crosley, Jr., of the Cincinnati Reds organization. Crosley was an energetic tinkerer and an entrepreneurial risk taker, a talent that drove him into various enterprises that eventually made him a millionaire. He was involved with a variety of products and business ventures in the Cincinnati area, but the most visible and profitable for him were his patented "Shelvador" refrigerators and the radio business. When radio grew in quantum leaps in the 1920s, Crosley, like Henry Ford, produced affordable radio sets that were eagerly purchased by millions. He not only built receivers, he served time as an announcer and eventually purchased his own station, WLW, the most powerful voice in the Cincinnati area. When he took over the floundering Reds, his knowledge of baseball operations was minimal at best, but he quickly applied his energy and acumen to give the franchise a new lease on life. He hired one of the most promising young executives in baseball, Larry MacPhail, to administer the reborn Reds with rare imagination and innovation.

Crosley and MacPhail not only gambled with night baseball, but they also introduced travel by air on occasion for the team and lured the golden voice of Red Barber to describe Reds games on the radio. The home park, Redlands Field, was renamed Crosley Field and numerous cosmetic improvements were introduced, including a bright new color scheme and a new partially electric scoreboard. MacPhail and Barber were lost to Brooklyn as the decade ended, but their departure was upstaged by two consecutive pennants under Bill McKechnie.

It seemed an unfortunate irony that once the doldrums of the Great Depression settled in, the two "grand old men" of the American League, Connie Mack and Clark Griffith, felt the financial pinch with more pain than many other newer club owners. The careers of both men dated all the way back to the formation of the league itself in 1901. But, unlike the newer breed of owners who jumped into baseball with ready-made fortunes at hand, Mack and Griffith depended on their baseball operations alone to make ends meet. Thus, existing from one season to the next without incurring insurmountable debts forced these clubs to operate on an often ultra-conservative agenda. Not that either man was by nature particularly innovative or daring in his stewardship, nevertheless their predicament helps to explain their often unpopular sale of proven stars for cash. Without farm system empires and cash reserves, Mack and Griffith gambled on their own instincts and the advice of their scouts to reassemble winning teams from scratch—a formula that failed miserably for both clubs. Both Mack and Griffith were enriched with baseball savvy and years of experience, but to their discredit they conducted their affairs as autocrats and were reluctant to delegate decisions to general managers with a more up-to-date sense of what was needed to resurrect a failing franchise.

Cardinals' executive Branch Rickey pioneered the idea of a vast farm system that was eventually copied by other clubs.

New Cincinnati owner Powell Crosley amassed a fortune in various enterprises and successful innovative products like the Crosley SHELVADOR refrigerator—as depicted in the ad on the right.

this much more in a SHELVADOR

EXCLUSIVELY IN CROSLEY ELECTRIC REFRIGERATORS

Crosley's imaginative GM, Larry MacPhail, was instrumental in bringing night baseball to the major leagues in 1935.

Clark Griffith was an American League legend, but his conservative one-man rule of the Washington club gave them one lone pennant in the '30s.

Connie Mack ruled the roost in Philadelphia, but it was 1937 before he became president of the Athletics.

Frank Navin, Tiger owner until his death in 1935, was an influential force in league affairs.

Navin's chief partner, W. O. Briggs (left), bankrolled the purchase of superstar Mickey Cochrane (right) in late 1933. Cochrane immediately justified the expenditure with a pennant-winning season in 1934.

New Red Sox owner Tom Yawkey (left) and his VP, Eddie Collins (right), beam over the acquisition of star player/manager Joe Cronin (center) in 1935.

Frank Navin of the Detroit club was another surviving "dinosaur" from the early years of the American League. But even though he ran a tightly budgeted ship, he was devoted to baseball and was committed to the quest of another championship for the Motor City. He also had the good fortune of having the wealthy industrialist Walter O. Briggs as a major partner. Briggs, like Navin, lusted for a winning combination and when star players Goose Goslin and Mickey Cochrane were offered to the highest bidder, he offered to back up the asking price and Navin went ahead with the deals. Much to the delight of Tiger fandom, the acquisition of Goslin and Cochrane was the catalyst in the transformation of the Bengals into pennant winners. Tiger attendance soared to new levels and Navin confidently made grandiose plans to enlarge Navin Field to accommodate the new windfall of loyal fans. After Navin's death in late 1935, new owner Briggs continued the expansion project to its conclusion in 1938, then renamed the place Briggs Stadium. A similar scenario took place in Boston, where new wealthy owner Tom Yawkey and his baseball-wise VP, Hall of Famer Eddie Collins, renovated Fenway Park and forked out huge sums for a handful of star players with hopes of revitalizing a comatose Red Sox team into contention. On paper, the acquisition of already legendary stars like Lefty Grove, Jimmy Foxx, and Joe Cronin alone seemed enough to "lock up" the AL championship for beleaguered Boston fans. Unfortunately, the chemistry just wasn't there and the Bosox were unable to even pull themselves out of the second division. Yawkey and Collins were obviously dismayed but remained determined that sooner or later an upward surge was inevitable. Since nothing was lost but Yawkey money, he was never chastised by Boston fans and remained one of baseball's most popular owners. Meanwhile, over at Braves Field, Judge Emil Fuchs, the eccentric owner who actually took over as field manager in 1929, had the ultimate wisdom to hire a real manager, Bill McKechnie, to try to magically transform losers into front runners. McKechnie's managerial skill elevated a mediocre collection to .500 status but he finally ran out of mirrors and the Tribe plummeted to the basement in 1935. Not even the magical presence of Babe Ruth could save this team from its manifest destiny. Bob Quinn, an experienced baseball executive who had only recently guided the Red Sox fortunes, took over in 1936 and his sole memorable legacy was to try to disguise the hopeless franchise behind a new nickname, Bees.

The New York Giants were fortunate in maintaining an able executive following the death of owner Charles Stoneham in 1934—namely, his 32-year-old son Horace.

The conservative Stoneham style of administration marched on through the balance of the decade uninterrupted. Neither Charles nor Horace were very imaginative but were adequately dedicated and blessed with strong, competitive teams with entertaining stars like Hubbell, Ott, and player/manager Bill Terry. Horace continued his father's stubborn blackout of radio coverage and his resistance to night baseball until the inevitability of both became obvious by 1939. The Stoneham style, for better or worse, kept decision-making at the ownership level and the Giants were one of the few clubs that never employed a general manager in their front office. Over in Brooklyn, the franchise muddled through the thirties with confusing ownership-by-committee at the top. Finally in 1938, they had the good fortune to hire a fiery shortstop and field manager, Leo Durocher, along with an aggressive and creative executive, Larry MacPhail. Both men were instrumental in initiating a new winning formula in Flatbush that gave them winning seasons in the 1940s. MacPhail gave Dodger fans night baseball in '38 and then finally ended the NYC radio blackout and gave Brooklyn its legendary voice, Red Barber.

Judge Emil Fuchs gave Babe Ruth his "last hurrah" in 1935 with the Braves.

Bob Quinn succeeded Fuchs and renamed the team as Bees.

Charles Stoneham gave Giants fans a flag in 1933 and some big heroes like Terry, Ott, and Hubbell.

Horace Stoneham inherited the club presidency upon his father's death in 1935.

SPRING TRAINING SITES 1930-39

BOSTON BRAVES/BEES	St. Petersburg FL 1930-37, Bradenton FL 1938-39
BOSTON RED SOX	Pensacola FL 1930-31, Savannah GA 1932, Sarasota FL 1933-39
BROOKLYN DODGERS	Clearwater FL 1930-32, 1936-39; Miami FL 1933, Orlando FL 1934-35
CHICAGO CUBS	Catalina Island, CA 1930-39
CHICAGO WHITE SOX	San Antonio TX 1930-32, Pasadena CA 1933-39
CINCINNATI REDS	Orlando FL 1930, Tampa FL 1931-39 (also San Juan PR in 1936)
CLEVELAND INDIANS	New Orleans LA 1930-39
DETROIT TIGERS	Tampa FL 1930, Sacramento CA 1931, Palo Alto CA 1932, San Antonio TX 1933, Lakeland FL 1934-39
NEW YORK GIANTS	San Antonio TX 1930-31, Los Angeles CA 1932-33, Miami Beach FL 1934-35, Pensacola FL 1936, Havana CUBA 1937, Baton Rouge LA 1938-39
NEW YORK YANKEES	St. Petersburg FL 1930-39
PHILADELPHIA ATHLETICS	Ft. Myers FL 1930-36, Mexico City 1937, Lake Charles, LA 1938-39
PHILADELPHIA PHILLIES	Winter Haven FL 1930-37, Biloxi MS 1938, New Braunfels TX 1939
PITTSBURGH PIRATES	Paso Robles CA 1930-34, San Bernardino CA 1935, 1937-39; San Antonio TX 1936
ST. LOUIS BROWNS	West Palm Beach FL 1930-36, San Antonio TX 1937-39
ST. LOUIS CARDINALS	Bradenton FL 1930-36, Daytona Beach FL 1937, St. Petersburg FL 1938-39
WASHINGTON NATIONALS	Biloxi MS 1930-35, Orlando FL 1936-39

THE NEGRO LEAGUES

Organized baseball's shameful policy of excluding Negroes could not suppress the game's popularity with millions of blacks, principally in the urban centers of the eastern U.S. Despite the enormous built-in obstacles of outright racism along with the economic hard times that hit the black population even harder than the average white, the Negro leagues were able to field talented teams that entertained a black audience (and indeed a white audience when their opponents were white) throughout the thirties. Some of the shrewder and more powerful franchises even managed a modest profit. Everywhere they went they faced a myriad of difficulties that organized baseball did not have to deal with. They traveled in their own buses and had to stay in sub-standard hotels and eat only in establishments that would serve blacks. They were welcomed in some major league parks and higher-level minor league parks, but very often were forced to use aging, outmoded facilities. Lacking the established infrastructure of organized baseball to support them, they were forced to play a more limited schedule of only 40 or 50 dates, often improvised as the summer progressed. Their competition was a mixture of other Negro league teams and exhibition games with all-white clubs, either official minor league franchises or local semi-pros. The whole structure of black baseball in the thirties was unstable at best, with a "revolving door" of teams representing the major eastern and southern cities with sizable black populations. Three of the more successful clubs were the Kansas City Monarchs, the Pittsburgh Crawfords, and the Homestead Grays. Players like Satchel Paige, Josh Gibson, and Cool Papa Bell enjoyed star billing wherever they played. The closest they came to major league levels of competition were occasional post-season exhibitions with barnstorming big league all-stars and they generally fared well. In retrospect, a sizable stable of potential stars was denied the opportunity to perform before a major league audience throughout the thirties. The baseball Hall of Fame has honored many of the Negro league greats in a noble effort to atone for their lengthy exclusion, but the almost non-existent statistical data from the Negro leagues has made the selection process sometimes totally reliant on recollected opinions.

The most legendary name in Negro baseball was the lanky hurler, Satchel Paige.

THE COMMISSIONER

Baseball's commissioner, Judge Kenesaw Mountain Landis, ruled the game with unchallenged authority in the 1930s. Landis was devoted to the sport and, for better or worse, acted on his personal interpretation of "the best interests of baseball." To his credit, he encouraged stability in the status quo, even when failing franchises like the St. Louis Browns might have been temporarily better off relocating to a new market. He remained neutral on the somewhat revolutionary concept of night baseball and on individual club policies toward radio broadcasting of games. He opposed the growth of farm systems and their subsequent "hoarding" of player talent. Unfortunately, he willfully perpetuated the ongoing discrimination against blacks in organized baseball and only after his death in 1945 was this shameful barrier ended.

ADMINISTRATION OF BASEBALL

Josh Gibson scoring for the Homestead Grays

KENESAW MOUNTAIN LANDIS Commissioner 1930-39

LESLIE O'CONNOR Secretary-Treasurer to the Commissioner 1930-39

LEW FONSECA Motion Picture Promotion

NAPBL (minor leagues) Presidents: M. H. SEXTON 1930-32 WM. G. BRAMHAM 1933-39 GEO. M. TRAUTMAN (VP)

NATIONAL LEAGUE

JOHN A. HEYDLER
President,
Secretary/Treasurer
1930-34
Chairman 1935-37

FORD C. FRICK
NL Service Bureau 1934
President 1935-39

BARNEY DREYFUSS
VP 1930-31

HARVEY TRABAND
Secretary-Treasurer, VP
1930-39

CULLEN CAIN
NL Service Bureau
1932-33

BILL BRANDT
NL Service Bureau
1935-39

SAM BREADON
VP 1936-39

NATIONAL LEAGUE UMPIRES

Field Umpires:

Supervisory Umpires:

BOB EMSLIE
Advisor
1930-35

HANK O'DAY
Advisor
1930-35

BILL KLEM 1930-39

GEORGE MAGERKURTH
1930-39

CHARLES MORAN
1930-39

JOHN "BEANS" REARDON
1930-39

ERNEST QUIGLEY
Supervisor
1937-38

LEE BALLANFANT 1936-39
GEORGE BARR 1931-39
WILLIAM CAMPBELL 1939
ROBERT M. CLARKE 1930-31
CHARLES DONNELLY 1931-32
MICHAEL DONOHUE 1930
THOMAS DUNN 1939
LARRY GOETZ 1936-39
LOU JORDA 1930-31
HARRY "TED" McGREW 1930-31, 1933-34
GEORGE PARKER 1936-38
CHAS. "CY" PFIRMAN 1930-36
"BABE" PINELLI 1935-39
JACK POWELL 1933
ERNEST QUIGLEY 1930-36

BILL STEWART
1933-39

ALBERT STARK
1930-39

CHARLES RIGLER 1930-35
JAMES SCOTT 1930-31
JOHN "ZIGGY" SEARS 1934-39

AMERICAN LEAGUE

ERNEST S. BARNARD
President/Treasurer
1930-31

WILLIAM HARRIDGE
Secretary 1930-31
President/Secy./Treas.
1931-39

FRANK J. NAVIN
VP 1930-35

JACOB RUPPERT
VP 1936-38

HENRY P. EDWARDS
AL Service Bureau
1932-39

L. C. McEVOY
Supervisor
Radio Broadcasting
1936-39

DOROTHY HUMMEL
Secretary to President
1930-39

EARL HILLIGAN
Public Relations

AMERICAN LEAGUE UMPIRES

Supervisory Umpire:

Field Umpires:

TOM CONNOLLY
Chief of Staff
1932-39

HARRY GIESEL
1930-39

BILL McGOWAN
1930-39

GEORGE MORIARTY
1930-39

EMMET "RED" ORMSBY
1930-39

STEVE BASIL 1936-39
WILLIAM CAMPBELL 1930-31
TOM CONNOLLY 1930-31
BILL DINNEEN 1930-37
CHARLES DONNELLY 1934-35
BILL GRIEVE 1938-39
WILLIAM GUTHRIE 1930-32
GEORGE HILDEBRAND 1930-34
CAL HUBBARD 1936-39
CHARLES JOHNSTON 1936-37
LOU KOLLS 1933-39

RICHARD NALLIN 1930-32
CLARENCE "BRICK" OWENS 1930-37
GEORGE PIPGRAS 1938-39
JOHN QUINN 1935-39
ED ROMMEL 1938-39
JOSEPH RUE 1938-39
BILL SUMMERS 1933-39
ROY VAN GRAFLAN 1930-33

THE CITIES & THE BALLPARKS

BOSTON 1930-39

View of city and Charles River basin

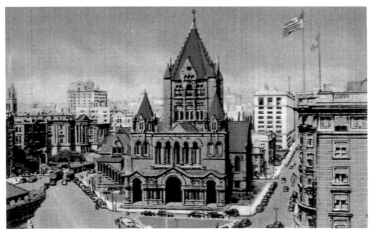

Trinity Church in Copley Square

West Boston Bridge

Soldiers Field, the home of Harvard football, shown during a 1936 game versus Dartmouth

Park Street Church and Tremont Street, 1936

An aerial view of Boston Fish Pier in 1936

BOSTON 1930-39 (continued)

THE NEWSPAPERS:

THE BASEBALL REPORTERS:

JOE CASHMAN
American, Record

JOHN FENTON
Herald

JOHN MALANEY
Post

JAMES O'LEARY
Globe

A. J. ROONEY
Traveler

PAUL SHANNON
Post

BURT WHITMAN
Herald

JAMES BAGLEY *INS*
WALTER S. BARNES, Jr. *Globe*
JACK BARNWELL *Post*
JOHN BROOKS *Record*
GEORGE CARENS *Transcript*
SAM CARRICK *American*
SAM COHEN *Advertiser, Record*
JOHN CONWAY *American*
AL COUGHLIN *Record*
BOB COYNE *Post*

BILL CUNNINGHAM *Post*
JOHN DROHAN *Traveler*
DAVE EGAN *Globe*
NICK FLATLEY *American*
A. LIND FOWLER *Transcript*
JOHN GARRO *La Notizia*
BILL GRIMES *American*
GEORGE GRIMM *American, Advertiser*
JOHN HALLAHAN *Globe*
W. C. HARVEY *CSM*
GEORGE HOLMES *CSM*
EDDIE HURLEY *Advertiser, Record*
HY HURWITZ *Globe*
VICTOR JONES *Globe*
HAROLD KAESE *Transcript*
WALTER KILEY *American*
W. R. KING *AP*
AUSTEN LAKE *Transcript*
FRED LANE *American*
GENE MACK *Globe*

S. J. MAHONEY *Advertiser, Record*
THOMAS McCABE *Herald*
MIKE McNAMEE *Record, Advertiser*
GERRY MOORE *Transcript, Globe*
W. J. MORSE *CSM*
JERRY NASON *Globe*
PARKE O'BRIEN *Advertiser*
HOWARD REYNOLDS *Post*
ED RUMMILL *CSM*
ARTHUR SAMPSON *Herald*
ABE SAVRANN *Traveler*
FORD SAWYER *Globe*
ARTHUR SIEGEL *Traveler*
LESLIE STOUT *Advertiser, Record*
VICTOR STOUT *Traveler*
MELVILLE WEBB *Globe*
W. A. WHITCOMB *Globe*

THE BROADCASTERS:

FRED HOEY
WAAB, WNAC
(YANKEE network)
1930-38

BILL WILLIAMS

JACK ONSLOW

BOB EVANS
ERNIE LABRANCH
DICK McDONOUGH
FRANK RYAN
JACK STEVENS
JAY WESLEY
ROLAND WINTERS

FRANKIE FRISCH
WAAB
(COLONIAL network)
1939

BOSTON—Braves Field/National League Park

An aerial view of cozy Braves Field

The ticket office and main entrance building behind the right field bleachers

Raising the flag in right center field at opening day 1931

A postcard view from inside the "Wigwam"

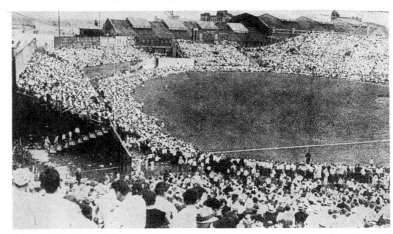

A view from the left field corner shows an overflow crowd of almost 60,000 that witnessed an important September game versus the league-leading Giants in 1933.

BOSTON—Fenway Park

A 1912 architect's drawing of the new home of the Red Sox

A postcard view from the left field corner

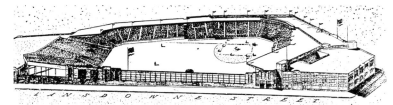

Another architect's drawing from a different angle showing the totally renovated 1934 version

An overflow crowd of 48,000 jammed the new Fenway Park to pay tribute to old Boston favorite Babe Ruth in his final season (1934) with the visiting Yankees.

A view looking toward the right field corner in 1937

The massive reconstruction of Fenway during the winter of 1933-34

BROOKLYN 1930-39

The famous Brooklyn Bridge, connecting the borough to Manhattan (in background)

Brooklyn's monumental arch in the late 1930s

A lunchtime crowd relaxes in the small park in front of Borough Hall.

Part of Brooklyn's extensive waterfront

BROOKLYN 1930-39 (continued)

THE NEWSPAPERS:

THE BASEBALL REPORTERS:

WM. McCULLOUGH
*Daily Times,
Times-Union, Eagle*

GARY SCHUMACHER
NY Eve Journal

HAROLD PARROTT
Eagle

CARLETON BLOCK *Std. Union*
HAROLD BURR *Eagle*
FRANK CASALE *Std. Union*
CLAY COTTER *Daily Times*
E. M. DARROW *Boys Club*
JAMES DEMPSEY *Citizen*
FRANK ECK *Queens News*
WM. FALVY *L. I. Press*
FRANK FARRELL *Times-Union*
FRANK FERGUSON *L. I. City Star*
JAMES FORBES *Eagle*
WM. GRANGER *Citizen*
WM. HICKS *Eagle*
CLINT HOARD *Citizen*
TOMMY HOLMES *Eagle*
ED HUGHES *Eagle*
GUS IHLMANN *Std. Union*

WM. JUENST *Eagle*
FRANK KEARNS *Daily Times, Times-Union, Eagle*
WM. KIRSCHENBAUM *NY Eve Journal*
BERNIE KREMENKO *Times-Union*
ANDREW LANG *Std. Union*
JOSEPH LEE *Times-Union*
JAMES MURPHY *Eagle*
THOMAS MURPHY *L. I. Press*
BUD NELSON *Times-Union*
LOU NISS *Times-Union, Eagle*
LOUIS O'NEILL *N.S. Journal, L.I. Star*
AL PALMA *NY Eve Journal*
JOHN PALMER *Citizen*
FRANK REIL *Eagle*
THOMAS RICE *Eagle*
JOSEPH ROBERTS *L.I. Press*
MURRAY ROBINSON *Std. Union*
I. ROSENBLATT *Times-Union*
LEE SCOTT *Citizen*
CHARLES VACKNER *Times-Union*
GEORGE VANDERGRIFT *N.S. Journal*
PAUL WARBURG *Eagle*
JAMES WOOD *Daily Times, Times-Union, Eagle*
LEN WOOSTER *Daily Times, Times-Union*
ABE YAGER *Eagle*

THE BROADCASTERS:

RED BARBER
WOR, WHN
1939

AL HELFER
WHN
1939

DICK FISHELL

BROOKLYN—Ebbets Field

An aerial view of Ebbets Field in the mid-'30s before the light towers were installed

A 1933 crowd gathers around the main entrance.

A street-level exterior view of the RF corner grandstand

In early 1931, the left and center field stand was double-decked—shown above nearing completion in April of that year.

An opening game crowd fills the new left field stand in 1933.

The first night game in 1938. Reds hurler Vander Meer is pitching his second consecutive no-hit game.

Another aerial view showing the newly added light towers

CHICAGO 1930-39

Outer Drive and North Shore skyline

The skyline of Chicago's "Loop" from a lakefront parking lot in 1932. The famous Wrigley Building and Tribune Tower are on the extreme right.

The Wabash Avenue drawbridge opens over the Chicago River. The Wrigley Building is in the background.

Midsummer bathers escape the heat in Lake Michigan's waters at Oak Street near Chicago's "Gold Coast."

THE NEWSPAPERS:

The Avenue of Flags at the spectacular Century of Progress fair in 1933

CHICAGO 1930-39 (continued)

THE BASEBALL REPORTERS:

WARREN BROWN
Her.-Ex.

ED BURNS
Tribune

RALPH CANNON
Daily News

JOHN CARMICHAEL
Daily News

JAMES CRUISINBERRY
Daily News

JAMES GALLAGHER
American

ED GEIGER
American

JOHN HOFFMAN
Daily News, INS, Times

HOWARD MANN
Daily News

W. M. McCARTHY
Daily Times

EDGAR MUNZEL
Her.-Ex.

WAYNE OTTO
Her.-Ex.

FRANCIS POWERS
Cons. PA

ED PRELL
American

HERB SIMONS
Daily Times

IRVING VAUGHAN
Tribune

ARCH WARD
Tribune

FRED BAILEY *UP*
E. G. BRANDS *BB World*
W. S. BRONS *INS*
CLARENCE CAREY *Her.-Ex.*
E. W. COCHRANE *American*
JAMES CORCORAN *American*
BERT DEMBY *UP*
HOWARD DENBY *Her.-Ex.*
CHAS. DUNKLEY *AP*
HENRY P. EDWARDS *ALSB*
LEO FISCHER *American*
JOE FOLEY *Daily Times*

WM. FORMAN *Daily News*
KENNETH FRY *Post, UP*
FRANK HICKS *BB World*
EARL HILLIGAN *AP*
FRED HOWE *Howe NB*
IRWIN HOWE *Howe NB*
ED JOHNSON *Post*
JAMES KEARNS *Daily News*
CLAIRE KELLY *American*
GENE KESSLER *Daily Times*
JOHN KEYES *Daily News*
GEORGE KIRKSEY *UP*

IRV KUPCINET *Times*
DAVID LAWLER *Post*
LLOYD LEWIS *Daily News*
WINTHROP LYMAN *UP*
WM. MARGOLIS *Daily Times*
DON MAXWELL *Tribune*
RONALD McINTYRE *Daily Times*
HARRY McNAMARA *Her.-Ex.*
PAUL MICKELSON *AP*
GEO. MORIARTY *NAPA*
MICHAEL MURPHY *Daily News*
FORREST MYERS *Daily News*

HARRY NEILY *American*
ROY NELSON *Daily News*
STEWART OWEN *Tribune*
JOHN PHILLIPS *Howe NB*
SAM POHN *Evanston NI*
HENRY RENNWALD *UP*
HOWARD ROBERTS *Daily News*
TOM SILER *AP*
CHUNG TONG *Howe NB*
HAL TOTTEN *Daily News*
WM. WEEKS *AP*
VERN WHITNEY *American*
HARVEY WOODRUFF *Tribune*
CHESTER YOULL *INS*

THE BROADCASTERS:

BOB ELSON
WGN, MUTUAL
1930-39

HAROLD "SPEED" JOHNSON
WIBO
1930

JOHNNY O'HARA
WCFL, WIND
1930-34

PAT FLANAGAN
WBBM, CBS
1930-39

JOHN HARRINGTON
WGN, WJJD, WBBM
1934-39

TRIS SPEAKER
WENR, WLS
1931

DUTCH REAGAN
(WHO—Des Moines)

HAL TOTTEN
WMAQ, WCFL, NBC
1930-38

LEW FONSECA
WJJD 1939

RUSS HODGES
WIND 1935-38

JIMMY DUDLEY
WIND, WCFL
1938-39

HAL BERGER
HARRY CREIGHTON
DON KELLEY

CHARLEY GRIMM
WBBM, WJJD
1938-39

QUIN RYAN

FRED LINDSTROM
WLS 1939

BOB HAWK

CHICAGO—Comiskey Park

An aerial view illustration of Comiskey Park as it was configured in the early thirties

An internal postcard view of the grandstand with a packed house

A workman prepares the outfield for the opening game of 1930. The left field scoreboard is in the background.

A 1931 footrace, won by the visiting Yanks' Ben Chapman. This snapshot provides a pretty good view of the center field bleachers of that period.

In 1934, the outfield distances were shortened by moving home plate 14 feet toward center field.

Comiskey Park gave South Side fans their first night game in 1939.

CHICAGO—Wrigley Field

The familiar exterior sign still in use today first appeared in 1937.

A packed grandstand at the 1932 World Series. Note the high vertical backstop.

A postcard drawing shows the outfield wall and bleacher arrangement in the early thirties.

The famous center field scoreboard was part of the outfield and bleacher reconstruction of 1937.

The Addison side of the grandstand during the 1938 World Series

A 1933 view from behind home plate. Direct center field was 436 feet away.

A street-level view looking down Waveland Avenue toward the center field bleachers

34,520 Cub fans filled the "Friendly Confines" to watch Dizzy Dean face off against the mighty Yanks in the '38 Fall Classic. Note the lower profile design of the backstop screen.

CINCINNATI 1930-39

The Cincinnati skyline and Ohio River as seen from the nearby Kentucky hills

Central Parkway, downtown Cincinnati

The main lobby of Cincinnati's Union Terminal

Mt. Adams and its famed inclined-plane rail cars

CINCINNATI 1930-39 (continued)

THE BASEBALL REPORTERS:

FRANK GRAYSON
Times-Star

BOB NEWHALL
Comm. Trib.

JOE NOLAN
Enquirer

JACK RYDER
Enquirer

BOB SAXTON
Enquirer

LOU SMITH
Enquirer

TOM SWOPE
Post

W. J. ANSCHUTZ *City News*
MAX BLOOM *City News*
WALTER BRINKMAN *Times-Star*
NIXSON DENTON *Times-Star*
CHARLES O'CONNOR *Times-Star*
HAROLD RUSSELL *Enquirer*

THE NEWSPAPERS:

YANK HOMERS VANQUISH REDS, 7-3

THE BROADCASTERS:

HARRY HARTMAN
WFBE, WCPO
1930-39

RED BARBER
WLW, WSAI, MUTUAL
1934-38

ROGER BAKER
WSAI 1939

DICK BRAY

TOM STULL

C. O. "OATMEAL" BROWN
PAUL HODGES
BOB NEWHALL
ALLEN STOUT
RED THORNBURGH

CINCINNATI—Redland/Crosley Field

A postcard aerial view from the mid-late '30s

Ground-level view from directly behind home plate, circa 1939

The right field corner bleachers in 1931

The scoreboard and battery of loudspeakers as they looked in 1933

Crosley Field gave the major leagues its first game under the arc lights in 1935.

Street-level view from the corner of Findlay & Western

A view toward right center field during the 1940 World Series

Owner Powell Crosley hastily added a rooftop press row and double-decked the right and left field pavilions just in time for the 1939 World Series (below).

CLEVELAND 1930-39

A high-level aerial shot of Cleveland's lakefront in 1932—showing the elaborate breakwater, the Cuyahoga Channel, and new Municipal Stadium on the left edge of the photo

Euclid Avenue, looking west in downtown Cleveland

Another aerial view from 1937 shows the giant stadium and, just beyond it, the grounds of the Great Lakes Exposition.

Cleveland's Terminal Tower, still a downtown landmark

The main thoroughfare for the magnificent Great Lakes Exposition of 1937, on the lakefront

CLEVELAND 1930-39 (continued)

THE NEWSPAPERS:

STOCKS
RACES
THE NEWS
BOX SCORE EDITION

VOL. 91—NO. 190.   CLEVELAND, FRIDAY, AUGUST 19, 1932.   Stocks, Markets (Complete) Pages 15-16-17   PRICE THREE CENTS

CLEVELAND PLAIN DEALER
SPORTS

97TH YEAR—NO. 107   CLEVELAND, SUNDAY MORNING, APRIL 17, 1938   124 PAGES   TEN CENTS

The Cleveland Press
HOME EDITION

Weather—Cloudy, warmer tonight and tomorrow.

ISSUE NO. 17134   CLEVELAND, WEDNESDAY, APRIL 20, 1933   PRICE THREE CENTS

THE BASEBALL REPORTERS:

ED BANG
News

STUART BELL
Press

WM. BRAUCHER
NEA, CPA

HENRY P. EDWARDS

CHAS. BANG *News*
J. BRONDFIELD *NEA*
NORMAN BROWN *CPA*
CLAIRE BURCKY *NEA*
GORDON COBBLEDICK *Plain Dealer*
JOHN DIETRICH *Plain Dealer*
JIMMY DONAHUE *NEA*
JAMES DOYLE *Plain Dealer*
WM. DVORAK *Press*
EARLE FERRIS *NNR*
FRANK GIBBONS *Press*
BOB GODLEY *Press*
HERM GOLDSTEIN *News*
EDWARD GOMBOS *Cons. Press*
HARRY GRAYSON *NEA*
HENRY HENSON *UP*
AL KRENZ *NEA*
ALVIN KRIEG *INS*
ERNEST LANIGAN *News*
WERNER LAUFER *NEA*

FRANKLIN LEWIS *Press*
ED McCAULEY *News*
CHARLES MEARS *News*
MEADE MONROE *UP*
SAM OTIS *Plain Dealer*
HOWARD PRESTON *News*
TOM QUINN *Press, News*
WILLIAM RITT *CPA*
CARL SHATTO *Press*
CHESTER SMITH *Press*
NAYLOR STONE *Press*
DAN TAYLOR *News*
BEN WARFIELD *Press*
ELMER WEINER *News*
EUGENE WHITNEY *Plain Dealer*
BEN WILLIAMSON *Press*
DAN WOOTON *Press*
MILTON YELSKY *Plain Dealer*
ALEX ZIRIN *Plain Dealer*

THE BROADCASTERS:

TOM MANNING
WTAM, NBC
1930-39

ELLIE VANDERPYLE
WHK, WGAR
1930-35

JACK GRANEY
WHK, WJAY, WCLE
1932-39

EARL HARPER
WHK 1933

FRANKLIN "WHITEY" LEWIS
BOB NEAL
GEORGE SUTHERLAND

CLEVELAND—League Park

A long-distance aerial photo of cozy League Park, the Tribe's on-again/off-again home field in the 1930s

The crowd spills onto the field following the 1932 home opener. The Tigers spoiled the day with a 2-1 win before 23,000 fans. Two months later, the new lakefront stadium was inaugurated.

A postcard view of the left field bleachers

A closer look at the Indians' alternate home playground. The concrete and steel version replaced the old wooden structure in 1910.

Another postcard view from behind home plate

CLEVELAND—Municipal Stadium 1932-39

The gigantic new oval as it appeared on its inauguration as a baseball facility—June 30, 1932. Over 80,000 fans watch the Athletics defeat the Tribe and Mel Harder 1-0.

Part of the 80,000 leaving the site after the historic baptism, wending their way across the pedestrian overpasses toward downtown

A magnificent wide-angle view of the 1932 opener, looking toward dead center field

A similar wide-angle shot from the opposite direction (from dead center) of another near-capacity throng witnessing the 1935 All-Star game

DETROIT 1930-39

The Ambassador Bridge, spanning the Detroit River, connects Canada (foreground) with the city of Detroit.

Griswold Street in downtown Detroit—featuring the Stott Building (center) and Penobscot Building (on right)

Grand Circus Park was Detroit's "hotel row"—the Statler (center) and Tuller (right) are shown here.

The Detroit Institute of Art on Woodward Avenue, the principal artery in the Motor City

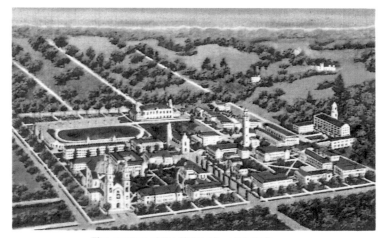

The campus of the University of Detroit

DETROIT 1930-39 (continued)

THE NEWSPAPERS:

THE BASEBALL REPORTERS:

SAM GREENE	LEO MacDONELL	H. G. SALSINGER	BUD SHAVER	CHARLES WARD
News	*Times*	*News*	*Times*	*Free Press*

H. H. BARCUS *News*
E. A. BATCHELOR, Jr. *News*
E. A. BATCHELOR, Sr. *Sat. Night*
GLENN BIRCHARD *City News*
RAY BOUSLOG *Daily*
HARRY BULLION *Free Press*
F. J. CARVETH *Free Press*
VERN DEGEER *BCS, Windsor Star*
M. F. DRUKENBROD *Free Press, Times*
L. B. DUNNIGAN *Free Press*
W. W. EDGAR *Free Press*
LESLIE HARROP *UP*
EDGAR HAYES *Times*
DOC HOLST *Times, Free Press*
HAROLD KAHL *Times*
ROBT. LABLOND *UP*
HARRY LEDUC *News*
FRANK MacDONELL *Times*

CY MANN *INS*
SAM McGUIRE *Times*
BOB MURPHY *Times*
LLOYD NORTHARD *News*
JAMES RENICK *Free Press*
TOD ROCKWELL *Free Press*
STEPHEN ROGIENSKI *INS*
JOHN SECHLER *Daily*
DALE STAFFORD *AP*
HARRY WADE *News*
BERT WALKER *Times*
LEWIS WALTER *Daily, Times*
DAVID WILKE *AP*
JAMES ZERILLI *News*

THE BROADCASTERS:

TY TYSON
WWJ, NBC
1930-39

HARRY HEILMANN
WXYZ, Mich. Network
1934-39

AL NAGLER

JOE GENTILE
CKLW, MUTUAL
1939

JIM STEPHENSON

BOB McLEAN
BILL STANLEY
HARRY WISMER

GEORGE SUTHERLAND

DETROIT—Navin Field/Briggs Stadium

Navin Field as it looked in 1930, looking east toward the Michigan/National corner

An aerial view taken during the 1935 World Series. The huge open bleacher in left field was temporary—erected for both Fall Classics of '34 and '35.

Ticket-seekers mill around the Michigan & Trumbull "corner," hoping to gain entrance to the 1934 World Series.

The newly completed Briggs Stadium awaits the home opener in April 1938.

The new center field scoreboard, high atop the upper deck center field bleachers

An aerial view of the Tigers' home field as it looked in 1939. Cherry Street was forcibly detoured to make room for park expansion in left field.

NEW YORK 1930-39

The Manhattan skyline, as viewed across the East River from Brooklyn's waterfront

Flushing Meadows was the site of the ambitious and spectacular New York World's Fair of 1939-40.

A far-reaching aerial photo of NYC and the western end of Long Island

NYC's main air terminal, LaGuardia Field

The world's tallest skyscraper, the Empire State Building, erected in 1931

NEW YORK 1930-39 (continued)

THE NEWSPAPERS:

THE BASEBALL REPORTERS:

CLIFFORD BLOODGOOD — *BB Mag.*

BILL CORUM — *Journal-Amer.*

DAN DANIEL — *Telegram, World-Tel.*

JAMES DAWSON — *Times*

JACK FOSTER — *Cons. Press*

N. M. GERSTENZANG — *Post*

FRANK GRAHAM — *Sun*

WALT HUDSON — *Mirror*

MAX KASE — *Journal-Amer.*

JACK KOFOED — *Post, Journal*

F. C. LANE — *BB Mag.*

FRED LIEB — *Post*

NEW YORK 1930-39 (continued)

ROSCOE McGOWAN
Times

TOM MEANY
Telegram, World-Tel.

SID MERCER
*American,
Journal-Amer.*

ED MURPHY
Sun

FRANK O'NEILL
Journal

CHARLES PARKER
World-Tel.

GEORGE PHAIR
American

R. F. POTTS
BB Mag.

JIMMY POWERS
Daily News

RUD RENNIE
Her.-Trib.

GRANTLAND RICE
NAM, Her.-Trib.

CHARLES SEGAR
Mirror

WM. SLOCUM
American

KEN SMITH
Graphic, Mirror

ED SODEN
BB Mag.

GERALD SYLVESTER
Post

RICHARDS VIDMER
Her.-Trib.

JOE VILA
Sun

FRANK WALLACE
Mirror, Daily News

CHRISTY WALSH
Walsh Synd.

DAVIS WALSH
INS

JOE WILLIAMS
Telegram, World-Tel.

WILBUR WOOD
Sun

HARRY FORBES *Daily News*
STANLEY FRANK *Post*
ED FRAYNE *American*
FORD FRICK *Journal, NLSB*
HARRY FRIEND *World, Press Pub.*
F. FUKUMOTO *Mainichi*
PEDRO GALIANA *Diario*
PAUL GALLICO *Daily News*
FRANK GETTY *UP*
JAMES GIAUQUE *Times*
HARRY GLASER *Journal*
LESTER GOODMAN *AMEBB*
MURRAY GOODMAN
HERB GOREN *Sun*
ALAN GOULD *AP*
DILLON GRAHAM *AP*
DAVE GROSSBERG *AMEBB*
BERT GUMPERT *Bronx News*
BILLY HANNA *Her.-Trib.*
CLAIRE HARE *Post*
JAMES HARRISON *Telegraph*
WM. HENNIGAN *World, Mirror*
WALTER HOBAN *Mirror*
CHAS. HOERTER *Daily News*
LEONARD HOWARD *Telegraph*
MARSHALL HUNT *Daily News*
JAMES HURLEY *Mirror*
C. W. HUSTON *Post*
HERBERT IGOE *Journal-Amer.*
KEVIN JONES *Daily News*
JAMES KAHN *Graphic, Sun*
RAYMOND KELLY *Times*
GEORGE KENNEY *Daily News*
JOHN KIERAN *Times*

GEO. KIRKSEY *UP*
AL LANEY *Her.-Trib.*
HAL LANIGAN *Telegraph*
FRANK LEONARD *Adams*
PEDRO LLANUZA *World-Tel., United*
STAN LOMAX *Bronx News*
ARTHUR MANN *Post, World*
ALEX MAVER *United*
PAT McDONOUGH *World-Tel.*
W. O. McGEEHAN *Her.-Trib.*
JOSEPH McGURK *American*
HENRY McLEMORE *UP*
FRANK MENKE *King*
DREW MIDDLETON *AP*
JACK MILEY *AP, King*
PIERRE MINER *UP*
JERRY MITCHELL *Post*
JOHN MONAHAN *Post*
ART MOND *Telegraph*
MORTON MOSS *INS*
WILLARD MULLIN *World-Tel.*
SAM MURPHY *Sun*
WILL MURPHY *Daily News*
FEG MURRAY *MNS, Cons. Pl.*
HARRY NASH *Post*
ED NEAL *AP*
HARRY NEWMAN *Box. World*
GEORGE PALMER *Telegraph*
TOM PAPROCKI *AP*
DAN PARKER *Mirror*
ART PATTERSON *Her.-Trib.*
WESTBROOK PEGLER *Chi. Trib.*
ART PERRIN *Her.-Trib.*
ROY POPKIN *Daily Worker*

JAMES RAHN *Daily News*
JOHN REARDON *Times*
QUENTIN REYNOLDS *Collier's*
PAT ROBINSON *Daily News, INS*
LESTER RODNEY *Daily Worker*
PAT ROSA *Post*
DAMON RUNYON *American, King*
GARRY SCHUMACHER *Journal-Amer.*
HARRY SCHUMACHER *Daily News*
IRA SEEBACHER *Telegraph*
HENRY SINGER *Bronx News*
JACK SMITH *Daily News*
LAWRENCE SPIKER *Times*
J. B. STARKEY *Telegraph*
GUS STEIGER *World, Mirror*
F. A. STEIMER *Sun*
DIXON STEWART *UP*
HENRY SUPER *UP*
SABURO SUZUKI *Mainichi*
GAYLE TALBOT *AP*
HOMER THORNE *Post*
GEORGE TREVOR *Sun*
WALT TRUMBULL *NAPA*
HY TURKIN *Daily News*
MURRAY TYNAN *Her.-Trib.*
GUS UHLMAN *Post*
JOE VAL *World-Tel.*
VERNON VAN NESS *Times*
WILL WEDGE *Sun*
JOHN WHEELER *Bell*
STAN WOODWARD *Her.-Trib.*
ED ZELTNER *Mirror*

J. P. ABRAMSON *Her.-Trib.*
JACK ABROMOWITZ *Forward*
CASWELL ADAMS *Her.-Trib.*
LES AVERY *UP*
BUGS BAER *American*
WOOD BALLARD *World*
HERB BARKER *AP*
BRYAN BELL *AP*
JOE BIHLER *Walsh Synd.*
ROGER BIRTWELL *Daily News*
CHRISTIE BOHNSACK *Radio News*
HUGH BRADLEY *Post*
CARL BRANDEBURY *AP*

WM. BRANDT *Times*
ED BRIETZ *AP*
WM. BRIORDY *Times*
BOZEMAN BULGER *World*
HARDIN BURNLEY *King*
HAROLD BURR *Post*
LEWIS BURTON *American*
NOEL BUSCH *Daily News*
T. M. BYRNE *Post*
CULLEN CAIN *NLSB*
FOREST CAIN *World*
DAVID CAMERER *World-Tel.*
L. S. CAMERON *UP*

HARRY CAPLAN *Graphic*
MAX CASE *Journal*
LEONARD COHEN *Post*
BOB CONSIDINE *Mirror*
ROBT. COOKE *Her.-Trib.*
HARRY CROSS *Her.-Trib.*
JACK CUDDY *UP*
ROBT. CURTIS *Times*
ARTHUR DALEY *Times*
GEORGE DALEY *World, Her.-Trib.*
G. HERB DALEY *World*
CHAS. DEXTER *Daily Worker*
PETER DOLAN *Sun*

ED DOOLEY *Sun*
JOHN DREBINGER *Times*
JOHN EBINGER *Daily News*
GUS EDSON *Post*
LOUIS EFFRAT *Times*
AL MUNRO ELIAS *AMEBB*
WALTER ELIAS *AMEBB*
WILTON FARNSWORTH *Journal*
SID FEDER *AP*
H. FERELSON *UP*
GEORGE FINLEY *King*
NAT FLEISCHER *Ring Mag.*
ADOLFO FONT *El Pais*

THE BROADCASTERS:

GRAHAM McNAMEE
NBC, WJZ, WEAF
1930-39

FORD BOND
NBC
-1934-

TED HUSING
CBS, WABC
1930-39

BOAKE CARTER
NBC
-1935-

MAJOR NETWORKS (NYC BASED):
Columbia Broadcasting System (CBS)
National Broadcasting Company (NBC)
MUTUAL Radio Network

ARCH McDONALD
WABC 1939

MEL ALLEN
WABC 1939

GARNETT MARKS
WABC 1939

PAT BARNES
RALPH DUMKE
DON DUNPHY
WAITE HOYT
ANDREW STANTON
BILL STERN
DON WILSON

NEW YORK—Polo Grounds

The Giants' fabled horseshoe served as home for some pretty good teams and outstanding players in the 1930s.

A view of the 1934 All-Star game crowd, looking across to the main grandstand and the heights of Coogan's Bluff from distant center field

A close-up scene of the grandstand near the right field corner

Action in the 1933 World Series between Washington and the "Jints," as seen from behind home plate

A closer look at dead center field and clubhouse building in 1934, before it featured its prominent advertising sign of later years

NEW YORK—Yankee Stadium

A bird's-eye view of the "House that Ruth built" in 1932, when the Babe was still a Yankee

A view from the right field corner during the 1937 World Series—Yanks vs. Giants

A giant right center field scoreboard was among the largest in the majors, posting complete line scores of games in both leagues.

The right field bleachers, or "Ruthville" in 1933

A tense moment in the 1939 All-Star game with Bob Feller on the mound and Arky Vaughan at bat

A 1939 aerial view clearly shows the 1936 CF bleacher reconstruction and the 1937 extension of the grandstand around the RF corner (lighter colored roof)

PHILADELPHIA 1930-39

The city skyline from Rittenhouse Square

The new Post Office and Pennsylvania RR station

Philadelphia's Municipal Airport in the 1930s

Market Street looking west toward City Hall

The new Delaware River Bridge, connecting Philadelphia and Camden, New Jersey

PHILADELPHIA 1930-39 (continued)

THE BASEBALL REPORTERS:

WM. BRANDT
Ledger

WM. DOOLY
Record

JAMES ISAMINGER
Inquirer

IVAN PETERMAN
Bulletin, Inquirer

JOE TUMELTY
Ledger

DON BASSENFELDER *Camden Courier*
STAN BAUMGARTNER *Inquirer*
CHAS. BELL *Inquirer*
PAUL BUSCH *Tageblatt*
JOE DAY *Bulletin*
ED DELANEY *Daily News*
DONALD DONAGHEY *Bulletin*
JOE DUGAN *Record*
WM. DUNCAN *Ledger*
JAMES GANTZ *Ledger, Record*
NORMAN GINSBERG *Jewish World*
J. HERBERT GOOD *Main Line*
S. O. GRAULEY *Inquirer*
CLAIRE HARE *Ledger*
RAY HILL *Bulletin*
EDDIE HOGAN *Record*

AL HOROWITZ *Ledger*
MYRON HUFF *Ledger*
OTIS HULLEBERG *Record*
MANLEY JACKSON *Record*
ROSS KAUFFMAN *Bulletin*
JOHN KOLBMAN *Ledger, Record*
SAM LAIRD *Record*
LEON LEVIN *Polish World*
GORDON MACKAY *Record*
FRANK McCRACKEN *Ledger*
LANSING McCURLEY *Daily News*
JOE McGLYNN *Ledger*
JOHN McINTYRE *Daily News*
STONEY McLINN *Ledger, Record*
JOHN NOLAN *Bulletin*
ROBERT PAUL *Daily News*

WM. PHILLIPS *Reach Guide*
E. J. POLLOCK *Ledger*
HARRY ROBERT *Bulletin*
FRANK RYAN *Camden Post*
TOM RYAN *Camden Post*
BOB SENSENDERFER *Bulletin*
TOM SHRIVER *Record*
W. W. SMITH *Record*
T. VON ZIEKURSCH *Daily News*
CHAS. VOORHIS *Ledger*
DAVIS WALSH *Record*
JOE WASNEY, Jr. *UP*
JOHN WEBSTER *Inquirer*
ART WEST *Record*
F. W. YEUTTER *Bulletin*

THE NEWSPAPERS:

THE BROADCASTERS:

BILLY DYER
WCAU 1930-39

JOHN KOLBMANN

STONY McLINN
WIP 1935-39

DOLLY STARK
WIP 1936

BYRUM SAAM
WIP, WCAU
1938-39

JOE TUMELTY

ANDREW STANTON

SAM BALTAR
DICK CAUFFMAN
HAROLD DAVIS

LANCE McCURLEY
HAL SIMONDS
IRA WALSH

PHILADELPHIA—Baker Bowl 1930-38

An aerial photo clearly reveals the disproportionately short RF wall

An older postcard view from the teens shows how little the park had changed through the years.

The main entrance to the grandstand at Huntingdon & 15th—an octagonal tower structure that dated back to the 19th century

The left field corner, adjacent to Lehigh St.

Brooklyn's Dolph Camilli, an ex-Phillie, celebrates his return to Baker Bowl with an opening day homer in 1938, the old park's final season of existence.

The Broad Street entrance to the grandstand (below)

The celebrated LIFEBUOY billboard that covered the high right field wall until it was painted over in 1935

PHILADELPHIA—Shibe Park

An aerial view of Shibe Park c. 1929 before the main grandstand was enlarged and heightened in 1930

An exterior view of the main entrance behind home plate c. 1930

An older postcard view illustrates the attractive architectural appeal of the park's exterior.

Up to 1935, the rows of flats facing the RF fence provided a "free" view of game action.

Looking down at a packed grandstand over the 3rd base dugout during the 1930 World Series

A virtually empty grandstand was all too common a sight during the dark days of the Great Depression and losing Philadelphia teams.

Finally in 1935, A's management blocked the free view with a high fence in RF. Note the cluster of speaker horns above the scoreboard—Babe Ruth was cheated of a home run in 1930 when he bounced a long drive off these horns for a ground rule double.

PITTSBURGH 1930-39

A view of the city from Castle Shannon incline

Liberty Bridge and tunnel entrance

Allegheny Municipal Airport from the air

Pitt Stadium, home of the University of Pittsburgh's gridiron Panthers

Allegheny Airport Terminal Building

PITTSBURGH 1930-39 (continued)

THE NEWSPAPERS:

THE BASEBALL REPORTERS:

ED BALINGER
Post-Gazette

HAVEY BOYLE
Post-Gazette

CHAS. DOYLE
Sun-Tel.

HARRY KECK
Sun-Tel.

JAMES LONG
Sun-Tel.

CHESTER SMITH
Press

VOLNEY WALSH
Press

ALBERT ABRAMS *Post-Gazette*
FRED ALGER *Post-Gazette*
DAN BENJAMIN *Sun-Tel.*
JACK BERGER *Press*
LES BIEDERMAN *Press*
TOM BIRKS *Sun-Tel.*
CLAIRE BURCKY *Press*
JOHN CARNEY *Tri-State*
JESS CARVER *Sun-Tel.*
RALPH DAVIS *Press*
WM. FARRELL *Press*
W. W. FORSTER *Press*
R. H. GALLIVAN *Press*
JOHN GRUBER
JOHN HERNON *Tri-State*
JOE HUHN *Tri-State, Press*
GEORGE JENNINGS *Jennings NB*

PAUL KURTZ *Press*
FRED LANDUCCI *Press*
JULIUS LEVIN *Sun-Tel.*
JAMES McSHANE *E. L. Trib.*
JAMES MILLER *Sun-Tel.*
JAMES MURRAY *Press*
ROBT. PFARR *UP*
GILBERT REMLEY *Post-Gazette*
W. P. SCHRAGEN *Jennings NB*
JACK SELL *Post-Gazette*
CARL SHATTO *Sun-Tel.*
JOHN SIKES *Press*
BERT TAGGART *Post-Gazette*
REGIS WELSH *Tri-State, Press*
FRED WERTENBACH *Press*

THE BROADCASTERS:

WALT SICKLES
WWSW 1934

JIMMY MURRAY
KQV, WCAE 1934-39

PAT PATTERSON
KQV 1935

JACK CRADDOCK
WWSW 1936

JACK HOLLISTER
CHESTER SMITH
JOE TUCKER

TONY WAKEMAN
KDKA
1933-36

ED SPRAGUE

ROSEY ROWSWELL
KDKA, WWSW
1939

PITTSBURGH—Forbes Field

A postcard view of Forbes Field, one of the early classic parks—opened for business in 1909

An aerial view, probably from the '20s, showing some of the pleasant surroundings of Schenley Park

The main entrance at Bouquet & Sennott

An early 1909 scene from behind home plate just before construction was complete. The new steel beam framework details are clearly illustrated.

A 1933 view from over the right field fence. A bleacher section has been added in outfield territory.

ST. LOUIS 1930-39

An airplane view of the downtown business section looking northwest

The double-decked Free Bridge over the Mississippi, connecting St. Louis and Illinois. It was later renamed the MacArthur Bridge.

Sunken Gardens, Christ Church Cathedral, and the Public Library

The then-new St. Louis Arena

ST. LOUIS 1930-39 (continued)

THE NEWSPAPERS:

THE BASEBALL REPORTERS:

RICHARD FARRINGTON *Times, Sp. News*   **JAMES GOULD** *Post-Disp.*   **MARTIN HALEY** *Globe-Dem.*   **SID KEENER** *Star, Star-Times*   **J. G. T. SPINK** *Sp. News*

J. ROY STOCKTON *Post-Disp.*   **GLEN WALLER** *Globe-Dem.*   **ED WRAY** *Post-Disp.*

FRANKLYN ADAMS *Sp. News*
L. H. ADDINGTON *Sp. News*
FRED BAILEY *UP*
DON BASENFELDER *Sp. News*
EARL BRADY *E. St. L. Journal*
E. G. BRANDS *Sp. News*
ROBT. BURNES *Globe-Dem.*
LELAND CHESLEY *UP*
CHAS. COMFORT *Times*
GEORGE CRISSEN *UP*
L. C. DAVIS *Post-Disp.*
ALFRED DEPAULI *Sp. News*
JUSTIN FAHERTY *Globe-Dem.*
C. T. FELKER *Sp. News*
RAY GILLESPIE *Star, Star-Times*
DAMON KERBY *Post-Disp.*
GENE KESSLER *Sp. News*
ERNEST LANIGAN *Sp. News*

RALPH LEON *Globe-Dem.*
W. J. McGOOGAN *Post-Disp.*
HARRY McKANNA *Post-Disp.*
L. A. McMASTERS *Post-Disp.*
DENT McSKIMMING *Post Disp.*
ROBT. MORRISON *Post-Disp.*
SAM MUCHNICK *Times*
ALBERT OFFER *Star*
MARION PARKER *Globe-Dem.*
ARTHUR PLAMBECK *Sp. News*
ALAN PRICE *Globe-Dem.*
E. L. RAY *Globe-Dem.*
RALPH RAYFIELD *Globe-Dem.*
GEORGE REDMOND *Star*
CHARLES REGAN *Star, Star-Times*
FRANCIS REILLEY *Globe-Dem.*
PAUL RICKART *Sp. News*
R. L. RUTLEDGE *Globe-Dem.*
JOHN SHERIDAN *Star-Times*
MAURICE SHEVLIN *Globe-Dem.*
CULLEN SMITH *UP*
RAYMOND SMITH *Globe-Dem.*
WALTER SMITH *Star*
W. V. TIETJEN *Star-Times*
ELLIS VEECH *E. St. L. Journal*
HERMAN WECKE *Post-Disp.*
FRANZ WIPPOLD *Star-Times*

THE BROADCASTERS:

BOB THOMAS KWK 1930-34   **TOM PATRICK**   **DAVE PARKS** WIL   **JOHNNY O'HARA** KWK 1939

FRANCE LAUX KMOX, CBS 1930-39

JOHN HARRINGTON KWK 1935

GEORGE SISLER KWK 1936
RAY SCHMIDT KWK 1934-36

DON BASENFELDER
JIM BOTTOMLEY
CY CASPER
JIMMY CONZELMAN
BILL DURNEY
FRANK ESCHEN

HERB MacGREADY
LLOYD McMASTER
NEIL NORMAN
BART SLATTERY
J. ROY STOCKTON

ST. LOUIS—Sportsman's Park

A hand-colored postcard view of the Browns' & Cardinals' home field

A special day of tribute was the occasion in 1938 for visiting Phils rookie Emmett Mueller, a St. Louis native son. The brand-new giant scoreboard in left field is clearly on display in the background.

A packed house in 1932 paid tribute to newly named Cardinal pilot Frankie Frisch.

A staged footrace in 1931 was won by Brooklyn's rookie Van Lingle Mungo (on far right). The background reveals a good view of the left field corner and old scoreboard.

An overflow crowd in 1931 is encouraged by Cards outfielder George Watkins to move back along the RF fence so the game could commence.

This view looking toward CF in 1931 shows Browns first baseman Jack Burns about to complete a circuit clout.

By 1940, the already huge scoreboard was enlarged even further with added billboards and new clock advertisement.

WASHINGTON D.C. 1930-39

The Washington Mall as it looked in 1937, looking west

Capitol Park Fountain and the Capitol Building

Children and their toy boats alongside the reflecting pool in the shadow of the Lincoln Memorial

Washington's National Airport terminal as it looked in the thirties

Union Station as seen from Capitol Park

WASHINGTON D.C. 1930-39 (continued)

THE NEWSPAPERS:

THE BASEBALL REPORTERS:

| VINCENT FLAHERTY *Herald* | JOHN KELLER *Star* | SHIRLEY POVICH *Post* | DENMAN THOMPSON *Star* | GARRETT WATERS *Times* | FRANK YOUNG *Post* |

LEWIS ATCHISON *Post*
JAMES BERRYMAN *Star*
BOB CONSIDINE *Herald*
AL COSTELLO *Herald*
FRANCIS CRONAN *Daily News, Herald*
TIM DOERER *Star*
BEN DULANEY *Post*
GEORGE GARNER *Herald*
ED GILMORE *AP*
WM. GOODE *Daily News*
DILLON GRAHAM *AP*
WALTER HAIGHT *Post*
B. C. HARTER *Herald*
KEN HARTER *Times*

BURTON HAWKINS *Star*
DICK HOLLANDER *Daily News*
JOE HOLMAN *Herald*
WM. HOTTEL *Star*
SID KATZELL *Times*
CHARLES KENNY *Times*
RICHARD McCANN *Daily News*
BOB McCORMICK *Daily News*
KIRK MILLER *Times*
DICK MOORE *Daily News*
BRYAN MORSE *Herald*
RAY MOULDEN *Daily News*
FRANK O'NEILL *Times*
JOHN O'ROURKE *Daily News*

A. A. POVICH *Post*
AL RECK *Daily News*
ROCKFORD RILEY *Daily News*
HENRY RODIER *Bulletin*
ROBT. RUARK *Daily News*
SAM RUBINTON *Herald*
GINO SIMI *Times*
GEORGE SIMPSON *Times*
FRANCIS STAN *Star*
ED SUSSDORF *Herald*
R. D. THOMAS *Star*
JACK TULLOCH *Alex. Gaz.*

THE BROADCASTERS:

ARCH McDONALD
WJSV 1934-38

WALTER JOHNSON
WMAL, WJSV 1936-39

RUSS HODGES
-1938-

BILL COYLE
WMAL

WASHINGTON—Griffith Stadium

Griffith Stadium, originally rebuilt in steel and concrete after a disastrous fire razed its wooden predecessor in 1911. It had the longest LF line in major league baseball.

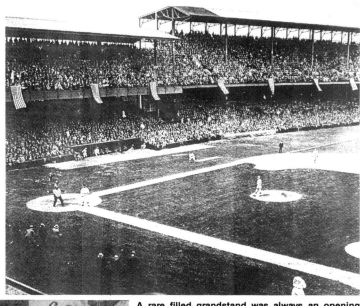

A rare filled grandstand was always an opening-game treat for the usually hapless Nationals.

A view from the RF corner in 1931. Note the loudspeaker racks on the grandstand roof.

A 1931 game action shot gives a glimpse of some outfield billboards of that period.

Another view from 1931 shows the mammoth left field bleacher section in the background.

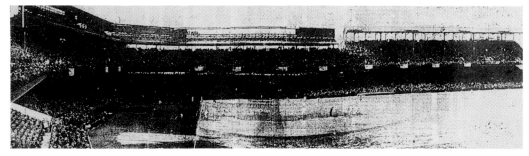

A temporary press deck was built on the grandstand roof to accommodate the media during the 1933 pennant-winning season. It remained for several more seasons.

Players scramble for FDR's opening-game toss in 1936.

THE TEAMS

Boston Braves/Bees

FRONT OFFICE:

EMIL FUCHS
President
1930-35

CHARLES F. ADAMS
VP 1930-33

FRED MITCHELL
Business Mgr.
1930-35

ALBERT M. LYON
Treasurer 1930-33

E. P. CUNNINGHAM
Secretary 1930-35

WESTON W. ADAMS
VP 1934-35
Traveling
Secretary 1933

BRUCE WETMORE
Treasurer 1933-35

PAUL G. CURLEY
Traveling Secretary
1934-35

RALPH DELOID
Asst. Treasurer
1936-39

JOHN J. QUINN
Secretary 1936-39

J. A. "BOB" QUINN
President 1936-39

LEO GOULSTON
VP 1936-39

OSCAR L. HORTON
Treasurer 1936-39

C. H. INNES
VP 1936-39

GEORGE "DUFFY" LEWIS
Traveling Secretary
1937-39

FIELD MANAGERS:

BILL McKECHNIE
1930-37

CASEY STENGEL
1938-39

COACHES:

GEORGE SISLER 1930
HANK GOWDY 1930-37
JOHNNY EVERS 1931-32
DUFFY LEWIS 1931-35
JEWEL ENS 1934
MIKE KELLY 1937-39
GEORGE KELLY 1938-39

THE PLAYERS:

BILLY RHIEL
third baseman
1930

JIM WELSH
outfielder
1930

GEORGE SISLER
first baseman 1930

**RALPH
"BUZZ" BOYLE**
outfielder
1930

HANK GOWDY
catcher 1930

**WILLIAM
"RED" ROLLINGS**
infielder
1930

KEN JONES
pitcher 1930

BILL DUNLAP
outfielder 1930

Boston Braves/Bees (continued)

BURLEIGH GRIMES
pitcher 1930

BERNIE JAMES
second baseman
1930

BUSTER CHATHAM
infielder 1930-31

JOHNNY NEUN
first baseman
1930-31

BILL CRONIN
catcher
1930-31

WALLY BERGER
outfielder 1930-37

HARRY
"SOCKS" SEIBOLD
pitcher 1930-33

LANCE RICHBOURG
outfielder 1930-31

GENE ROBERTSON
third baseman 1930

BRUCE
CUNNINGHAM
pitcher
1930-32

BEN CANTWELL
pitcher 1930-36

JOHNNY COONEY
pitcher 1930
first base, outfield
1938-39

FRED MAGUIRE
second baseman
1930-31

ED BRANDT
pitcher
1930-35

BILL SHERDEL
pitcher 1930-32

BAILEY
"EARL" CLARK
outfielder
1930-33

TOM ZACHARY
pitcher 1930-34

BOB BROWN
pitcher 1930-36

BOB SMITH
pitcher
1930, 1933-37

FRED FRANKHOUSE
pitcher 1930-35, 1939

Boston Braves/Bees (continued)

RANDY MOORE
utility 1930-35

**WALTER
"RABBIT" MARANVILLE**
infielder 1930-33, 1935

AL SPOHRER
catcher 1930-35

AL BOOL
catcher
1931

EARL SHEELY
first baseman 1931

BILL URBANSKI
shortstop 1931-37

BUCKY WALTERS
infielder 1931-32

BILL HUNNEFIELD
second baseman 1931

RAY MOSS
pitcher
1931

BILL McAFEE
pitcher 1931

**ROBERT "RED"
WORTHINGTON**
outfielder
1931-34

BILL DREESEN
third baseman
1931

HAL HAID
pitcher
1931

PAT VELTMAN
catcher 1931

JOHN SCALZI
pinch hitter 1931

CHARLIE WILSON
third baseman
1931

WES SCHULMERICH
outfielder 1931-33

**THOMAS
"BILL" AKERS**
infielder
1932

FRED LEACH
outfielder 1932

Boston Braves/Bees (continued)

JOHN SCHULTE
catcher 1932

OSCAR
"OX" ECKHARDT
outfielder 1932

HORACE
"HOD" FORD
infielder
1932-33

ED FALLENSTEIN
(VALESTIN)
pitcher 1933

ART SHIRES
first baseman
1932

HUB PRUETT
pitcher 1932

WILFRED
"FRITZ" KNOTHE
infielder 1932-33

WILLIAM
"PINKY" HARGRAVE
catcher 1932-33

BUCK JORDAN
first baseman
1932-37

PINKY WHITNEY
third baseman
1933-36

RAY STARR
pitcher 1933

HAROLD LEE
outfielder
1933-36

HUCK BETTS
pitcher
1932-35

LEO MANGUM
pitcher 1932-35

ROBERT
"DUTCH" HOLLAND
outfielder
1932-33

AL WRIGHT
second baseman
1933

DICK GYSELMAN
infielder
1933-34

JOE MOWRY
outfielder
1933-35

Boston Braves/Bees (continued)

SHANTY HOGAN
catcher 1933-35

MARTY McMANUS
infielder 1934

DAN McGEE
shortstop 1934

**JAMES
"JUMBO" ELLIOTT**
pitcher 1934

FLINT RHEM
pitcher 1934-35

LES MALLON
utility 1934-35

BABE RUTH
outfielder 1935

RAY MUELLER
catcher 1935-38

**RUPERT
"TOMMY" THOMPSON**
first base, outfield
1933-36

**RICHARD OLIVER
(BARRETT)**
pitcher 1934

**CLARENCE
PICKREL**
pitcher 1934

ELBIE FLETCHER
first baseman 1934-39

**JOHNNIE TYLER
(TYLKA)**
outfielder 1934-35

**JAMES
"TINY" CHAPLIN**
pitcher 1936

ED MORIARTY
second baseman
1935-36

LARRY BENTON
pitcher 1935

JOE COSCARART
infielder 1935-36

**AL BLANCHE
(BELANGIO)**
pitcher 1935-36

BILL LEWIS
catcher 1935-36

Boston Braves/Bees (continued)

DANNY
MacFAYDEN
pitcher
1935-39

ANDY PILNEY
pinch-hitter 1936

FABIAN KOWALIK
pitcher 1936

JOHN BABICH
pitcher 1936

GENE MOORE
outfielder 1936-38

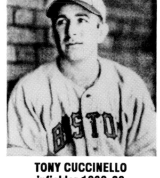

GUY BUSH
pitcher
1936-37

TONY CUCCINELLO
infielder 1936-39

MICKEY HASLIN
infielder 1936

WAYNE OSBORNE
pitcher 1936

AL LOPEZ
catcher
1936-39

HAROLD
"RABBIT" WARSTLER
infielder 1936-39

BOB REIS
utility
1936-38

JOHN LANNING
pitcher
1936-39

ART DOLL
catcher, pitcher
1935-36, 1938

AMBY MURRAY
pitcher 1936

JAMES
"IRISH" McCLOSKEY
pitcher 1936

GENE FORD
pitcher 1936

ERLING
"SWEDE" LARSEN
second baseman
1936

KEN WEAFER
pitcher 1936

RAY BENGE
pitcher 1936

WILLIAM
"ROY" WEIR
pitcher
1936-39

TOMMY
THEVENOW
shortstop 1937

FRANK McGOWAN
outfielder 1937

VIC FRASIER
pitcher 1937

IRA HUTCHINSON
pitcher 1937-38

Boston Braves/Bees (continued)

GIL ENGLISH
third baseman
1937-38

VINCE DiMAGGIO
outfielder 1937-38

LOU FETTE
pitcher
1937-39

DEBS GARMS
third base, outfield
1937-39

JOE WALSH
shortstop
1938

BOB KAHLE
infielder
1938

JIM TURNER
pitcher
1937-39

MILT SHOFFNER
pitcher 1937-39

RALPH McLEOD
outfielder 1938

JOHNNY NIGGELING
pitcher 1938

CHARLES "BUTCH" SUTCLIFFE
catcher 1938

JOHNNY RIDDLE
catcher 1937-38

ART KENNEY
pitcher 1938

JOE STRIPP
third baseman
1938

HARL MAGGERT
outfielder 1938

JIM HITCHCOCK
shortstop 1938

FRANK GABLER
pitcher 1937-38

ROY JOHNSON
outfielder
1937-38

EDDIE MAYO
infielder
1937-38

TOMMY REIS
pitcher 1938

Boston Braves/Bees (continued)

MAX WEST
outfielder
1938-39

**AL
"HIKER" MORAN**
pitcher 1938-39

**JOHN
"RED" BARKLEY**
infielder 1939

AL SIMMONS
outfielder 1939

JOHN HILL
infielder
1939

BILL POSEDEL
pitcher 1939

RALPH HODGIN
outfielder 1939

BUDDY HASSETT
first base, outfield
1939

**RICHARD
"LIEF" ERRICKSON**
pitcher 1938-39

TOM EARLEY
pitcher 1938-39

PHIL MASI
catcher 1939

SIBBY SISTI
infielder
1939

OTTO HUBER
infielder 1939

MIKE BALAS
pitcher 1938

CHET ROSS
outfielder
1939

AL VEIGEL
pitcher 1939

CHET CLEMENS
outfielder 1939

JOE SULLIVAN
pitcher 1939

Boston Braves/Bees (continued)

EDDIE MILLER
shortstop 1939

**WHITEY
WIETELMANN**
shortstop 1939

BILL SCHUSTER
infielder 1939

**STAN ANDREWS
(ANDRUSKEWICZ)**
catcher 1939

JIMMY OUTLAW
outfielder 1939

**CARVEL
"BAMA" ROWELL**
outfielder 1939

HANK MAJESKI
third baseman
1939

**GEORGE
BARNICLE**
pitcher 1939

JOE CALLAHAN
pitcher 1939

UNIFORMS:

1930 sleeve patch

1930

Boston Red Sox

FRONT OFFICE:

J. A. "BOB" QUINN
President 1930-33
Treasurer 1930-33

E. M. SCHOENBORN
VP 1930-33

HIRAM W. MASON
Secretary 1930-33

JOHN J. QUINN
Secretary 1931-33

THOMAS YAWKEY
President 1933-39

PHILIP TROY
Secretary 1930-33
Traveling Secretary
1934-39

FREDERICK DEFOE
Secretary 1933-39

EDDIE COLLINS
Vice President,
Treasurer, Gen. Mgr.
1933-39

FIELD MANAGERS:

HEINIE WAGNER
1930

SHANO COLLINS
1931-32

MARTY McMANUS
1932-33

BUCKY HARRIS
1934

JOE CRONIN
1935-39

COACHES:

JACK McCALLISTER 1930
RUDY HULSWITT 1931-33
HUGH DUFFY 1932
TOM DALY 1933-39
BIBB FALK 1934
JACK ONSLOW 1934
AL SCHACHT 1935-36
HERB PENNOCK 1936-39
BING MILLER 1937

THE PLAYERS:

PHIL TODT
first baseman
1930

BILL REGAN
second baseman
1930

JOHN HEVING
catcher 1930

FRANK BUSHEY
pitcher 1930

JIM GALVIN
pinch-hitter
1930

BILL BARRETT
outfielder 1930

GEORGE SMITH
pitcher 1930

JOE CICERO
third base,
outfield
1930

Boston Red Sox (continued)

CHARLES
"RED" RUFFING
pitcher 1930

JACK RUSSELL
pitcher
1930-32, 1936

BILL SWEENEY
first baseman
1930-31

MILT GASTON
pitcher 1930-31

HOD LISENBEE
pitcher 1930-32

OTIS MILLER
utility 1930-32

EARL WEBB
outfielder
1930-32

"TOM" JOHN WINSETT
outfielder
1930-31, 1933

CEDRIC DURST
outfielder 1930

BILL NARLESKI
infielder 1930

HAL RHYNE
shortstop
1930-32

BOBBY REEVES
utility 1930-31

CHARLEY BERRY
catcher 1930-32

ED CONNOLLY
catcher 1930-32

BEN SHIELDS
pitcher 1930

CHARLIE SMALL
outfielder 1930

ED MORRIS
pitcher 1930-31

RUSS SCARRITT
outfielder 1930-31

JACK ROTHROCK
utility 1930-32

HAROLD
"RABBIT" WARSTLER
infielder 1930-33

Boston Red Sox (continued)

DANNY MacFAYDEN
pitcher
1930-32

TOM OLIVER
outfielder
1930-33

ED "BULL" DURHAM
pitcher 1930-32

AL VAN CAMP
utility 1931-32

JIM BRILLHEART
pitcher 1931

BILL McWILLIAMS
pinch-hitter 1931

MARTY McMANUS
infielder 1931-33
(manager 1932-33)

MARV OLSON
second baseman
1931-33

HOWIE STORIE
catcher 1931-32

BOB KLINE
pitcher
1930-33

ALBERT "OLLIE" MARQUARDT
second baseman
1931

BILL MARSHALL
second baseman
1931

JOHN SMITH
first baseman
1931

HAROLD "MUDDY" RUEL
catcher 1931

EUGENE RYE (MERCANTELLI)
outfielder
1931

URBANE PICKERING
infielder 1931-32

PAT CREEDEN
second baseman
1931

GEORGE STUMPF
outfielder
1931-33

Boston Red Sox (continued)

WILCY MOORE
pitcher 1931-32

LARRY BOERNER
pitcher 1932

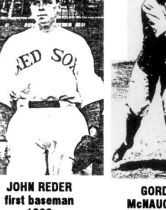

JOHN REDER
first baseman
1932

GORDON McNAUGHTON
pitcher 1932

ROY JOHNSON
outfielder
1932-35

JUD McLAUGHLIN
pitcher 1931-33

JOHN LUCAS
outfielder
1931-32

ED GALLAGHER
pitcher 1932

ANDY SPOGNARDI
infielder 1932

JOHN MICHAELS
pitcher 1932

JOHN WATWOOD
first base, outfield
1932-33

BOB WEILAND
pitcher 1932-34

DALE ALEXANDER
first baseman
1932-33

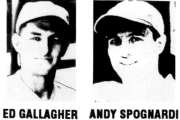

JOHN WELCH
pitcher
1932-36

PETE APPLETON (JABLONOWSKI)
pitcher 1932

IVY ANDREWS
pitcher 1932-33

BENNIE TATE
catcher 1932

PETE DONOHUE
pitcher 1932

REGIS LEHENY
pitcher 1932

Boston Red Sox (continued)

SMEAD JOLLEY
outfielder
1932-33

JOHNNY GOOCH
catcher 1933

JOHN G.
"DUSTY" RHODES
pitcher 1932-35

BARNEY
FRIBERG
utility 1933

JOHNNY
HODAPP
infielder
1933

LLOYD BROWN
pitcher 1933

CURT
FULLERTON
pitcher
1933

LOU LEGETT
catcher
1933-35

ALLEN
"DUSTY" COOKE
outfielder
1933-36

GREG MULLEAVY
infielder 1933

GEORGE PIPGRAS
pitcher 1933-35

FRED MULLER
infielder
1933-34

BUCKY WALTERS
infielder 1933-34

JOE JUDGE
first baseman
1933-34

BOB FOTHERGILL
outfielder 1933

BOB SEEDS
outfielder
1933-34

MIKE MEOLA
pitcher
1933, 1936

MERVYN SHEA
catcher 1933

HANK JOHNSON
pitcher 1933-35

Boston Red Sox (continued)

RICK FERRELL
catcher 1933-37

BILL WERBER
infielder 1933-36

CHALMER
"BILL" CISSELL
infielder
1934

LYN LARY
infielder
1934

JOE MULLIGAN
pitcher 1934

DANIEL
"GORDIE" HINKLE
catcher 1934

ARTHUR
"SKINNY" GRAHAM
outfielder
1934-35

DICK PORTER
outfielder 1934

MEL ALMADA
outfielder 1933-37

ED MORGAN
first baseman
1934

DONALD
"RED" KELLETT
infielder
1934

WES FERRELL
pitcher 1934-37

GEORGE
"RUBE" WALBERG
pitcher 1934-37

GEORGE HOCKETTE
pitcher 1934-35

HERB PENNOCK
pitcher 1934

JOHN
"SPIKE" MERENA
pitcher 1934

AL NIEMIEC
second baseman
1934

CARL REYNOLDS
outfielder
1934-35

Boston Red Sox (continued)

MAX BISHOP
infielder
1934-35

**JULIUS
"MOOSE" SOLTERS**
outfielder
1934-35

LEFTY GROVE
pitcher 1934-39

JOHN KRONER
infielder
1935-36

**EDMUND
"BING" MILLER**
outfielder
1935-36

JOE CRONIN
shortstop 1935-39
(manager 1935-39)

**JOE
CASCARELLA**
pitcher
1935-36

**ELLSWORTH
"BABE" DAHLGREN**
first baseman
1935-36

**HY
VANDENBERG**
pitcher 1935

**EDWIN
"DIB" WILLIAMS**
infielder
1935

**FRITZ
OSTERMUELLER**
pitcher 1934-39

DOC FARRELL
second baseman
1935

GEORGE DICKEY
catcher 1935-36

MOE BERG
catcher 1935-39

JACK WILSON
pitcher
1935-39

Boston Red Sox (continued)

OSCAR MELILLO
second baseman
1935-37

JENNINGS
POINDEXTER
pitcher 1936

JIMMY FOXX
first baseman
1936-39

ERIC McNAIR
infielder
1936-38

ROGER
"DOC" CRAMER
outfielder
1936-39

STEWART BOWERS
pitcher 1935-37

W. BYRON
HUMPHREYS
pitcher 1936

HEINIE MANUSH
outfielder 1936

JOHN MARCUM
pitcher 1936-38

BUSTER MILLS
outfielder 1937

BOB DAUGHTERS
pinch-hitter
1937

BOBBY DOERR
second baseman
1937-39

GEORGE
EMERSON DICKMAN
pitcher 1936, 1938-39

JIM HENRY
pitcher
1936-37

FABIAN GAFFKE
outfielder 1936-39

TED OLSON
pitcher
1936-38

JOE GONZALES
pitcher 1937

ALPHONSE
"TOMMY" THOMAS
pitcher 1937

Boston Red Sox (continued)

BUCK NEWSOM
pitcher 1937

**DOMINIC
DALLESANDRO**
outfielder 1937

JOHNNY PEACOCK
catcher 1937-39

LEE ROGERS
pitcher 1938

JIM BAGBY, Jr.
pitcher 1938-39

**LEO "RED"
NONNENKAMP**
outfielder
1938-39

JOE HEVING
pitcher 1938-39

GENE DESAUTELS
catcher 1937-39

**WILLIAM
"BEN" CHAPMAN**
outfielder 1937-38

PINKY HIGGINS
third baseman
1937-38

**RICHARD
MIDKIFF**
pitcher
1938

BILL HARRIS
pitcher 1938

BILL LEFEBVRE
pitcher 1938-39

JOE VOSMIK
outfielder
1938-39

**LOUIS
"BOZE" BERGER**
infielder
1939

ARCHIE McKAIN
pitcher 1937-38

AL BAKER
pitcher 1938

JIM TABOR
third baseman
1938-39

**CHARLIE
WAGNER**
pitcher
1938-39

Boston Red Sox (continued)

TED WILLIAMS
outfielder
1939

MONTE WEAVER
pitcher 1939

LOU FINNEY
first base, outfield
1939

JAKE WADE
pitcher 1939

BILL SAYLES
pitcher 1939

WOODY RICH
pitcher 1939

**THOMAS
"SCOOPS" CAREY**
infielder
1939

DENNY GALEHOUSE
pitcher 1939

ELDON AUKER
pitcher 1939

UNIFORMS:

1930 sleeve patch

Brooklyn Robins/Dodgers

FRONT OFFICE:

FRANK B. YORK
President 1930-32

HARRY DEMOTT
VP 1930-36

S. W. McKEEVER
VP/Treasurer 1930-32
President 1933-37

DAVID DRISCOLL
Business Mgr.
1930-33

J. A. GILLEAUDEAU
Secretary 1930-32
VP/Treasurer 1933-39

JOHN GORMAN
Traveling Secy. 1930-35
Business Mgr. 1936-37

JAMES MULVEY
Asst. Treas. 1932
VP/Secy. 1933-39

J. A. "BOB" QUINN
Gen. Mgr. 1934-35

LARRY MacPHAIL
Executive VP
General Manager
1938-39

GEORGE BARNEWALL
VP 1939

JOHN McDONALD
Traveling Secy.
1939

FIELD MANAGERS:

WILBERT ROBINSON
1930-31

MAX CAREY
1932-33

CASEY STENGEL
1934-36

BURLEIGH GRIMES
1937-38

LEO DUROCHER
1939

COACHES:

IVY OLSEN 1930-31
OTTO MILLER 1930-36
JIMMY JOHNSTON 1931
CASEY STENGEL 1932-33
ZACK TAYLOR 1936
ANDY HIGH 1937-38
JESSE HAINES 1938
BABE RUTH 1938
CHUCK DRESSEN 1939
BILL KILLEFER 1939

THE PLAYERS:

BUCK NEWSOM
pitcher 1930

CLISE DUDLEY
pitcher 1930

JAMES "JUMBO" ELLIOTT
pitcher 1930

HAROLD LEE
outfielder 1930

JOHNNY MORRISON
pitcher 1930

GRAHAM "EDDIE" MOORE
utility 1930

JIM FAULKNER
pitcher 1930

Brooklyn Robins/Dodgers (continued)

HANK DeBERRY
catcher 1930

BABE HERMAN
outfielder 1930–31

DEL BISSONETTE
first baseman
1930–31, 1933

GORDON SLADE
shortstop 1930–32

NEAL "MICKEY" FINN
second baseman
1930–32

JAKE FLOWERS
utility 1930–31, 1933

HARVEY HENDRICK
outfielder 1930–31

RAY MOSS
pitcher
1930–31

RAY PHELPS
pitcher
1930–32

WALLY GILBERT
third baseman
1930–31

WILLIAM
"CY" MOORE
pitcher
1930–32

ISAAC
"IKE" BOONE
outfielder
1930–32

RAYMOND
"RUBE" BRESSLER
outfielder 1930–31

JACK WARNER
infielder 1930–31

ADOLFO LUQUE
pitcher 1930–31

FRED HEIMACH
pitcher 1930–33

DAZZY VANCE
pitcher
1930–32, 1935

Brooklyn Robins/Dodgers (continued)

JOHNNY FREDERICK
outfielder
1930-34

WILLIAM "WATTY" CLARK
pitcher
1930-33, 1934-37

HOLLIS "SLOPPY" THURSTON
pitcher 1930-33

LEFTY O'DOUL
outfielder
1931-33

ERNIE LOMBARDI
catcher 1931

JACK QUINN (PICUS)
pitcher
1931-32

AL COHEN
outfielder
1931-32

AL LOPEZ
catcher
1930-35

GLENN WRIGHT
shortstop 1930-33

EARL MATTINGLY
pitcher 1931

CLYDE DAY
pitcher 1931

MAX ROSENFELD
outfielder 1931-33

VAL PICINICH
catcher 1930-33

DENNY SOTHERN
outfielder 1931

FRESCO THOMPSON
infielder 1931-32

PHIL GALLIVAN
pitcher 1931

BOB REIS
utility
1931-32, 1935

Brooklyn Robins/Dodgers (continued)

JOE SHAUTE
pitcher
1931-33

JOHN
"BUD" CLANCY
first baseman
1932

CLYDE
SUKEFORTH
catcher
1932-34

WAITE HOYT
pitcher
1932, 1937-38

HACK WILSON
outfielder
1932-34

DAN TAYLOR
outfielder
1932-36

GEORGE KELLY
first baseman
1932

FAY THOMAS
pitcher 1932

BRUCE CALDWELL
first baseman 1932

TONY
CUCCINELLO
infielder
1932-35

VAN LINGLE
MUNGO
pitcher
1931-39

PAUL RICHARDS
catcher 1932

ED PIPGRAS
pitcher 1932

DICK SIEBERT
first base, outfield
1932, 1936

JOE STRIPP
first, third base
1932-37

CHICK OUTEN
catcher 1933

Brooklyn Robins/Dodgers (continued)

JOE JUDGE
first baseman
1933

RALPH
"BUZZ" BOYLE
outfielder
1933-35

RAY LUCAS
pitcher 1933-34

WALTER BECK
pitcher 1933-34

OWEN CARROLL
pitcher 1933-34

LINUS
"LONNY" FREY
infielder
1933-36

JOE HUTCHESON
outfielder 1933

LU BLUE
first baseman
1933

SAM LESLIE
first baseman
1933-35

JIM JORDAN
infielder 1933-36

HARRY SMYTHE
pitcher 1934

RAY BENGE
pitcher
1933-35

BERT DELMAS
second baseman
1933

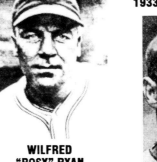

WILFRED
"ROSY" RYAN
pitcher
1933

EMIL
"DUTCH" LEONARD
pitcher 1933-36

GLENN
"PETE" CHAPMAN
utility 1934

CHARLIE PERKINS
pitcher 1934

Brooklyn Robins/Dodgers (continued)

TOM ZACHARY
pitcher 1934-36

ART HERRING
pitcher 1934

LES MUNNS
pitcher
1934-35

JOHN BABICH
pitcher 1934-35

JIM BUCHER
utility 1934-37

FRANK LAMANSKE
pitcher 1935

WALT MILLIES
catcher 1934

LEN KOENECKE
outfielder 1934-35

NICK TREMARK
outfielder
1934-36

RAY BERRES
catcher
1934, 1936

BUSTER MILLS
outfielder 1935

ROD DEDEAUX
shortstop 1935

BABE PHELPS
catcher 1935-39

PHIL PAGE
pitcher 1934

BERT HOGG
third baseman
1934

JOHNNY McCARTHY
first baseman
1934-35

FRANK SKAFF
infielder 1935

VINCE SHERLOCK
second baseman
1935

BOB LOGAN
pitcher 1935

JAMES
"ZACK" TAYLOR
catcher 1935

MANUEL ONIS
catcher 1935

HARVEY GREEN
pitcher 1935

Brooklyn Robins/Dodgers (continued)

STANLEY
"FRENCHY" BORDAGARAY
utility 1935-36

JOHNNY COONEY
first base, outfield
1935-37

ED BRANDT
pitcher 1936

HANK WINSTON
pitcher 1936

FRED LINDSTROM
outfielder 1936

HARRY
EISENSTAT
pitcher
1935-37

GEORGE WATKINS
outfielder 1936

BEN GERAGHTY
infielder 1936

ED WILSON
outfielder
1936-37

BOB BARR
pitcher 1935

GEORGE EARNSHAW
pitcher 1935-36

TOM BAKER
pitcher 1935-37

JACK RADTKE
second baseman
1936

RANDY MOORE
utility 1936-37

BUDDY HASSETT
first base, outfield
1936-38

Brooklyn Robins/Dodgers (continued)

GEORGE JEFFCOAT
pitcher 1936-37, 1939

JOHN
"TOM" WINSETT
outfielder
1936-38

ELMER KLUMPP
catcher 1937

JAKE DANIEL
first baseman
1937

TONY
MALINOSKY
infielder
1937

OSCAR
"OX" ECKHARDT
outfielder 1936

MAX BUTCHER
pitcher 1936-38

JOHN
"LINDSAY" BROWN
shortstop 1937

PAUL CHERVINKO
catcher 1937-38

NICK POLLY
(POLACHANIN)
third baseman
1937

HEINIE MANUSH
outfielder 1937-38

GIB BRACK
outfielder
1937-38

SID GAUTREAUX
catcher 1936-37

FRED FRANKHOUSE
pitcher 1936-38

JOHN HUDSON
infielder
1936-39

GEORGE CISAR
pitcher 1937

GEORGE
FALLON
second base
1937

EDWIN
"PEPPER" MORGAN
outfielder 1937

ROY SPENCER
catcher 1937-38

Brooklyn Robins/Dodgers (continued)

WOODY ENGLISH
infielder 1937-38

BERT HAAS
first baseman
1937-38

WILLIAM
"GILLY" CAMPBELL
catcher 1938

LUKE HAMLIN
pitcher 1937-39

FREDDY
FITZSIMMONS
pitcher 1937-39

BILL POSEDEL
pitcher 1938

HAZEN
"KIKI" CUYLER
outfielder
1938

ART PARKS
outfielder
1937, 1939

GOODY ROSEN
outfielder
1937-39

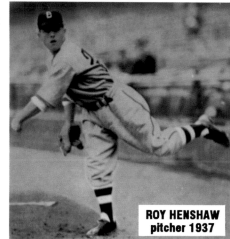

ROY HENSHAW
pitcher 1937

RALPH
BIRKOFER
pitcher 1937

LEE ROGERS
pitcher 1938

JIM WINFORD
pitcher 1938

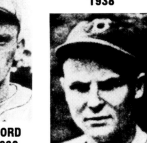

WAYNE
LAMASTER
pitcher 1938

MERVYN SHEA
catcher 1938

CHARLES
"GREEK" GEORGE
catcher 1938

ORIS HOCKETT
outfielder 1938-39

DYKES POTTER
pitcher 1938

COOKIE
LAVAGETTO
infielder
1937-39

BEN CANTWELL
pitcher 1937

JIM LINDSEY
pitcher 1937

JIM PETERSON
pitcher 1937

BUCK MARROW
pitcher 1937-38

WOODY WILLIAMS
shortstop 1938

PACKY ROGERS
(HAZINSKI)
infielder 1938

JOHN GADDY
pitcher 1938

Brooklyn Robins/Dodgers (continued)

LEO DUROCHER
shortstop 1938-39
(manager 1939)

PETE COSCARART
second baseman
1938-39

TONY LAZZERI
infielder 1939

MEL ALMADA
outfielder 1939

**FRED
"DIXIE" WALKER**
outfielder 1939

"TUCK" STAINBACK
outfielder 1938-39

TOT PRESNELL
pitcher 1938-39

ERNIE KOY
outfielder
1938-39

DOLPH CAMILLI
first baseman
1938-39

AL TODD
catcher
1939

VITO TAMULIS
pitcher 1938-39

RAY HAYWORTH
catcher 1938-39

FRED SINGTON
outfielder 1938-39

HUGH CASEY
pitcher 1939

GENE SCHOTT
pitcher 1939

**FRED
LINDSAY DEAL**
outfielder 1939

LYN LARY
infielder 1939

Brooklyn Robins/Dodgers (continued)

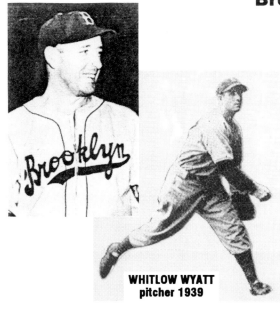

JIMMY RIPPLE
outfielder 1939

CHRIS HARTJE
catcher 1939

**AL
HOLLINGSWORTH**
pitcher 1939

GENE MOORE
outfielder 1939

IRA HUTCHINSON
pitcher 1939

**RUSSELL
"RED" EVANS**
pitcher 1939

CARL DOYLE
pitcher 1939

BILL CROUCH
pitcher 1939

**CLETUS "BOOTS"
POFFENBERGER**
pitcher 1939

UNIFORMS:

1938 sleeve patch

Chicago Cubs

FRONT OFFICE:

WM. WRIGLEY
Executive Chairman
1930-31

WM. L. VEECK, Sr.
President/Treasurer
1930-33

JOHN O. SEYS
VP 1930-37

WM. M. WALKER
VP 1930-33
President 1934

ROBERT C. LEWIS
Traveling Secy.
1930-39

MARGARET DONAHUE
Secretary 1930-39

CHARLES S. GRIMM
VP 1935

PHILIP K. WRIGLEY
Executive Chairman
1932-34
President 1935-39

CHARLES F. DRAKE
Public Relations
1935-39

CHARLES A. WEBER
Treasurer 1934
Treasurer/Bus. Mgr.
1935-37
VP/Treas. 1938-39

WM. L. VEECK, Jr.
Asst. Secy. 1938-39

FIELD MANAGERS:

JOE McCARTHY
1930

ROGERS HORNSBY
1930-32

CHARLIE GRIMM
1932-38

GABBY HARTNETT
1938-39

COACHES:

JIMMY BURKE 1930
RAY SCHALK 1930-31
CHARLEY O'LEARY 1931-33
RED CORRIDEN 1932-39
JOHNNY SCHULTE 1933
MIKE KELLY 1934
ROY JOHNSON 1935-39
GABBY HARTNETT 1938
TONY LAZZERI 1938

THE PLAYERS:

JESSE PETTY
pitcher 1930

CLIFF HEATHCOTE
outfielder 1930

CHARLES "MAL" MOSS
pitcher 1930

AL SHEALY
pitcher 1930

BILL McAFEE
pitcher 1930

GEORGE KELLY
first baseman 1930

BOB OSBORN
pitcher 1930

Chicago Cubs (continued)

GABBY HARTNETT
catcher 1930-39
(manager 1938-39)

CLYDE BECK
infielder 1930

CHICK TOLSON
first baseman
1930

PAT MALONE
pitcher 1930-34

ROGERS HORNSBY
utility 1930-32
(manager 1930-32)

CLARENCE
"FOOTSIE" BLAIR
infielder 1930-31

HAZEN
"KIKI" CUYLER
outfielder
1930-35

HAL CARLSON
pitcher 1930

DOC FARRELL
shortstop 1930

LESTER BELL
third baseman
1930-31

BUD TEACHOUT
pitcher 1930-31

RIGGS
STEPHENSON
outfielder
1930-34

LEWIS
"HACK" WILSON
outfielder
1930-31

Chicago Cubs (continued)

JAMES
"ZACK" TAYLOR
catcher 1930-33

JOHN
"SHERIFF" BLAKE
pitcher 1930-31

LYNN NELSON
pitcher 1930, 1933-34

CHARLIE GRIMM
first baseman 1930-36
(manager 1932-38)

LON WARNEKE
pitcher 1930-36

WOODY ENGLISH
infielder 1930-36

DAN TAYLOR
outfielder
1930-32

CHARLEY ROOT
pitcher 1930-39

GUY BUSH
pitcher
1930-34

JOHN WELCH
pitcher 1931

BOB SMITH
pitcher 1931-32

MIKE KREEVICH
outfielder 1931

ROBERT
"EARL" GRACE
catcher 1931

Chicago Cubs (continued)

JOHN MOORE
outfielder 1931-32

LANCE
RICHBOURG
outfielder
1932

BUCK NEWSOM
pitcher 1932

LES SWEETLAND
pitcher 1931

VINCE BARTON
outfielder 1931-32

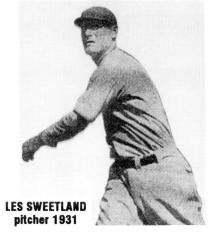

ROLLIE HEMSLEY
catcher 1931-32

BILLY HERMAN
second baseman
1931-39

MARV GUDAT
pitcher, outfield
1932

HARRY TAYLOR
first baseman 1932

JIMMY ADAIR
shortstop 1931

JAKIE MAY
pitcher 1931-32

ED BAECHT
pitcher 1931-32

BILLY JURGES
shortstop 1931-38

BURLEIGH
GRIMES
pitcher
1932-33

CARROLL YERKES
pitcher 1932-33

Chicago Cubs (continued)

MARK KOENIG
infielder 1932-33

STAN HACK
third base, first base
1932-39

FRANK DEMAREE
outfielder
1932-33, 1935-38

HARVEY HENDRICK
utility 1933

TAYLOR DOUTHIT
outfielder 1933

BABE PHELPS
catcher 1933-34

BUD TINNING
pitcher 1932-34

LEROY HERRMANN
pitcher 1932-33

**WILLIAM
"GILLY" CAMPBELL**
catcher 1933

JIM MOSOLF
outfielder
1933

DOLPH CAMILLI
first baseman
1933-34

BERYL RICHMOND
pitcher 1933

ROY HENSHAW
pitcher 1933-36

BABE HERMAN
outfielder 1933-34

Chicago Cubs (continued)

BENNIE TATE
catcher 1934

JIM WEAVER
pitcher 1934

BOB O'FARRELL
catcher 1934

PHIL CAVARETTA
first base, outfield
1934-39

AUGIE GALAN
second base,
outfielder
1934-39

JOHN GILL
outfielder
1935-36

DICK WARD
pitcher 1934

FRANK "DON" HURST
first baseman
1934

ROY JOINER
pitcher 1934-35

WALTER STEPHENSON
catcher 1935-36

CHARLES WIEDEMEYER
pitcher 1934

BILL LEE
pitcher
1934-39

CHUCK KLEIN
outfielder 1934-36

HUGH CASEY
pitcher 1935

"TUCK" STAINBACK
outfielder 1934-37

FRED LINDSTROM
third base, outfield
1935

FABIAN KOWALIK
pitcher 1935-36

Chicago Cubs (continued)

LARRY FRENCH
pitcher 1935-39

CLYDE SHOUN
pitcher 1935-37

GENE LILLARD
infielder, pitcher
1936, 1939

JOHN BOTTARINI
catcher
1937

JAMES A. "RIP" COLLINS
first baseman
1937-38

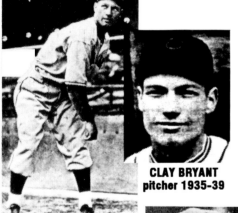

CLAY BRYANT
pitcher 1935-39

CURT DAVIS
pitcher 1936-37

ETHAN ALLEN
outfielder 1936

ROY PARMELEE
pitcher 1937

KEN O'DEA
catcher
1935-38

"TEX" CARLETON
pitcher 1935-38

LINUS "LONNY" FREY
infielder
1937

LAMBERT "DUTCH" MEYER
second baseman
1937

NEWT KIMBALL
pitcher 1937-38

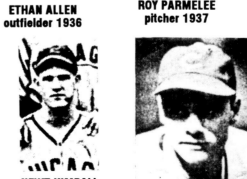

KIRBY HIGBE
pitcher 1937-39

JOE MARTY
outfielder
1937-39

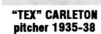

Chicago Cubs (continued)

BOB LOGAN
pitcher
1937-38

TONY LAZZERI
shortstop 1938

**COAKER
TRIPLETT**
outfielder
1938

STEVE MESNER
shortstop 1938-39

DIZZY DEAN
pitcher
1938-39

CARL REYNOLDS
outfielder 1937-39

AL EPPERLY
pitcher 1938

VANCE PAGE
pitcher 1938-39

BOBBY MATTICK
shortstop 1938-39

EARL WHITEHILL
pitcher 1939

BOB GARBARK
catcher 1937-39

JIM ASBELL
outfielder
1938

JACK RUSSELL
pitcher 1938-39

GUS MANCUSO
catcher 1939

Chicago Cubs (continued)

HANK LEIBER
outfielder 1939

DICK BARTELL
shortstop 1939

VERN OLSEN
pitcher 1939

**GLENN
"RIP" RUSSELL**
first baseman
1939

CLAUDE PASSEAU
pitcher 1939

BILL NICHOLSON
outfielder 1939

RAY HARRELL
pitcher 1939

JIM GLEESON
outfielder 1939

UNIFORMS:

1930
sleeve
patch
(road)

THE TEAMS

113

Chicago White Sox

FRONT OFFICE:

CHARLES COMISKEY
President 1930-31

J. LOUIS COMISKEY
VP/Treasurer 1930-31
President/Treasurer
1932-39

HARRY GRABINER
Secretary 1930-31
VP/Secretary 1932-39

LOUIS C. BARBOUR
Traveling Secretary
1930-31

JOSEPH BARRY
Traveling Secretary
1932-39

FIELD MANAGERS:

DONIE BUSH
1930-31

LEW FONSECA
1932-34

COACHES:

ED WALSH 1930
MIKE KELLY 1930-31
JOHNNY BUTLER 1932
BILL CUNNINGHAM 1932
JIMMY AUSTIN 1933-39
MUDDY RUEL 1935-39
BILLY WEBB 1935-39
MONTY STRATTON 1939

JIMMY DYKES
1934-39

THE PLAYERS:

JAMES W. "JIM" MOORE
pitcher, outfield
1930

JOE KLINGER
catcher, first base
1930

DUTCH HENRY
pitcher 1930

TED BLANKENSHIP
pitcher 1930

JOHN "BUD" CLANCY
first baseman
1930

CLYDE CROUSE
catcher 1930

BILL HUNNEFIELD
shortstop 1930

HAROLD McKAIN
pitcher 1930-32

HUGH WILLINGHAM
second base
1930

Chicago White Sox (continued)

**MARTIN
"CHICK" AUTRY**
catcher 1930

ERNIE SMITH
shortstop 1930

DAVE HARRIS
outfielder 1930

LUKE APPLING
shortstop 1930-39

MOE BERG
catcher 1930

**EMILE
"RED" BARNES**
outfielder
1930

**JOHN
"BLONDY" RYAN**
infielder 1930

BUTCH HENLINE
catcher 1930-31

CARL REYNOLDS
outfielder 1930-31

RED FABER
pitcher
1930-33

JOHN KERR
infielder
1930-31

ART SHIRES
first baseman
1930

GREG MULLEAVY
infielder 1930, 1932

**GARLAND
BRAXTON**
pitcher
1930-31

PAT CARAWAY
pitcher 1930-32

ED WALSH, Jr.
pitcher 1930, 1932

Chicago White Sox (continued)

JOHNNY RIDDLE
catcher 1930

TED LYONS
pitcher
1930-39

ALEX METZLER
outfielder 1930

BOB FOTHERGILL
outfielder 1930-32

BILL CISSELL
infielder
1930-32

**WILBER
"BIGGS" WEHDE**
pitcher 1930-31

BOB WEILAND
pitcher 1930-31

WILLIE KAMM
third baseman
1930-31

IRV JEFFRIES
infielder 1930-31

SMEAD JOLLEY
outfielder
1930-32

**JAMES S.
"JIM" MOORE**
pitcher
1930-32

BRUCE CAMPBELL
outfielder 1930-32

BENNIE TATE
catcher 1930-32

**ALPHONSE
"TOMMY" THOMAS**
pitcher 1930-32

JOHN WATWOOD
first base, outfielder
1930-32

Chicago White Sox (continued)

LEW FONSECA
first base, utility
1931-33
(manager 1932-34)

FRANK GRUBE
catcher
1931-33, 1935-36

MEL SIMONS
outfielder
1931-32

VIC FRASIER
pitcher
1931-33, 1939

BILL NORMAN
outfielder 1931-32

LOU GARLAND
pitcher 1931

GRANT BOWLER
pitcher 1931-32

LU BLUE
first baseman
1931-32

LES BARTHOLOMEW
pitcher 1932

PETE DAGLIA
pitcher 1932

FRED EICHRODT
outfielder 1931

HANK GARRITY
catcher 1931

BILLY SULLIVAN, Jr.
infielder, catcher
1931-33

JOHN F.
"BOB" POSER
pitcher 1932

FABIAN KOWALIK
pitcher 1932

HAROLD
ANDERSON
outfielder
1932

MINTER "JACKIE" HAYES
infielder
1932-39

CAREY SELPH
third baseman
1932

BUMP HADLEY
pitcher 1932

CHARLES BIGGS
pitcher 1932

JOHN HODAPP
outfielder 1932

BOB SEEDS
outfielder 1932

CLARENCE FIEBER
pitcher 1932

JACK ROTHROCK
outfielder 1932

CHARLIE BERRY
catcher 1932-33

LIZ FUNK
outfielder
1932-33

PAUL GREGORY
pitcher 1932-33

ARCHIE WISE
pitcher
1932

ART SMITH
pitcher 1932

CHARLIE ENGLISH
infielder 1932-33

CHAD KIMSEY
pitcher 1932-33

SAM JONES
pitcher 1932-35

RED KRESS
utility 1932-34

Chicago White Sox (continued)

MILT GASTON
pitcher 1932-34

ED "BULL" DURHAM
pitcher 1933

HAL HAID
pitcher 1933

MILT BOCEK
outfielder
1933-34

JIMMY DYKES
infielder 1933-39
(manager 1934-39)

EVAR SWANSON
outfielder 1932-34

JOHN STONEHAM
outfielder 1933

WALTER "JAKE" MILLER
pitcher 1933

PHIL GALLIVAN
pitcher 1932, 1934

HAL RHYNE
infielder 1933

EARL WEBB
outfielder 1933

WHITLOW WYATT
pitcher 1933-36

BILL CHAMBERLAIN
pitcher 1932

ART EVANS
pitcher 1932

GEORGE MURRAY
pitcher 1933

IRA HUTCHINSON
pitcher 1933

JOE HEVING
pitcher 1933-34

AL SIMMONS
outfielder 1933-35

LES TIETJE
pitcher 1933-36

MULE HAAS
outfielder 1933-37

Chicago White Sox (continued)

JOE CHAMBERLAIN
infielder 1934

MERVYN SHEA
catcher 1934-37

JOHN PASEK
catcher 1934

RIP RADCLIFF
outfield, first base
1934-39

HENRY "ZEKE" BONURA
first baseman
1934-37

FRENCHY BORDAGARAY
outfielder 1934

GEORGE CAITHAMER
catcher 1934

HARRY KINZY
pitcher 1934

BOB BOKEN
infielder 1934

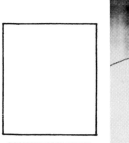

JOHN POMORSKI
pitcher 1934

CHARLIE UHLIR
outfielder 1934

HUGO KLAERNER
pitcher 1934

FRENCHY UHALT
outfielder 1934

ED MADJESKI (MAJEWSKI)
catcher 1934

MUDDY RUEL
catcher 1934

MARSHALL MAULDIN
third baseman
1934

Chicago White Sox (continued)

MONTY STRATTON
pitcher 1934-38

MARTY HOPKINS
third baseman
1934-35

GEORGE EARNSHAW
pitcher 1934-35

CARL FISCHER
pitcher 1935

RAY PHELPS
pitcher 1935-36

ITALO CHELINI
pitcher
1935-37

VERN KENNEDY
pitcher 1934-37

JOCKO CONLAN
outfielder 1934-35

GLENN WRIGHT
shortstop 1935

BUD HAFEY
outfielder
1935

SLOAN "GEORGE" WASHINGTON
outfielder 1935-36

MIKE KREEVICH
outfielder 1935-39

LEE STINE
pitcher 1934-35

FRED TAUBY (TAUBENSEE)
outfielder 1935

SANDY VANCE
pitcher 1935

TONY PIET (PIETRUSZKA)
infielder
1935-37

JOHN WHITEHEAD
pitcher 1935-39

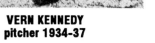

JACK SALVESON
pitcher 1935

Chicago White Sox (continued)

LUKE SEWELL
catcher 1935-38

BILL SHORES
pitcher 1936

LARRY ROSENTHAL
outfielder 1936-39

CLINT BROWN
pitcher 1936-39

BILL DIETRICH
pitcher 1936-39

LOUIS "BOZE" BERGER
infielder 1937-38

RUSSELL "RED" EVANS
pitcher 1936

GEORGE STUMPF
outfielder 1936

MERRITT "SUGAR" CAIN
pitcher 1936-38

HANK STEINBACHER
outfielder 1937-39

THORNTON LEE
pitcher 1937-39

LES ROCK (SCHWARZROCK)
first baseman 1936

FRED "DIXIE" WALKER
outfielder 1936-37

JO-JO MORRISSEY
infielder 1936

BILL COX
pitcher 1937-38

JOHN RIGNEY
pitcher 1937-39

GEORGE GICK
pitcher 1937-38

MERV CONNORS
infielder 1937-38

Chicago White Sox (continued)

TONY RENSA
catcher 1937-39

JOE MARTIN
third baseman
1938

GEORGE MEYER
second baseman 1938

JACK KNOTT
pitcher 1938-39

**GERALD
"GEE" WALKER**
outfielder 1938-39

JOE KUHEL
first baseman
1938-39

BOB UHLE
pitcher 1938

MARVIN OWEN
third baseman
1938-39

MIKE TRESH
catcher 1938-39

JOHN GERLACH
infielder 1938-39

HARRY BOYLES
pitcher 1938-39

**NORM
SCHLUETTER**
catcher 1938-39

GENE FORD
pitcher 1938

FRANK GABLER
pitcher 1938

JESSE LANDRUM
second baseman 1938

**RUPERT
"TOMMY" THOMPSON**
outfield, first base
1938-39

ERIC McNAIR
infielder 1939

KEN SILVESTRI
catcher 1939

Chicago White Sox (continued)

ART HERRING
pitcher 1939

JOHN MARCUM
pitcher 1939

JESS DOBERNIC
pitcher 1939

BOB KENNEDY
third baseman 1939

OLLIE BEJMA
infielder 1939

VALLIE EAVES
pitcher 1939

EDGAR SMITH
pitcher 1939

UNIFORMS:

Cincinnati Reds

FRONT OFFICE:

SIDNEY WEIL
President
1930-33

GUS H. HILB
VP 1930-32

L. C. WIDRIG
Treasurer
1930-32

W. J. FRIEDLANDER
VP 1930

FRANK J. BEHLE
Business Mgr. 1930

BILL ROURKE
Scout/Asst. to Pres.
1930-31

JOSEPH MEAGHER
Secretary 1930-32
Secy./Treas. 1933

MEYER UHLFELDER
Traveling Secy.
1930-33

JAMES RESTON
Traveling Secy.
1934

POWEL CROSLEY, Jr.
President 1933-39

LARRY MacPHAIL
VP/Gen. Mgr.
1933-36

T. M. CONROY
Secy./Treas.
1934-39

GENE KARST
Information Dir./
Traveling Secy.
1935-36

JOHN McDONALD
Asst. GM 1935-36
Traveling Secy.
1937

FRANK LANE
Asst. Gen. Mgr.
1937-39

W. P. BRAMHAM
Asst. Secy./Treas.
1937-39

WARREN GILES
VP/Gen. Mgr.
1937-39

GABE PAUL
Info. Director
1937
Traveling Secy.
1938-39

FIELD MANAGERS:

DAN HOWLEY
1930-32

DONIE BUSH
1933

BOB O'FARRELL
1934

BURT SHOTTON
(interim) 1934

CHUCK DRESSEN
1934-37

BOBBY WALLACE
(interim) 1937

BILL McKECHNIE
1938-39

COACHES:

OTTO WILLIAMS 1930
BOBBY WALLACE 1930-31
MICKEY DOOLAN 1930-32
HARRY HEILMANN 1932
JEWEL ENS 1933
VAL PICINICH 1934
BURT SHOTTON 1934
GEORGE KELLY 1935-37
TOM SHEEHAN 1935-37
IVEY WINGO 1936
EDD ROUSH 1938
HANK GOWDY 1938-39
JIMMY WILSON 1939

THE PLAYERS:

PAT CRAWFORD
infielder 1930

ETHAN ALLEN
outfielder 1930

ARCHIE CAMPBELL
pitcher 1930

BOB MEUSEL
outfielder 1930

PETE DONOHUE
pitcher 1930

Cincinnati Reds (continued)

HARRY HEILMANN
first base, outfield
1930, 1932

CURT WALKER
first base, outfield
1930

KEN ASH
pitcher
1930

JOHNNY GOOCH
catcher 1930

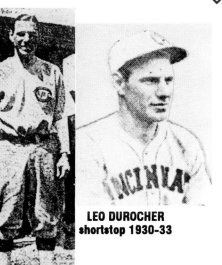

LEO DUROCHER
shortstop 1930-33

HUGH CRITZ
second baseman
1930

EVAR SWANSON
outfielder 1930

BIFF WYSONG
pitcher 1930-32

**MARTY
CALLAGHAN**
outfielder 1930

CHUCK DRESSEN
infielder 1930-31
(manager 1934-37)

**TONY
CUCCINELLO**
infielder
1930-31

GEORGE KELLY
first baseman 1930

HARRY RICONDA
infielder 1930

JAKIE MAY
pitcher 1930

SI JOHNSON
pitcher 1930-36

AL ECKERT
pitcher 1930-31

LENA STYLES
catcher 1930-31

Cincinnati Reds (continued)

JOE STRIPP
infielder
1930-31

LARRY BENTON
pitcher 1930-34

CLYDE
SUKEFORTH
catcher 1930-31

EPPA RIXEY
pitcher
1930-33

EDD ROUSH
outfielder
1931

GENE MOORE
outfielder 1931

CLYDE BECK
infielder 1931

ED STRELECKI
pitcher 1931

HENRY
"NICK" CULLOP
outfielder
1930-31

RED LUCAS
pitcher 1930-33

DOUG McWEENY
pitcher 1930

OWEN CARROLL
pitcher 1930-32

CLIFF HEATHCOTE
outfielder 1931-32

MICKEY HEATH
first baseman
1931-32

HORACE
"HOD" FORD
infielder
1930-31

BENNY FREY
pitcher
1930-31, 1932-36

RAY KOLP
pitcher
1930-34

FRANK SIGAFOOS
infielder 1931

WALTER ROETTGER
outfielder
1931, 1932-33

Cincinnati Reds (continued)

CASPER ASBJORNSON
catcher 1931–32

TAYLOR DOUTHIT
outfielder 1931–33

ESTEL CRABTREE
utility 1931–32

BABE HERMAN
first base, outfield
1932, 1935–36

ERNIE LOMBARDI
catcher 1932–39

WHITEY HILCHER
pitcher 1931–32, 1935–36

JACK OGDEN
pitcher 1931–32

WALLY GILBERT
third baseman 1932

GEORGE GRANTHAM
infielder 1932–33

CHICK HAFEY
outfielder
1932–35, 1937

CLYDE "PETE" MANION
catcher 1932–34

JACK QUINN
pitcher 1933

HARVEY HENDRICK
first baseman 1931–32

JIM SHEVLIN
first baseman
1932, 1934

ANDY HIGH
infielder 1932–33

OTTO BLUEGE
infielder 1932–33

JO-JO MORRISSEY
infielder 1932–33

JACK CROUCH
catcher 1933

TONY ROBELLO
infielder 1933–34

Cincinnati Reds (continued)

PAUL DERRINGER
pitcher 1933-39

JOHN MOORE
outfielder 1933-34

SPARKY ADAMS
infielder 1933-34

ALLYN STOUT
pitcher 1933-34

JUNIE BARNES
pitcher 1934

BOB SMITH
pitcher
1933

BERYL
RICHMOND
pitcher
1934

JIM BOTTOMLEY
first baseman 1933-35

HARRY RICE
third base, outfield
1933

ROLLIE HEMSLEY
catcher 1933

HARRY McCURDY
first baseman 1934

MARK KOENIG
infielder 1934

BILL MARSHALL
second baseman 1934

SYL JOHNSON
pitcher 1934

Cincinnati Reds (continued)

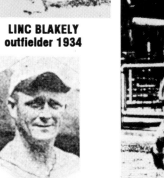

LINC BLAKELY
outfielder 1934

DAZZY VANCE
pitcher 1934

BOB O'FARRELL
catcher 1934
(manager 1934)

ALEX KAMPOURIS
second baseman
1934-38

TONY PIET
(PIETRUSZKA)
utility 1934-35

WES
SCHULMERIC
outfielder
1934

LEE GRISSOM
pitcher 1934-39

JIM LINDSEY
pitcher 1934

IVEY SHIVER
outfielder 1934

JAKE FLOWERS
infielder 1934

JOE SHAUTE
pitcher 1934

FRANK McCORMICK
first baseman
1934, 1937-39

GORDON SLADE
utility 1934-35

SHERMAN
EDWARDS
pitcher 1934

WHITEY
WISTERT
pitcher
1934

TONY FREITAS
pitcher 1934-36

HARLIN POOL
outfielder
1934-35

ADAM
COMOROSKY
outfielder
1934-35

TED KLEINHANS
pitcher 1934, 1937-38

TED PETOSKEY
outfielder 1934-35

Cincinnati Reds (continued)

DON BRENNAN
pitcher 1934-37

LEW RIGGS
infielder
1935-39

SAMMY BYRD
outfielder 1935-36

BILLY MYERS
infielder 1935-39

LEE GAMBLE
outfielder
1935, 1938-39

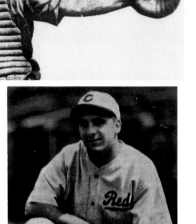

**WILLIAM
"GILLY" CAMPBELL**
catcher, utility
1935-37

HANK ERICKSON
catcher 1935

LEROY HERRMANN
pitcher 1935

GEORGE NELSON
pitcher 1935-36

**HAZEN
"KIKI" CUYLER**
outfielder
1935-37

LES SCARSELLA
first baseman
1935-37, 1939

BILLY SULLIVAN, Jr.
infielder 1935

**DANNY
MacFAYDEN**
pitcher
1935

CALVIN CHAPMAN
utility 1935-36

IVAL GOODMAN
outfielder 1935-39

GENE SCHOTT
pitcher 1935-38

**AL
HOLLINGSWORTH**
pitcher 1935-38

Cincinnati Reds (continued)

LEE HANDLEY
second baseman
1936

TOMMY THEVENOW
infielder
1936

RAY DAVIS
pitcher 1936-39

HUB WALKER
utility 1936-37

BILL HALLAHAN
pitcher 1936-37

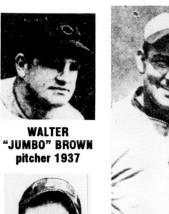

CHARLIE GELBERT
infielder 1937

WALTER "JUMBO" BROWN
pitcher 1937

ALBERT "DUTCH" MELE
outfielder
1937

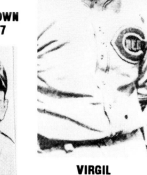

VIRGIL "SPUD" DAVIS
catcher
1937-38

GEORGE McQUINN
first baseman 1936

LEE STINE
pitcher 1936

EDDIE MILLER
shortstop 1936-37

CHARLIE ENGLISH
infielder 1937

"DOUBLE JOE" DWYER
pinch-hitter
1937

GUS BRITTAIN
catcher 1937

DEE MOORE
pitcher, catcher
1936-37

JAKE MOOTY
pitcher 1936-37

LLOYD "WHITEY" MOORE
pitcher 1936-39

EDDIE JOOST
infielder
1936-37, 1939

ARNIE MOSER
pinch-hitter
1937

PAUL GEHRMAN
pitcher 1937

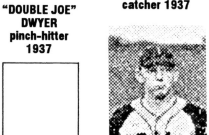

CARL "PINKY" JORGENSEN
outfielder
1937

Cincinnati Reds (continued)

JOHNNY
VANDER MEER
pitcher
1937-39

BAXTER
"BUCK" JORDAN
first baseman
1937-38

GEORGE
"KIDDO" DAVIS
outfielder
1937-38

DUSTY COOKE
outfielder 1938

JIM WEAVER
pitcher 1938-39

DICK WEST
catcher, outfield
1938-39

NINO
BONGIOVANNI
outfielder
1938-39

PHIL WEINTRAUB
outfielder 1937

JIMMY OUTLAW
third baseman
1937-38

RAY BENGE
pitcher 1938

JUSTIN STEIN
infielder 1938

WILLARD
HERSHBERGER
catcher 1938-39

CHARLES
"RED" BARRETT
pitcher
1937-39

JOE
CASCARELLA
pitcher
1937-38

HARRY CRAFT
outfielder
1937-39

LINUS
"LONNY" FREY
infielder
1938-39

DON LANG
infielder 1938

BUCKY WALTERS
pitcher 1938-39

CLIFFORD "NOLEN"
RICHARDSON
shortstop 1938-39

WALLY BERGER
outfielder 1938-39

Cincinnati Reds (continued)

WES LIVENGOOD
pitcher 1939

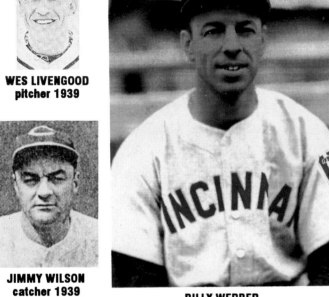

JIMMY WILSON
catcher 1939

BILLY WERBER
infielder 1939

ART JACOBS
pitcher 1939

EUGENE "JUNIOR" THOMPSON
pitcher 1939

HANK JOHNSON
pitcher 1939

UNIFORMS:

ELMER RIDDLE
pitcher 1939

VINCE DiMAGGIO
outfielder 1939

BUD HAFEY
outfielder 1939

JOHNNY NIGGELING
pitcher 1939

FRENCHY BORDAGARAY
utility 1939

PETE NAKTENIS
pitcher 1939

MILT SHOFFNER
pitcher 1939

MILT GALATZER
first baseman 1939

AL SIMMONS
outfielder 1939

Cleveland Indians

FRONT OFFICE:

ALVA BRADLEY
President/Treasurer
1930-39

BILLY EVANS
VP/Gen. Mgr.
1930-35

JOSEPH HOSTETTLER
Secretary 1931-39

W. H. McNICHOLS
Business Mgr.
1930-34
Bus. Mgr./Trav. Secy.
1935-36

CY SLAPNICKA
Asst. to Pres. 1936-37
VP 1938-39

FRANK KOHLBECKER
Traveling Secy. 1937
Business Mgr. 1938-39

LEWIS MUMAW
Traveling Secy. 1939

FIELD MANAGERS:

ROGER PECKINPAUGH
1930-33

WALTER JOHNSON
1933-35

STEVE O'NEILL
1935-37

OSSIE VITT
1938-39

COACHES:

GROVER HARTLEY 1930
MICKEY O'NEIL 1930
HOWIE SHANKS 1930-32
EARL WOLGAMOT 1931-33
BIBB FALK 1933
PATSY GHARRITY 1933-35
STEVE O'NEILL 1935
GEORGE UHLE 1936-37
WALLY SCHANG 1936-38
JOHNNY BASSLER 1938-39
OSCAR MELILLO 1939
LUKE SEWELL 1939

THE PLAYERS:

JOE SHAUTE
pitcher 1930

CARL LIND
infielder
1930

GROVER HARTLEY
catcher 1930

SAL GLIATTO
pitcher 1930

RAY GARDNER
shortstop 1930

GLENN MYATT
catcher 1930-35

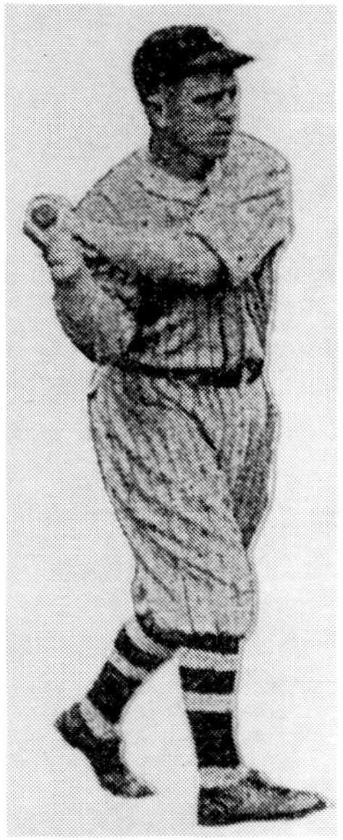

JOE SEWELL
third baseman
1930

LES BARNHART
pitcher 1930

Cleveland Indians (continued)

EARL AVERILL
outfielder 1930-39

ROXIE LAWSON
pitcher 1930-31

BIBB FALK
outfielder
1930-31

JOE VOSMIK
outfielder
1930-36

**RALPH
WINEGARNER**
utility
1930, 1932, 1934-36

KEN HOLLOWAY
pitcher 1930

MILT SHOFFNER
pitcher 1930-31

MEL HARDER
pitcher 1930-39

JAKE MILLER
pitcher 1930-31

LEW FONSECA
first baseman
1930-31

JOHN BURNETT
infielder 1930-34

LUKE SEWELL
catcher
1930-32, 1939

GEORGE DETORE
infielder 1930-31

**EDWARD C.
"ED" MORGAN**
first base, outfield
1930-33

CLINT BROWN
pitcher 1930-35

JONAH GOLDMAN
shortstop 1930-31

Cleveland Indians (continued)

JOE SPRINZ
catcher
1930-31

WILLIS HUDLIN
pitcher 1930-39

BILL BEAN
pitcher
1930-31, 1933-35

WES FERRELL
pitcher, outfield
1930-33

ED MONTAGUE
infielder 1930-32

BOB SEEDS
outfielder
1930-32, 1934

PETE DONOHUE
pitcher 1931

**BRUCE
CONNATSER**
first baseman
1931-32

**PETE APPLETON
(JABLONOWSKI)**
pitcher 1930-32

DICK PORTER
outfielder 1930-34

JOHN HODAPP
second baseman
1930-32

**CHARLIE
JAMIESON**
outfielder
1930-32

FAY THOMAS
pitcher 1931

BILL HUNNEFIELD
shortstop 1931

Cleveland Indians (continued)

WILLIE KAMM
third baseman
1931-35

**ORAL
HILDEBRAND**
pitcher
1931-36

MOE BERG
catcher
1931, 1934

**HOWARD
CRAGHEAD**
pitcher
1931, 1933

**ELLIS
"MIKE" POWERS**
outfielder
1932-33

MONTE PEARSON
pitcher 1932-35

**GEORGE "SARGE"
CONNALLY**
pitcher 1931-34

**ARVEL ODELL
"BAD NEWS" HALE**
infielder
1931, 1933-39

JACK RUSSELL
pitcher 1932

FRANK PYTLAK
catcher 1932-39

JOHN OULLIBER
outfielder 1933

LEO MOON
pitcher
1932

JOE BOLEY
shortstop 1932

**LOUIS
"BOZE" BERGER**
infielder
1932, 1935-36

BILL CISSELL
infielder 1932-33

**ELMER
HARLEY BOSS**
first baseman
1933

ROY SPENCER
catcher 1933-34

Cleveland Indians (continued)

THORNTON LEE
pitcher 1933-36

MILT GALATZER
first base, outfield
1933-36

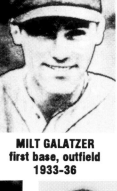

**HAL TROSKY
(TROYAVESKY)**
first baseman
1933-39

**DENNY
GALEHOUSE**
pitcher
1934-38

**BILL
KNICKERBOCKER**
shortstop
1933-36

BILL BRENZEL
catcher 1934-35

BOB GARBARK
catcher 1934-35

LLOYD BROWN
pitcher 1934-37

BILL PERRIN
pitcher 1934

BOB WEILAND
pitcher 1934

**GRAHAM
"EDDIE" MOORE**
second baseman
1934

SAM RICE
outfielder
1934

**WALTER
"KIT" CARSON**
outfielder
1934-35

**ROBERT
"DUTCH" HOLLAND**
outfielder
1934

Cleveland Indians (continued)

WALTER STEWART
pitcher 1935

**ALBERT O.
"AB" WRIGHT**
outfielder
1935

EDDIE PHILLIPS
catcher 1935

PAUL KARDOW
pitcher 1936

**GEORGE
BLAEHOLDER**
pitcher 1936

BOB FELLER
pitcher 1936-39

BRUCE CAMPBELL
outfielder 1935-39

**CHARLES
"GREEK" GEORGE**
catcher 1935-36

GEORGE UHLE
pitcher 1936

JOE BECKER
catcher 1936-37

ROY WEATHERLY
outfielder 1936-39

ROY HUGHES
infielder 1935-37

JIM GLEESON
outfielder 1936

BILLY SULLIVAN, Jr.
catcher 1936-37

BILL ZUBER
pitcher
1936, 1938-39

AL MILNAR
pitcher
1936, 1938-39

Cleveland Indians (continued)

JEFF HEATH
outfielder
1936-39

BLAS MONACO
second baseman 1937

WHITLOW WYATT
pitcher 1937

IVY ANDREWS
pitcher 1937

BILL SODD
outfielder
1937

JOHNNY ALLEN
pitcher 1936-39

EARL WHITEHILL
pitcher 1937-38

HUGH ALEXANDER
pitcher 1937

LYN LARY
shortstop
1937-39

KEN KELTNER
third baseman
1937-39

CARL FISCHER
pitcher 1937

JOE HEVING
pitcher
1937-38

MOOSE SOLTERS
outfielder 1937-39

JOHN KRONER
infielder
1937-38

KEN JUNGELS
pitcher 1937-38

Cleveland Indians (continued)

JAMES "SKEETER" WEBB
shortstop 1938-39

CLAY SMITH
pitcher 1938

CHUCK WORKMAN
outfielder 1938

RAY MACK (MICKOVSKY)
second baseman 1938-39

CHARLES SUCHE
pitcher 1938

JOHNNY HUMPHRIES
pitcher 1938-39

UNIFORMS:

HANK HELF
catcher 1938

LOU BOUDREAU
infielder 1938-39

JOE DOBSON
pitcher 1939

MIKE NAYMICK
pitcher 1939

HARRY EISENSTAT
pitcher 1939

FLOYD STROMME
pitcher 1939

TOMMY IRWIN
shortstop 1938

LLOYD RUSSELL
infielder 1938

OSCAR GRIMES
infielder 1938-39

ROLLIE HEMSLEY
catcher 1938-39

PAUL SULLIVAN
pitcher 1939

BEN CHAPMAN
outfielder 1939

JIM SHILLING
second baseman 1939

TOM DRAKE
pitcher 1939

JOHN BROACA
pitcher 1939

Detroit Tigers

THE PLAYERS:

FRONT OFFICE:

FRANK NAVIN
President 1930-35

WALTER O. BRIGGS
VP 1930-35
President 1936-39

ARTHUR SHEEHAN
Business Mgr. 1930-31
Traveling Secy. 1932-39

CHARLES NAVIN
Secy./Treas. 1930-35
Bus. Mgr. 1936-37
Secretary 1938

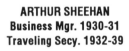

W. O. "SPIKE" BRIGGS
Asst. Secy./Treas. 1937
Treasurer 1938
VP/Treas. 1939

GORDON S. COCHRANE
VP/Field Mgr. 1936-38

JACK ZELLER
Minor League Dir. 1938
Secy./GM 1939

FIELD MANAGERS:

BUCKY HARRIS
1930-33

DEL BAKER
(interim 1933, 36, 37)
1938-39

MICKEY COCHRANE
1934-38

COACHES:

BENNY MEYER 1930
WISH EGAN 1930
ROGER BRESNAHAN 1930-31
JEAN DUBUC 1930-31
JEWEL ENS 1932
BOB COLEMAN 1932
DEL BAKER 1933-38
CY PERKINS 1934-38
BING MILLER 1938-39
MERV SHEA 1939

BOB FOTHERGILL
outfielder 1930

ELIAS
"LIZ" FUNK
outfielder
1930

GUY CANTRELL
pitcher 1930

HUGH WISE
catcher 1930

JIMMY SHEVLIN
first baseman 1930

OWEN CARROLL
pitcher 1930

Detroit Tigers (continued)

CHARLEY GEHRINGER
second baseman
1930-39

HARRY RICE
outfielder
1930

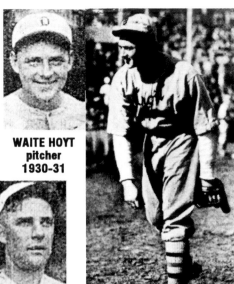

WAITE HOYT
pitcher
1930-31

CHARLIE SULLIVAN
pitcher 1930-31

DALE ALEXANDER
first baseman
1930-32

GEORGE UHLE
pitcher 1930-33

RAY HAYWORTH
catcher 1930-38

PAUL EASTERLING
outfielder
1930

GEORGE "TONY" RENSA
catcher 1930

PHIL PAGE
pitcher 1930

JOHN WATSON
shortstop 1930

JOE SAMUELS
third baseman
1930

PINKY HARGRAVE
catcher 1930

GEORGE "YATS" WUESTLING
shortstop
1930

THOMAS "BILL" AKERS
infielder
1930-31

MARK KOENIG
infielder, pitcher
1930-31

WHITLOW WYATT
pitcher 1930-33

Detroit Tigers (continued)

FRANK DOLJACK
outfielder 1930-34

MARTY McMANUS
infielder 1930-31

ROY JOHNSON
outfielder 1930-32

HANK GREENBERG
first baseman
1930, 1933-39

GENE DESAUTELS
catcher 1930-33

VIC SORRELL
pitcher 1930-37

EARL WHITEHILL
pitcher 1930-32

ART HERRING
pitcher 1930-33

TOM HUGHES
outfielder
1930

TOMMY BRIDGES
pitcher 1930-39

JOHNNY STONE
outfielder
1930-33

Detroit Tigers (continued)

**ELON
"CHIEF" HOGSETT**
pitcher 1930-36

BILLY ROGELL
shortstop 1930-39

GEORGE QUELLICH
outfielder 1931

JOHN GRABOWSKI
catcher 1931

**GERALD
"GEE" WALKER**
outfielder
1931-37

BUCKY HARRIS
second baseman 1931
(manager 1930-33)

WALLY SCHANG
catcher 1931

JOE DUGAN
third baseman
1931

LOU BROWER
shortstop 1931

MARVIN OWEN
third baseman
1931, 1933-37

**HARVEY
"HUB" WALKER**
outfielder
1931, 1935

**CLIFFORD
"NOLEN" RICHARDSON**
third baseman 1931-32

ORLIN COLLIER
pitcher 1931

IVEY SHIVER
outfielder 1931

**HAROLD
"MUDDY" RUEL**
catcher 1931-32

**TRUETT
"RIP" SEWELL**
pitcher 1932

Detroit Tigers (continued)

BILL LAWRENCE
outfielder 1932

IZZY GOLDSTEIN
pitcher 1932

GEORGE SUSCE
catcher 1932

**JOYNER
"JO-JO" WHITE**
outfielder
1932-38

BILL RHIEL
utility 1932-33

FIRPO MARBERRY
pitcher 1933-35

BUCK MARROW
pitcher 1932

HARRY DAVIS
first baseman
1932-33

EARL WEBB
outfielder
1932-33

HEINIE SCHUBLE
infielder 1932-35

ROXIE LAWSON
pitcher 1933, 1935-39

Detroit Tigers (continued)

ERVIN
"PETE" FOX
outfielder
1933-39

VIC FRASIER
pitcher
1933-34

FRANK REIBER
catcher 1933-36

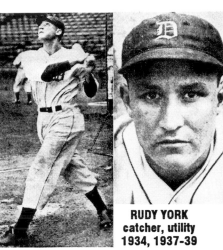

RUDY YORK
catcher, utility
1934, 1937-39

LYNWOOD
"SCHOOLBOY" ROWE
pitcher 1933-39

JOHN PASEK
catcher 1933

HERMAN CLIFTON
infielder 1934-37

CY PERKINS
catcher 1934

CARL FISCHER
pitcher 1933-35

LUKE HAMLIN
pitcher 1933-34

FRANCIS
"BOTS" NEKOLA
pitcher 1933

STEVE LARKIN
pitcher 1934

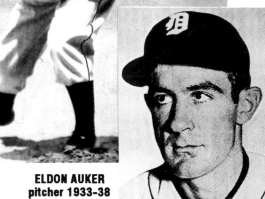

ELDON AUKER
pitcher 1933-38

GEORGE WILSON
pinch-hitter
1934

Detroit Tigers (continued)

GORDON "MICKEY" COCHRANE
catcher 1934-37
(manager 1934-38)

GOOSE GOSLIN
outfielder
1934-37

AL SIMMONS
outfielder
1936

ALVIN "GENERAL" CROWDER
pitcher 1934-36

RED PHILLIPS
pitcher 1934, 1936

HUGH SHELLEY
outfielder 1935

JOE SULLIVAN
pitcher 1935-36

GLENN MYATT
catcher 1936

CHICK MORGAN
outfielder 1935, 1938

CLYDE HATTER
pitcher 1935, 1937

JAKE WADE
pitcher
1936-38

Detroit Tigers (continued)

JACK BURNS
first baseman
1936

GIL ENGLISH
infielder
1936-37

JACK RUSSELL
pitcher 1937

PAT McLAUGHLIN
pitcher 1937

**CLETUS "BOOTS"
POFFENBERGER**
pitcher 1937-38

BABE HERMAN
outfielder 1937

SALTY PARKER
infielder 1936

BIRDIE TEBBETTS
catcher 1936-39

CHARLIE GELBERT
shortstop 1937

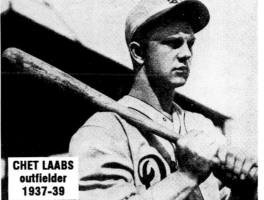

CHET LAABS
outfielder
1937-39

JOE ROGALSKI
pitcher 1938

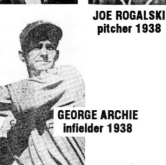

DON ROSS
third baseman
1938

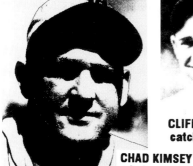

CHAD KIMSEY
pitcher 1936

CLIFF BOLTON
catcher 1937

BOB LOGAN
pitcher 1937

GEORGE GILL
pitcher 1937-39

GEORGE COFFMAN
pitcher 1937-39

GEORGE ARCHIE
infielder 1938

TONY PIET
(PIETRUSZKA)
third baseman
1938

VERN KENNEDY
pitcher 1938-39

ROY CULLENBINE
outfielder 1938-39

AL BENTON
pitcher 1938-39

FLOYD GIEBELL
pitcher 1939

BEAU BELL
outfielder
1939

PAUL
"DIZZY" TROUT
pitcher
1939

BOB HARRIS
pitcher 1938-39

BENNY McCOY
infielder 1938-39

JIM WALKUP
pitcher 1939

COTTON PIPPEN
pitcher 1939

WOODROW
"BABE" DAVIS
pitcher 1938

HARRY
EISENSTAT
pitcher
1938-39

MARK CHRISTMAN
shortstop 1938-39

FRED
"DIXIE" WALKER
outfielder
1938-39

FRANK CROUCHER
shortstop 1939

RED KRESS
shortstop 1939

MERVYN SHEA
catcher 1939

HAROLD NEWHOUSER
pitcher
1939

FRED HUTCHINSON
pitcher 1939

UNIFORMS:

BUD THOMAS
pitcher 1939

ED "DIXIE" PARSONS
catcher 1939

BUCK NEWSOM
pitcher 1939

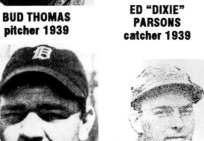

LESLIE H. "MOE" FLEMING
outfielder 1939

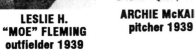

ARCHIE McKAIN
pitcher 1939

BARNEY McCOSKY
outfielder 1939

PINKY HIGGINS
third baseman
1939

RED LYNN
pitcher 1939

EARL AVERILL
outfielder 1939

New York Giants

FRONT OFFICE:

CHARLES A. STONEHAM
President 1930-35

HORACE STONEHAM
President 1936-39

JOHN J. McGRAW
VP/Field Mgr. 1930-32
VP 1933-34

LEO BONDY
Treasurer 1930-35
VP/Treas. 1936-39

JAMES TIERNEY
Secretary 1930-35

ED BRANNICK
Traveling Secy. 1931-32
Asst. Secy. 1933-35
Secretary 1936-39

FIELD MANAGERS:

JOHN McGRAW
1930-32

BILL TERRY
1932-39

COACHES:

IRISH MEUSEL 1930
DAVE BANCROFT 1930-32
TOMMY CLARKE 1930-35, 38
CHIEF BENDER 1931
GEORGE J. BURNS 1931
IVY OLSEN 1932
CLARENCE MITCHELL 1932-33
AL SMITH 1933
BILLY SOUTHWORTH 1933
FRANK SNYDER 1933-39
ADOLFO LUQUE 1935-38
TRAVIS JACKSON 1939

THE PLAYERS:

DAVE BANCROFT
shortstop 1930

WALLY ROETTGER
outfielder 1930

PETE DONOHUE
pitcher 1930-31

JO-JO MOORE
outfielder
1930-39

LARRY BENTON
pitcher 1930

JOE GENEWICH
pitcher 1930

PAT CRAWFORD
infielder 1930

HARRY ROSENBERG
outfielder
1930

HUB PRUETT
pitcher 1930

ANDY REESE
third base, outfield
1930

RALPH JUDD
pitcher 1930

WILLARD MORRELL
pitcher 1930-31

New York Giants (continued)

FRED LEACH
outfielder 1930-31

FRANCIS HEALY
catcher, outfield
1930-32

CHICK FULLIS
outfielder
1930-32

CARL HUBBELL
pitcher
1930-39

BILL WALKER
pitcher 1930-32

ROY PARMELEE
pitcher 1930-35

HUGH CRITZ
second baseman
1930-35

JAMES
"TINY" CHAPLIN
pitcher 1930-31

RAY LUCAS
pitcher
1930-31

CLARENCE
MITCHELL
pitcher
1930-32

BOB O'FARRELL
catcher 1930-32

SHANTY HOGAN
catcher 1930-32

TRAVIS JACKSON
shortstop 1930-36

JOE HEVING
pitcher 1930-31

BILL TERRY
first baseman
1930-36
(manager 1932-39)

New York Giants (continued)

MEL OTT
outfield, third base
1930-39

FRED FITZSIMMONS
pitcher 1930-37

HAL SCHUMACHER
pitcher 1931-39

JIM MOONEY
pitcher 1931-32

WAITE HOYT
pitcher
1932

SAM GIBSON
pitcher 1932

DOC MARSHALL
infielder 1930-32

SAM LESLIE
first baseman
1930-33, 1936-38

JACK BERLY
pitcher 1931

GIL ENGLISH
infielder
1931-32

PAT VELTMAN
catcher 1932

**GRAHAM
"EDDIE" MOORE**
shortstop
1932

ETHAN ALLEN
outfielder 1930-32

FRED LINDSTROM
third base, outfield
1930-32

JOHNNY VERGEZ
third baseman
1931-34

EMIL PLANETA
pitcher 1931

BILL HUNNEFIELD
second baseman 1931

ART McLARNEY
shortstop 1932

**JOHN M.
"TIP" TOBIN**
pinch-hitter
1932

New York Giants (continued)

LEN KOENECKE
outfielder 1932

RAY STARR
pitcher 1933

CHUCK DRESSEN
third baseman 1933

BILL SHORES
pitcher 1933

HOMER PEEL
outfielder
1933-34

JOE MALAY
first baseman
1933, 1935

GLENN SPENCER
pitcher 1933

GEORGE UHLE
pitcher 1933

**ROBERT
"BERNIE" JAMES**
infielder 1933

LEFTY O'DOUL
outfielder 1933-34

**GEORGE
"KIDDO" DAVIS**
outfielder
1933, 1935-37

**HERMAN
"HI" BELL**
pitcher
1932-34

ADOLFO LUQUE
pitcher 1932-35

HANK LEIBER
outfielder 1933-38

PAUL RICHARDS
catcher 1933-35

GUS MANCUSO
catcher
1933-38

**JOHN
"BLONDY" RYAN**
infielder
1933-34, 1937-38

New York Giants (continued)

JACK SALVESON
pitcher 1933-34

PHIL WEINTRAUB
outfield, first base
1933-35, 1937

FRESCO THOMPSON
infielder 1934

AL SMITH
pitcher
1934-37

LEON CHAGNON
pitcher 1935

DICK BARTELL
shortstop 1935-38

EUEL MOORE
pitcher 1935

HARRY DANNING
catcher 1933-39

WILLIAM "WATTY" CLARK
pitcher
1933-34

JOE BOWMAN
pitcher 1934

GLENN MYATT
catcher 1935

MARK KOENIG
infielder
1935-36

ALLYN STOUT
pitcher 1935

CHARLIE ENGLISH
second baseman
1936

AL CUCCINELLO
infielder 1935

JIM SHEEHAN
catcher 1936

GEORGE WATKINS
outfielder 1934

GEORGE GRANTHAM
infielder 1934

CLYDELL "SLICK" CASTLEMAN
pitcher 1934-39

HARRY GUMBERT
pitcher 1935-39

FRANK GABLER
pitcher 1935-37

FIRPO MARBERRY
pitcher 1936

WILLIAM "JOE" MARTIN
third baseman
1936

New York Giants (continued)

EDDIE MAYO
third baseman
1936

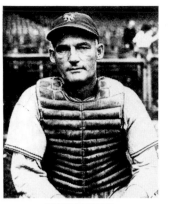

ROY SPENCER
catcher 1936

**SAMUEL
"DICK" COFFMAN**
pitcher 1936-39

WALLY BERGER
outfielder 1937-38

**HY
VANDENBERG**
pitcher 1937-39

LOU CHIOZZA
utility 1937-39

**BURGESS
WHITEHEAD**
infielder
1936-37, 1939

**NORMAN
"BABE" YOUNG**
first baseman
1936, 1939

**JAMES
"DON" BRENNAN**
pitcher 1937

TOM BAKER
pitcher
1937-38

MICKEY HASLIN
infielder 1937-38

JIMMY RIPPLE
outfielder 1936-39

JOHNNY McCARTHY
first baseman 1936-39

**WALTER
"JUMBO" BROWN**
pitcher 1937-39

BEN CANTWELL
pitcher 1937

**ED
MADJESKI
(MAJEWSKI)**
catcher 1937

BILL LOHRMAN
pitcher 1937-39

CLIFF MELTON
pitcher 1937-39

New York Giants (continued)

BOB SEEDS
outfielder
1938-39

JOHN WITTIG
pitcher 1938-39

ALEX KAMPOURIS
second baseman
1938-39

TONY LAZZERI
third baseman
1939

JOHNNY DICKSHOT
(DICKSUS)
outfielder 1939

UNIFORMS:

BILL CISSELL
infielder
1938

LES POWERS
first baseman
1938

FRANK DEMAREE
outfielder 1939

FRANK SCALZI
infielder 1939

BILLY JURGES
shortstop 1939

1939

1938 sleeve patch

GEORGE MYATT
infielder
1938-39

OSCAR GEORGY
pitcher 1938

RED LYNN
pitcher 1939

TOM HAFEY
third baseman
1939

ZEKE BONURA
first baseman
1939

TOM GORMAN
pitcher 1939

RAY HAYWORTH
catcher 1939

AL GLOSSOP
second baseman
1939

MANUEL SALVO
pitcher 1939

KEN O'DEA
catcher 1939

New York Yankees

FRONT OFFICE:

GEORGE RUPPERT
VP 1930-39

JACOB RUPPERT
President 1930-38

ALBERT BRENNAN
Treasurer 1930-39

ED BARROW
Secy./Bus. Mgr. 1930-38
President 1939

MARK ROTH
Traveling Secy.
1930-39

GEORGE WEISS
Secretary 1939

FIELD MANAGERS:

BOB SHAWKEY
1930

JOE McCARTHY
1931-39

COACHES:

CHARLEY O'LEARY 1930
ART FLETCHER 1930-39
JIMMY BURKE 1931-33
CY PERKINS 1932-33
JOE SEWELL 1934-35
JOHNNY SCHULTE 1934-39
EARLE COMBS 1936-39

THE PLAYERS:

WAITE HOYT
pitcher 1930

TOM ZACHARY
pitcher 1930

CEDRIC DURST
outfielder 1930

FRANK BARNES
pitcher 1930

KEN HOLLOWAY
pitcher 1930

HARRY RICE
outfielder 1930

HANK KARLON
outfielder 1930

SAM GIBSON
pitcher 1930

**FOSTER
"EDDIE" EDWARDS**
pitcher 1930

**BILL
HENDERSON**
pitcher 1930

**GEORGE "YATS"
WUESTLING**
shortstop 1930

New York Yankees (continued)

MARK KOENIG
shortstop 1930

OWEN CARROLL
pitcher 1930

BENNY BENGOUGH
catcher 1930

BABE RUTH
outfielder, pitcher
1930-34

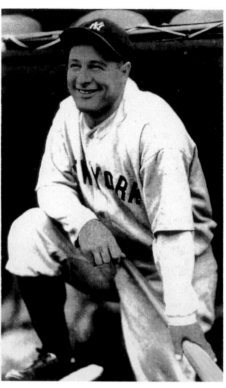

**JIMMY REESE
(SOLOMON)**
second baseman
1930-31

LOU GEHRIG
first baseman
1930-39

**EUGENE
"BUBBLES" HARGRAVE**
catcher 1930

EDDIE WELLS
pitcher
1930-32

LOU McEVOY
pitcher 1930-31

**JOHN G.
"DUSTY" RHODES**
pitcher 1930-32

**WILLIAM
"BEN" CHAPMAN**
utility 1930-36

SAMMY BYRD
outfielder 1930-34

HANK JOHNSON
pitcher 1930-32

ROY SHERID
pitcher 1930-31

EARLE COMBS
outfielder 1930-35

**CHARLES
"RED" RUFFING**
pitcher
1930-39

New York Yankees (continued)

BILL DICKEY
catcher
1930-39

HERB PENNOCK
pitcher 1930-33

BILLY WERBER
infielder 1930, 1933

JOE SEWELL
third baseman
1931-33

RED ROLFE
infielder
1931, 1934-39

**VERNON
"LEFTY" GOMEZ**
pitcher 1930-39

ARNDT JORGENS
catcher 1930-39

MYRIL HOAG
outfielder
1931-32, 1934-38

**FRED
"DIXIE" WALKER**
outfielder
1931, 1933-36

PHIL WEINERT
pitcher 1931

DUSTY COOKE
outfielder
1930-32

GEORGE PIPGRAS
pitcher 1930-33

TONY LAZZERI
infielder 1930-37

LYN LARY
shortstop, utility
1930-34

JIM WEAVER
pitcher 1931

CY PERKINS
catcher 1931

IVY ANDREWS
pitcher
1931-32, 1937-38

New York Yankees (continued)

ED PHILLIPS
catcher 1932

JOHNNY ALLEN
pitcher 1932-35

WILCY MOORE
pitcher 1932-33

FRANK CROSETTI
shortstop 1932-39

DOC FARRELL
infielder 1932-33

RUSS VANATTA
pitcher 1933-35

PETE APPLETON
(JABLONOWSKI)
pitcher 1933

LEROY SCHALK
second baseman
1932

JOHNNY MURPHY
pitcher 1932, 1934-39

JOE GLENN
(GURZENSKY)
catcher
1932-33, 1935-38

OTTO
SALTZGAVER
infielder
1932, 1934-37

GEORGE
"TONY" RENSA
catcher 1933

VITO TAMULIS
pitcher 1934-35

BURLEIGH GRIMES
pitcher 1934

JOHN BROACA
pitcher 1934-37

CHARLIE DEVENS
pitcher 1932-34

DANNY
MacFAYDEN
pitcher
1932-34

WALTER
"JUMBO" BROWN
pitcher
1932-33, 1935-36

JAMES
"DON" BRENNAN
pitcher 1933

GEORGE UHLE
pitcher 1933-34

JAMES
"ZACK" TAYLOR
catcher 1934

WILLIAM
"HARRY" SMYTHE
pitcher 1934

New York Yankees (continued)

GEORGE SELKIRK
outfielder 1934-39

JIM DESHONG
pitcher 1934-35

PAT MALONE
pitcher 1935-37

**KEMP WICKER
(WHICKER)**
pitcher 1936-38

BOB SEEDS
outfielder
1936

MONTE PEARSON
pitcher 1936-39

BABE DAHLGREN
first baseman
1937-39

DON HEFFNER
infielder
1934-37

**JOHN
"BLONDY" RYAN**
infielder
1935

STEVE SUNDRA
pitcher
1936, 1938-39

**IRVING
"BUMP" HADLEY**
pitcher 1936-39

ROY JOHNSON
outfielder
1936-37

JESSE HILL
outfielder
1935

**NOLEN
RICHARDSON**
shortstop 1935

**TED
KLEINHANS**
pitcher
1936

JOE DiMAGGIO
outfielder
1936-39

JAKE POWELL
outfielder
1936-39

TOMMY HENRICH
outfielder 1937-39

New York Yankees (continued)

JOE VANCE
pitcher 1937-38

SPUD CHANDLER
pitcher 1937-39

JOE GORDON
second baseman
1938-39

CHARLIE KELLER
outfielder 1939

UNIFORMS:

FRANK MAKOSKY
pitcher 1937

LEE STINE
pitcher 1938

WES FERRELL
pitcher 1938-39

ORAL HILDEBRAND
pitcher 1939

BUDDY ROSAR
catcher 1939

1938 sleeve patch

ATLEY DONALD
pitcher 1938-39

**BILL
KNICKERBOCKER**
infielder
1938-39

JOE BEGGS
pitcher
1938

MARIUS RUSSO
pitcher 1939

JOE GALLAGHER
outfielder 1939

Philadelphia Athletics

FRONT OFFICE:

THOMAS SHIBE
President 1930-35

JOHN SHIBE
VP/Secy. 1930-35
Treasurer 1933-35
President 1936

RUDOLPH VON OHL
Traveling Secy. 1930-36

ROBT. SCHROEDER
Business Mgr. 1932-36
Asst. Secy. 1937-39

CONNIE MACK
Treasurer/Field Mgr.
1930-39
President 1937-39

ROY MACK
VP 1936
VP/Secy. 1937-39

BEN McFARLAND
Traveling Secy.
1937-39

FRANK McFARLAND
Asst. Treas. 1937
Treasurer 1938

FIELD MANAGER:

CONNIE MACK
1930-39

COACHES:

EDDIE COLLINS 1930-32
KID GLEASON 1930-32
EARLE MACK 1930-39
CONNIE MACK, JR. 1932-
EDDIE ROMMEL 1933-34
LENA BLACKBURNE 1933-39
CHARLIE BERRY 1936-39
DAVE KEEFE 1939

THE PLAYERS:

EDDIE COLLINS, Sr.
pinch-hitter 1930

HOMER SUMMA
outfielder 1930

WALLY SCHANG
catcher 1930

JACK QUINN
(PICUS)
pitcher 1930

HOWARD EHMKE
pitcher 1930

GLENN LIEBHARDT, Jr.
pitcher 1930

AL MAHON
pitcher
1930

CHARLES
PERKINS
pitcher
1930

JIM KEESEY
first baseman
1930

ROY MAHAFFEY
pitcher 1930-35

Philadelphia Athletics (continued)

LEFTY GROVE
pitcher
1930-33

EDDIE ROMMEL
pitcher 1930-32

JOE BOLEY
shortstop
1930-32

GEORGE EARNSHAW
pitcher 1930-33

PINKY HIGGINS
third baseman
1930, 1933-36

ROGER
"DOC" CRAMER
outfielder
1930-35

CY PERKINS
catcher 1930

JIMMY DYKES
infielder 1930-32

MULE HAAS
outfielder
1930-32, 1938

SPENCER HARRIS
oufielder 1930

BILL SHORES
pitcher 1930-31

BING MILLER
outfielder 1930-34

Philadelphia Athletics (continued)

MICKEY COCHRANE
catcher 1930-33

AL SIMMONS
outfielder
1930-32

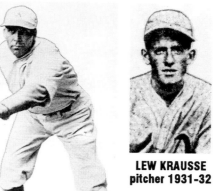

RUBE WALBERG
pitcher 1930-33

LEW KRAUSSE
pitcher 1931-32

JAMES W.
"JIM" MOORE
outfielder
1930-31

JIMMY FOXX
first baseman
1930-35

ERIC McNAIR
infielder 1930-35

JOHN HEVING
catcher 1931-32

DIB WILLIAMS
infielder 1930-35

MAX BISHOP
second baseman
1930-33

BUCK CARTER
pitcher 1931

JOE
PALMISANO
catcher 1931

PHIL TODT
first baseman
1931

Philadelphia Athletics (continued)

WAITE HOYT
pitcher 1931

LOU FINNEY
outfield, first base
1931, 1933-39

JIM DESHONG
pitcher 1932

**ED MADJESKI
(MAJEWSKI)**
catcher 1932-34

**MERRITT
"SUGAR" CAIN**
pitcher
1932-35

**TIM
McKEITHAN**
pitcher
1932-34

**JOHN W.
JONES**
outfielder
1932

JIM PETERSON
pitcher 1931, 1933

HANK McDONALD
pitcher 1931, 1933

JOE BOWMAN
pitcher 1932

TONY FREITAS
pitcher 1932-33

ED COLEMAN
outfielder
1932-35

BOBBY COOMBS
pitcher 1933

HANK WINSTON
pitcher 1933

OSCAR ROETTGER
first baseman 1932

AL REISS
shortstop
1932

ED CIHOCKI
outfield, shortstop
1932-33

EMILE ROY
pitcher 1933

**GOWELL
CLASET**
pitcher
1933

**RICHARD
TRACY BARRETT
(OLIVER)**
pitcher 1933

Philadelphia Athletics (continued)

BILL DIETRICH
pitcher 1933-36

JACK WILSON
pitcher 1934

JOE CASCARELLA
pitcher
1934-35

WHITEY WILSHERE
pitcher
1934-36

AL BENTON
pitcher
1934-35

BOB JOHNSON
outfielder 1933-39

GEORGE CASTER
pitcher
1934-35, 1937-39

JOE ZAPUSTAS
outfielder
1933

FRANK HAYES
catcher
1933-34, 1936-39

RABBIT WARSTLER
infielder 1934-36

DUTCH FLOHR
pitcher 1934

ROY VAUGHN
pitcher 1934

CHARLIE BERRY
catcher
1934-36, 1938

FURMAN OWENS
catcher 1935

JOHN MARCUM
pitcher 1933-35

HARRY MATUZAK
pitcher 1934, 1936

ED LAGGER
pitcher 1934

BOB KLINE
pitcher 1934

JERRY McQUAIG
outfielder 1934

**CHARLES C.
"CHARLIE" MOSS**
catcher 1934-36

AL VEACH
pitcher 1935

Philadelphia Athletics (continued)

PAUL RICHARDS
catcher 1935

GEORGE
BLAEHOLDER
pitcher 1935

ALEXANDER
HOOKS
first baseman
1935

SKEETER
NEWSOME
shortstop
1935-39

WILLIAM
"CARL" DOYLE
pitcher
1935-36

GEORGE
TURBEVILLE
pitcher
1935-37

PETE
NAKTENIS
pitcher
1936

GUIDO
MARTINI
pitcher
1935

VALLIE EAVES
pitcher 1935

BERNARD
SNYDER
infielder
1935

HERMAN FINK
pitcher 1935-37

JACK PEERSON
infielder 1935-36

WOODY UPCHURCH
pitcher 1935-36

JIM OGLESBY
first baseman
1936

CHARLES LIEBER
pitcher 1935-36

HOD
LISENBEE
pitcher
1936

BILL
FERRAZZI
pitcher 1935

BILL PATTON
catcher 1935

BILL CONROY
catcher
1935-37

WALLY MOSES
outfielder 1935-39

HANK JOHNSON
pitcher 1936

HAL LUBY
second baseman
1936

EMIL MAILHO
outfielder 1936

Philadelphia Athletics (continued)

BILL NICHOLSON
outfielder 1936

**ALFRED
"CHUBBY"
DEAN**
pitcher, first base
1936-39

RUSTY PETERS
infielder 1936-38

**RANDY
GUMPERT**
pitcher
1936-38

BUCK ROSS
pitcher
1936-39

BILL CISSELL
infielder 1937

EARLE BRUCKER
catcher 1937-39

**GEORGE
PUCCINELLI**
outfielder
1936

HARRY KELLEY
pitcher 1936-38

DOYT MORRIS
outfielder 1937

JACK ROTHROCK
outfielder 1937

RED BULLOCK
pitcher 1936

ED SMITH
pitcher
1936-39

BILL KALFASS
pitcher 1937

FRED ARCHER
pitcher 1936-37

AL NIEMIEC
second baseman
1936

**JOHN G.
"DUSTY" RHODES**
pitcher 1936

STUART FLYTHE
pitcher 1936

DICK CULLER
infielder 1936

WARREN HUSTON
infielder 1937

JESSE HILL
outfielder
1937

Philadelphia Athletics (continued)

BILLY WERBER
infielder 1937-38

GENE HASSON
first baseman
1937-38

HAL WAGNER
catcher 1937-39

IRV BARTLING
shortstop 1938

DICK SIEBERT
first baseman
1938-39

LYNN NELSON
pitcher 1937-39

BUD THOMAS
pitcher 1937-39

FLOYD YOUNT
outfielder 1937

BABE BARNA
outfielder
1937-38

**PAUL
EASTERLING**
outfielder
1938

NELSON POTTER
pitcher 1938-39

**DARIO
LODIGIANI**
infielder
1938-39

**CLARENCE
"ACE" PARKER**
shortstop 1937-38

**ALMON
WILLIAMS**
pitcher
1937-38

WAYNE AMBLER
second baseman
1937-39

**RALPH
BUXTON**
pitcher
1938

STAN SPERRY
second baseman
1938

DAVE SMITH
pitcher 1938-39

NICK ETTEN
first baseman
1938-39

Philadelphia Athletics (continued)

UNIFORMS:

SAM CHAPMAN
outfield, first base
1938-39

JIM RENINGER
pitcher 1938-39

AL BRANCATO
third baseman
1939

BOB McNAMARA
third baseman
1939

DEE MILES
outfielder
1939

ROY PARMELEE
pitcher 1939

COTTON PIPPEN
pitcher 1939

WALT MASTERS
pitcher 1939

BILL BECKMAN
pitcher 1939

BIL NAGEL
pitcher, infielder
1939

EDDIE COLLINS, Jr.
outfielder 1939

SAM PAGE
pitcher 1939

BOB JOYCE
pitcher 1939

BILL LILLARD
shortstop 1939

ERIC TIPTON
outfielder
1939

LES McCRABB
pitcher 1939

FRED CHAPMAN
shortstop 1939

SEP GANTENBEIN
infielder 1939

Philadelphia Phillies

FRONT OFFICE:

WILLIAM F. BAKER
President 1930

LEWIS C. RUCH
VP 1930
President
1931-32

ROBERT IRWIN
Secretary 1930-39

GERALD P. NUGENT
Bus. Mgr. 1930-32
President 1932-39

DOUGLAS NICHOLSON
VP 1931-34

MAE M. (MRS. G. P.) NUGENT
Asst. Secy. 1930
Treasurer 1931-34
VP 1935-39

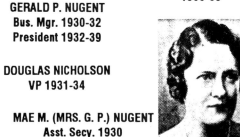

FIELD MANAGERS:

BURT SHOTTON
1930-33

JIMMY WILSON
1934-38

HANS LOBERT
(interim) 1938

DOC PROTHRO
1939

COACHES:

NEWT HUNTER 1930-31, 33
JACK ONSLOW 1931-32
DICK SPALDING 1934-36
HANS LOBERT 1934-39
CLARENCE JONNARD 1935
SYL JOHNSON 1937-39

THE PLAYERS:

CLAUDE WILLOUGHBY
pitcher 1930

GROVER ALEXANDER
pitcher 1930

TRIPP SIGMAN
outfielder 1930

CY WILLIAMS
outfielder 1930

LES SWEETLAND
pitcher 1930

HARRY SMYTHE
pitcher 1930

JIM SPOTTS
catcher
1930

LEFTY O'DOUL
outfielder 1930

Philadelphia Phillies (continued)

LOU KOUPAL
pitcher 1930

ALBERT PHILLIPS
pitcher 1930

MONK SHERLOCK
first baseman 1930

HOWARD ELLIOTT
pitcher 1930-32

TONY RENSA
catcher 1930-31

CHUCK KLEIN
outfielder
1930-33, 1936-39

PINKY WHITNEY
third baseman
1930-33, 1936-39

DENNY SOTHERN
outfielder 1930

FRESCO THOMPSON
second baseman 1930

FRANK "DON" HURST
first baseman
1930-34

SPUD DAVIS
catcher
1930-33, 1938-39

HAP COLLARD
pitcher 1930

HARRY McCURDY
catcher 1930-33

JOHN MILLIGAN
pitcher 1930-31

TOMMY THEVENOW
shortstop 1930

RAY BENGE
pitcher
1930-32, 1936

BARNEY FRIBERG
utility 1930-32

SNIPE HANSEN
pitcher
1930, 1932-35

PHIL COLLINS
pitcher 1930-35

Philadelphia Phillies (continued)

BYRON SPEECE
pitcher 1930

CHESTER NICHOLS
pitcher 1930-32

FRED BRICKELL
outfielder 1930-33

BUZZ ARLETT
first base, outfield
1931

DICK BARTELL
shortstop 1931-34

FRED KOSTER
outfielder 1931

ED HOLLEY
pitcher
1932-34

EDWARD FALLENSTEIN (VALESTIN)
pitcher 1931

BEN SHIELDS
pitcher 1931

JOHN "FRED" BLAKE
pitcher 1931

LES MALLON
second baseman
1931-32

STEWART BOLEN
pitcher 1931-32

FRANK WATT
pitcher 1931

DUTCH SCHESLER
pitcher
1931

LIL STONER
pitcher 1931

CLISE DUDLEY
pitcher 1931-32

HAROLD "SHERIFF" LEE
outfielder
1931-33

DOUG TAITT
outfielder
1931-32

CLIFF HEATHCOTE
outfielder
1932

HAROLD WILTSE
pitcher 1931

JIM ELLIOTT
pitcher
1931-34

BOB STEVENS
shortstop 1931

EUGENE CONNELL
catcher 1931

HUGH WILLINGHAM
second baseman
1931-33

ROBERT ADAMS
pitcher 1931-32

Philadelphia Phillies (continued)

GEORGE
"KIDDO" DAVIS
outfielder
1932, 1934

GEORGE
KNOTHE
second baseman
1932

FLINT RHEM
pitcher 1932-33

AL TODD
catcher
1932-35

ALTA COHEN
outfielder 1933

JOHN WARNER
infielder 1933

MICKEY HASLIN
infielder 1933-36

FRANK PEARCE
pitcher 1933-35

RUSS SCARRITT
outfielder 1932

RUBE BRESSLER
outfielder 1932

ED DELKER
infielder
1932-33

NEAL "MICKEY" FINN
second baseman
1933

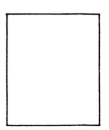

JIM McLEOD
infielder 1933

CLARENCE
PICKREL
pitcher 1933

CY MOORE
pitcher
1933-34

WES
SCHULMERIC
outfielder
1933-34

REG
GRABOWSKI
pitcher
1932-34

JOHN BERLY
pitcher
1932-33

JOHN
JACKSON
pitcher
1933

WILFRED
"FRITZ" KNOTHE
infielder 1933

GUS DUGAS
utility 1933

FRANK
RAGLAND
pitcher
1933

CHICK FULLIS
outfielder 1933-34

AD LISKA
pitcher 1932-33

Philadelphia Phillies (continued)

HACK WILSON
outfielder 1934

BILL LOHRMAN
pitcher 1934

IRV JEFFRIES
infielder 1934

ANDY HIGH
third baseman
1934

BUCKY WALTERS
pitcher, utility
1934-38

SYL JOHNSON
pitcher 1934-39

CURT DAVIS
pitcher
1934-36

FRED FRINK
outfielder
1934

BUD CLANCY
first baseman
1934

HARVEY HENDRICK
outfielder 1934

CY MALIS
pitcher
1934

ED BOLAND
outfielder
1934-35

TED KLEINHANS
pitcher 1934

MARTY HOPKINS
third baseman 1934

GEORGE DARROW
pitcher 1934

ART RUBLE
outfielder
1934

EUEL MOORE
pitcher
1934-35, 1936

JOE HOLDEN
catcher 1934-36

HENRY OANA
outfielder 1934

LOU CHIOZZA
utility 1934-36

Philadelphia Phillies (continued)

JIMMY WILSON
catcher 1934–38
(manager 1934–38)

DOLPH CAMILLI
first baseman
1934–37

**ALPHONSE
"TOMMY" THOMAS**
pitcher 1935

GEORGE WATKINS
outfielder 1935–36

**HAROLD
KELLEHER**
pitcher
1935–38

**JOHN
PEZZULLO**
pitcher
1935–36

TOM ZACHARY
pitcher 1936

JOHNNY MOORE
outfielder 1934–37

RAY PRIM
pitcher 1935

JIM BIVIN
pitcher
1935

ART BRAMHALL
infielder 1935

**JOSE
"CHILE" GOMEZ**
infielder
1935–36

JOHN VERGEZ
third baseman
1935–36

HUGH MULCAHY
pitcher 1935–39

ETHAN ALLEN
outfielder 1934–36

FRED LUCAS
outfielder 1935

**JOHN
"BLONDY" RYAN**
infielder 1935

**CLARENCE
"BUBBER" JONNARD**
catcher 1935

ORVILLE JORGENS
pitcher 1935–37

DINO CHIOZZA
shortstop 1935

JOE BOWMAN
pitcher 1935–36

**ROMAN
BERTRAND**
pitcher 1936

Philadelphia Phillies (continued)

ELMER BURKART
pitcher 1936-39

HERSHEL MARTIN
outfielder 1937-39

BILL ATWOOD
catcher 1936-39

HERB HARRIS
pitcher 1936

STAN SPERRY
second baseman 1936

**MORRIE
ARNOVICH**
outfielder
1936-39

**WAYNE
LaMASTER**
pitcher 1937-38

CHUCK SHEERIN
infielder 1936

CLAUDE PASSEAU
pitcher 1936-39

**EUGENE
CORBETT**
infielder
1936-38

**FRED TAUBY
(TAUBENSEE)**
outfielder 1937

**ROBERT
"EARL" GRACE**
catcher
1936-37

LEO NORRIS
infielder
1936-37

**WALT
BASHORE**
outfielder
1936

**FABIAN
KOWALIK**
pitcher
1936

**ERNEST
"DAVE" SULIK**
outfielder
1936

PETE SIVESS
pitcher 1936-38

LEON PETTIT
pitcher
1937

BOB ALLEN
pitcher 1937

**CHARLES
"LARRY" CRAWFORD**
pitcher 1937

**GEORGE
SCHAREIN**
shortstop
1937-39**

Philadelphia Phillies (continued)

DEL YOUNG
infielder
1937-39

BOB BURKE
pitcher 1937

HOWARD GORMAN
outfielder 1937-38

TUCK STAINBACK
outfielder 1938

**JOHN
"CAP" CLARK**
catcher 1938

**PHIL
WEINTRAUB**
first baseman
1938

**JAMES W.
"EARL" BROWNE**
first base, outfield
1937-38

**WALT
STEPHENSON**
catcher 1937

RAY STOVIAK
outfielder 1938

JUSTIN STEIN
infielder 1938

**EMMET
"HEINIE" MUELLER**
utility 1938-39

ED HEUSSER
pitcher 1938

MAX BUTCHER
pitcher 1938-39

**AL
HOLLINGSWORTH**
pitcher 1938-39

BILL ANDRUS
third baseman
1937

WALT MASTERS
pitcher 1937

**ART
REBEL**
outfielder
1938

ALEX PITKO
outfielder
1938

BILL HALLAHAN
pitcher 1938

BUCK JORDAN
first baseman
1938

TOM LANNING
pitcher 1938

TOM REIS
pitcher
1938

Philadelphia Phillies (continued)

GIB BRACK
outfielder
1938-39

**ALFRED
"AL" SMITH**
pitcher 1938-39

ED FEINBERG
utility 1938-39

KIRBY HIGBE
pitcher 1939

GUS SUHR
first baseman
1939

**LEN
GABRIELSON**
first baseman
1939

GENE SCHOTT
pitcher 1939

PINKY MAY
third baseman
1939

**WALTER
MILLIES**
catcher
1939

JIM SHILLING
infielder 1939

LES POWERS
first baseman
1939

JOHN WATWOOD
first baseman 1939

ROY HUGHES
shortstop 1939

BENNIE WARREN
catcher 1939

JOE MARTY
pitcher, outfield
1939

**BILL
KERKSIECK**
pitcher
1939

BILL HOFFMAN
pitcher 1939

**CHARLIE
LETCHAS**
second baseman
1939

BUD BATES
outfielder
1939

JOHN BOLLING
first baseman
1939

Philadelphia Phillies (continued)

WALTER BECK
pitcher 1939

DAVE COBLE
catcher 1939

**LEGRAND
SCOTT**
outfielder
1939

IKE PEARSON
pitcher 1939

**WALTER
"ROY" BRUNER**
pitcher 1939

JIM HENRY
pitcher 1939

BUD HAFEY
outfielder 1939

RAY HARRELL
pitcher 1939

**JENNINGS
POINDEXTER**
pitcher 1939

JOE KRACHER
catcher 1939

**STAN
BENJAMIN**
third base, outfield
1939

UNIFORMS:

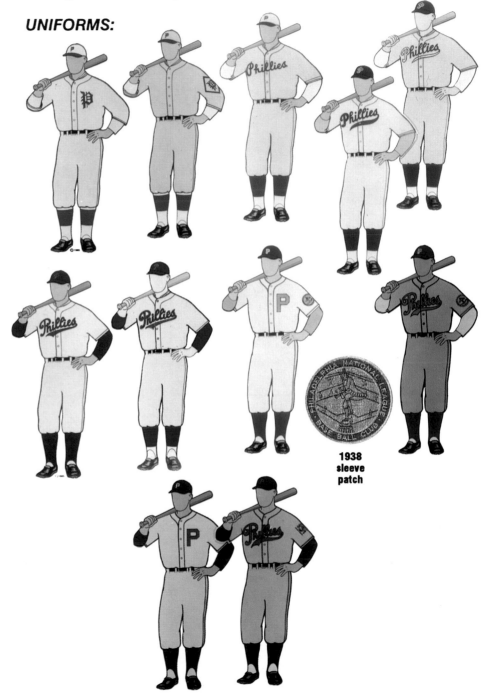

**1938
sleeve
patch**

Pittsburgh Pirates

FRONT OFFICE:

BARNEY DREYFUSS
President 1930-32

SAMUEL DREYFUSS
VP/Treas. 1930

O. B. HARSHMAN
VP 1930

SAMUEL WATTERS
Secretary 1930-39
VP 1932-39
Traveling Secy. 1937-39

WILLIAM E. BENSWANGER
Treasurer 1931-39
President 1932-39

JAMES LONG
Publicity 1937-39

JOE SCHULTZ
Field Director
1938-39

MRS. BARNEY DREYFUSS
Chairman 1932-39

FIELD MANAGERS:

JEWEL ENS
1930-31

PIE TRAYNOR
1934-39

GEORGE GIBSON
1932-34

COACHES:

MAX CAREY 1930
OSCAR STANAGE 1930-31
GROVER HARTLEY 1931-33
DOC CRANDALL 1931-34
HONUS WAGNER 1933-39
JEWEL ENS 1935-39
JOHNNY GOOCH 1937-39

THE PLAYERS:

FRED BRICKELL
outfielder 1930

AL BOOL
catcher
1930

RALPH ERICKSON
pitcher
1930

PERCY JONES
pitcher 1930

LIL STONER
pitcher 1930

JESSE PETTY
pitcher 1930

DENNIS SOTHERN
outfielder 1930

MARTIN LANG
pitcher 1930

IRA FLAGSTEAD
outfielder 1930

Pittsburgh Pirates (continued)

DICK BARTELL
shortstop 1930

CHARLES HARGREAVES
catcher 1930

WILLIAM "STU" CLARKE
second baseman 1930

GEORGE GRANTHAM
first, second base 1930-31

LLOYD WANER
outfielder 1930-39

PAUL WANER
outfield, first base 1930-39

ROLLIE HEMSLEY
catcher 1930-31

STEVE SWETONIC
pitcher 1930-33, 1935

CHARLES ENGLE
infielder 1930

HOWARD GROSKLOSS
infielder 1930-32

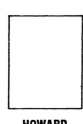

ERV BRAME
pitcher 1930-32

BEN SANKEY
infielder 1930-31

HEINIE MEINE
pitcher 1930-34

ANDY BEDNAR
pitcher 1930-31

CHARLES WOOD
pitcher 1930-31

RAY KREMER
pitcher 1930-33

GUS SUHR
first baseman 1930-39

PIE TRAYNOR
third baseman 1930-35, 1937
(manager 1934-39)

ADAM COMOROSKY
outfielder 1930-33

LARRY FRENCH
pitcher 1930-34

Pittsburgh Pirates (continued)

LEON CHAGNON
pitcher
1930, 1932-34

GLENN SPENCER
pitcher 1930-32

GEORGE GRANT
pitcher
1931

HAROLD FINNEY
catcher
1931-34, 1936

BOB OSBORN
pitcher 1931

ED PHILLIPS
catcher 1931

BILL HARRIS
pitcher 1931-34

JIM MOSOLF
pitcher, outfielder
1930-31

GUS DUGAS
outfielder
1930, 1932

ROBERT "EARL" GRACE
catcher
1931-35

CLAUDE WILLOUGHBY
pitcher 1931

JAMES "RED" BENNETT
outfielder 1931

TONY PIET (PIETRUSZKA)
second baseman
1931-33

ARKY VAUGHAN
shortstop 1932-39

BILL REGAN
second baseman 1931

PETE McCLANAHAN
pinch-hitter
1931

TOMMY THEVENOW
infielder
1931-35, 1938

BILL STEINECKE
catcher 1931

FORREST "WOODY" JENSEN
outfielder
1931-39

DAVE BARBEE
outfielder 1932

BILL BRENZEL
catcher 1932

TOM PADDEN
catcher 1932-37

Pittsburgh Pirates (continued)

**BILL
BRUBAKER**
third baseman
1932-39

BILL SWIFT
pitcher 1932-39

HAROLD SMITH
pitcher 1932-35

VAL PICINICH
catcher 1933

**LEMUEL
"PEP" YOUNG**
infielder
1933-39

WAITE HOYT
pitcher 1933-37

**LEO
NONNENKAMP**
outfielder 1933

**RALPH
BIRKOFER**
pitcher
1933-36

FRED LINDSTROM
outfielder 1933-34

RED LUCAS
pitcher 1934-38

BURLEIGH GRIMES
pitcher 1934

ED HOLLEY
pitcher 1934

WALLY ROETTGER
outfielder 1934

**CLARENCE
STRUSS**
pitcher 1934

PAT VELTMAN
catcher 1934

CY BLANTON
pitcher 1934-39

Pittsburgh Pirates (continued)

COOKIE LAVAGETTO
infielder 1934-36

BABE HERMAN
first base, outfield
1935

BUD HAFEY
outfielder
1935-36

GUY BUSH
pitcher
1935-36

EARL BROWNE
first base, outfield
1935-36

JIM WEAVER
pitcher 1935-37

RUSS BAUERS
pitcher 1936-39

AL TODD
catcher
1936-38

RAY BERRES
catcher 1937-39

JACK SALVESON
pitcher 1935

AUBREY EPPS
catcher 1935

MACE BROWN
pitcher 1935-39

FRED SCHULTE
outfielder 1936-37

JOHN WELCH
pitcher 1936

BILL SCHUSTER
shortstop 1937

LEE HANDLEY
infielder 1937-39

CLAUDE PASSEAU
pitcher 1935

WAYNE OSBORNE
pitcher 1935

JACK TISING
pitcher 1936

JOHNNY DICKSHOT (DICKSUS)
outfielder 1936-38

ED BRANDT
pitcher 1937-38

JOE BOWMAN
pitcher 1937-39

KEN HEINTZELMAN
pitcher 1937-39

JIM TOBIN
pitcher 1937-39

Pittsburgh Pirates (continued)

HEINIE MANUSH
outfielder
1938-39

JOHNNY RIZZO
outfielder 1938-39

BOB KLINGER
pitcher 1938-39

JOHN JUELICH
second baseman
1939

ELBIE FLETCHER
first baseman 1939

UNIFORMS:

BILL CLEMENSEN
pitcher 1939

JOHNNY GEE
pitcher 1939

RAY MUELLER
catcher 1939

FLOYD "EDDIE" YOUNT
outfielder 1939

MAURICE VAN ROBAYS
outfielder
1939

GEORGE SUSCE
catcher 1939

BOB ELLIOTT
outfielder 1939

TRUETT "RIP" SEWELL
pitcher
1938-39

JOE SCHULTZ
catcher 1939

CHUCK KLEIN
outfielder 1939

FERN BELL
outfielder
1939

OADIS SWIGART
pitcher 1939

ELMER "PEP" RAMBERT
pitcher 1939

FRANK GUSTINE
third baseman 1939

MAX BUTCHER
pitcher 1939

St. Louis Browns

FRONT OFFICE:

PHILIP BALL
President 1930-33

BILL FRIEL
Business Mgr.
1930-32

WILLIAM CADY
Treasurer 1934-36

E. M. JACOBY
Secretary 1934-36

L. CARLE McEVOY
VP 1930-36

LOUIS VON WEISE
Secretary 1930-33
President 1934-36

WILLIS JOHNSON
Traveling Secy. 1930-36

WALTER FRITSCH
VP 1931-33

WM. O. DEWITT
VP 1937-39
GM 1938-39

G. E. GILLILAND
Asst. VP 1937-39

CHARLES DEWITT
Traveling Secy. 1938-39

DONALD BARNES
President 1937-39

SAM McCLUNEY
Treasurer 1937-39

GEORGE FOSTER
Secretary 1937-39

GEORGE IRWIN
Traveling Secy. 1937

HOWARD STEPHENS
VP 1938-39

CY CASPER
Info. Dir. 1938

MARGARET MURPHY
Asst. Treasurer 1938-39

ROGER BACON
Info. Dir. 1939

FIELD MANAGERS:

BILL KILLEFER
1930-33

ALLAN SOTHORON
(interim) 1933

ROGERS HORNSBY
1933-37

JIM BOTTOMLEY
1937

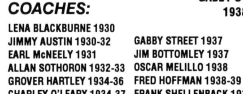

FRED HANEY
1939

GABBY STREET
1938

COACHES:

LENA BLACKBURNE 1930
JIMMY AUSTIN 1930-32
EARL McNEELY 1931
ALLAN SOTHORON 1932-33
GROVER HARTLEY 1934-36
CHARLEY O'LEARY 1934-37

GABBY STREET 1937
JIM BOTTOMLEY 1937
OSCAR MELILLO 1938
FRED HOFFMAN 1938-39
FRANK SHELLENBACK 1939

THE PLAYERS:

RED BADGRO
outfielder 1930

JOE HASSLER
shortstop 1930

HERMAN HOLSHOUSER
pitcher 1930

BUN HUNGLING
catcher 1930

ALEX METZLER
outfielder 1930

CLYDE MANION
catcher 1930

St. Louis Browns (continued)

ALVIN CROWDER
pitcher 1930

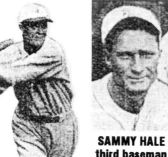

LU BLUE
first baseman
1930

SAMMY HALE
third baseman
1930

GEORGE BLAEHOLDER
pitcher 1930-35

RICK FERRELL
catcher 1930-33

LIN STORTI
infielder
1930-33

ROLLAND STILES
pitcher 1930-31, 1933

HEINIE MANUSH
outfielder 1930

CHAD KIMSEY
pitcher 1930-32

TED GULLIC
utility 1930, 1933

SAMUEL "DOLLY" GRAY
pitcher 1930-33

JIM LEVEY
shortstop
1930-33

JACK CROUCH
catcher
1930-31, 1933

GOOSE GOSLIN
outfielder
1930-32

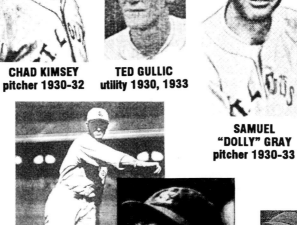

DICK COFFMAN
pitcher
1930-32, 1933-35

TOM JENKINS
outfielder 1930-32

FRED STIELY
pitcher 1930-31

FRED SCHULTE
outfielder 1930-32

St. Louis Browns (continued)

OSCAR MELILLO
second baseman
1930-35

RED KRESS
utility
1930-32, 1938-39

EARL McNEELY
first base, outfield
1930-31

RUSS YOUNG
catcher 1931

ED GRIMES
third baseman
1931-32

CARL FISCHER
pitcher 1932

DEBS GARMS
outfielder 1932-35

WALTER STEWART
pitcher 1930-32

HARRY COLLINS
pitcher 1930-31

**FRANK
O'ROURKE**
infielder
1930-31

WALLY HEBERT
pitcher 1931-33

**GARLAND
BRAXTON**
pitcher
1931, 1933

LOUIS POLLI
pitcher 1932

JOHN SCHULTE
catcher 1932

ART SCHAREIN
infielder
1932-34

BUCK STANTON
outfielder 1931

**LARRY
BETTENCOURT**
outfield, third base
1931-32

**BENNY
BENGOUGH**
catcher
1931-32

BOB COONEY
pitcher 1931-32

JACK BURNS
first baseman
1930-36

FRANK WADDEY
outfielder 1931

JOHN KLOZA
outfielder 1931-32

GEORGE FISHER
outfielder 1932

St. Louis Browns (continued)

BRUCE CAMPBELL
outfielder 1932-34

CARL REYNOLDS
outfielder 1933

MUDDY RUEL
catcher 1933

MERVYN SHEA
catcher 1933

JACK KNOTT
pitcher 1933-38

GROVER HARTLEY
catcher 1934

BAILEY "EARL" CLARK
outfielder 1934

BUMP HADLEY
pitcher 1932-34

SAM WEST
outfielder 1933-38

ROLLIE HEMSLEY
catcher 1933-37

BILL McAFEE
pitcher 1934

GEORGE PUCCINELLI
outfielder 1934

HOWARD MILLS
pitcher 1934, 1937-39

JIM WEAVER
pitcher 1934, 1938

HANK McDONALD
pitcher 1933

LLOYD BROWN
pitcher 1933

EDDIE WELLS
pitcher 1933-34

ROGERS HORNSBY
utility 1933-37
(manager 1933-37)

CHARLIE O'LEARY
pinch-hitter 1934

FRANK GRUBE
catcher 1934-35

RAY PEPPER
outfielder 1934-36

OLLIE BEJMA
infielder 1934-36

St. Louis Browns (continued)

BUCK NEWSOM
pitcher
1934-35, 1938-39

ALAN STRANGE
shortstop 1934-35

HARLOND CLIFT
third baseman
1934-39

HAL WARNOCK
outfielder 1935

JOHNNY BURNETT
infielder
1935

TOM HEATH
catcher
1935, 1937-38

TOM "SCOOPS" CAREY
infielder
1935-37

IVY ANDREWS
pitcher 1934-36

FAY THOMAS
pitcher 1935

BOB WEILAND
pitcher 1935

MIKE MAZZERA
outfielder
1935, 1937-39

ROY HANSEN
pitcher 1935

BEAU BELL
utility 1935-39

MOOSE SOLTERS
outfielder
1935-36, 1939

ROY MAHAFFEY
pitcher
1936

MIKE MEOLA
pitcher 1936

JIM WALKUP
pitcher 1934-39

CLARENCE HEINIE MUELLER
utility 1935

LYN LARY
shortstop
1935-36

BOB POSER
pitcher 1935

RUSS VAN ATTA
pitcher 1935-39

MERRITT "SUGAR" CAIN
pitcher
1935-36

EARL CALDWELL
pitcher
1935-37

ED COLEMAN
outfielder
1935-36

HARRY KIMBERLIN
pitcher
1936-39

SIG JAKUCKI
pitcher 1936

St. Louis Browns (continued)

GLENN LIEBHARDT
pitcher 1936, 1938

TONY GIULIANI
catcher 1936–37

WILLIAM F. MILLER
pitcher 1937

JOHN "FRED" BLAKE
pitcher 1937

TOM CAFEGO
outfielder 1937

BENNIE HUFFMAN
catcher 1937

BILL STRICKLAND
pitcher 1937

JOE VOSMIK
outfielder 1937

JIM BOTTOMLEY
first baseman 1936–37
(manager 1937)

CHIEF HOGSETT
pitcher 1936–37

GEORGE HENNESSEY
pitcher 1937

GERARD LIPSCOMB
pitcher, infield 1937

BILL TROTTER
pitcher 1937–39

BILL KNICKERBOCKER
shortstop 1937

EMIL BILDILLI
pitcher 1937–39

ALPHONSE "TOMMY" THOMAS
pitcher 1936–37

LES TIETJE
pitcher 1936–38

ED BAECHT
pitcher 1937

LOUIS KOUPAL
pitcher 1937

HARRY DAVIS
first baseman 1937

ORAL HILDEBRAND
pitcher 1937–38

JOHN "RED" BARKLEY
second baseman 1937

SAM HARSHANY
catcher 1937–39

St. Louis Browns (continued)

ETHAN ALLEN
outfielder
1937-38

JULIO
BONETTI
pitcher
1937-38

BOB MUNCRIEF
pitcher 1937, 1939

ED LINKE
pitcher
1938

DON HEFFNER
infielder 1938-39

JOE GRACE
outfielder
1938-39

BILLY SULLIVAN, Jr.
catcher 1938-39

ED SILBER
outfielder
1937, 1939

VITO TAMULIS
pitcher 1938

GEORGE McQUINN
first baseman 1938-39

ROY HUGHES
infielder 1938-39

BILL COX
pitcher
1938-39

ED COLE
(KISLEAUSKAS)
pitcher 1938-39

JOHNNY
LUCADELLO
infielder
1938-39

GLENN
McQUILLEN
outfielder
1938

BUSTER MILLS
outfielder 1938

SIG GRYSKA
shortstop
1938-39

FRED JOHNSON
pitcher 1938-39

MEL ALMADA
outfielder 1938-39

ROXIE LAWSON
pitcher 1939

St. Louis Browns (continued)

UNIFORMS:

VERN KENNEDY
pitcher 1939

HAROLD SPINDEL
catcher 1939

JOHN BERARDINO
second baseman
1939

HERBERT PYLE
pitcher
1939

JAKE WADE
pitcher 1939

JOHN WHITEHEAD
pitcher 1939

GEORGE GILL
pitcher 1939

MARK CHRISTMAN
shortstop 1939

CHET LAABS
outfielder
1939

JOE GLENN (GURZENSKY)
catcher 1939

JOHN MARCUM
pitcher 1939

LOY HANNING
pitcher 1939

MYRIL HOAG
outfield, pitcher
1939

JACK KRAMER
pitcher 1939

BOB HARRIS
pitcher 1939

RUPERT "TOMMY" THOMPSON
outfielder 1939

JOE GALLAGHER
outfielder
1939

BOB NEIGHBORS
shortstop 1939

1937-40 sleeve patch

St. Louis Cardinals

FRONT OFFICE:

SAM BREADON
President 1930-39

BRANCH RICKEY
VP/Bus. Mgr. 1930-39

CLARENCE LLOYD
Secretary 1930-36
Secy./Trav. Sec. 1937

WM. O. DEWITT
Treasurer 1930-35
Asst. Bus. Mgr. 1936

PHIL BARTELME
Asst. Bus. Mgr.
1930-35

A. M. DIEZ
Treasurer
1937-39

EUGENE KARST
Publicity 1931-34

WM. WALSINGHAM, Jr.
Treasurer 1936
Asst. VP 1937-39

ED STAPLES
Secretary 1938

LEO WARD
Traveling Secy.
1938-39

ED ROTH
Asst. Treas.
1938-39

FIELD MANAGERS:

GABBY STREET
1930-33

FRANKIE FRISCH
1933-38

MIKE GONZALES
1938

RAY BLADES
1939

COACHES:

RAY BLADES 1930-32
BUZZY WARES 1930-35,
37-39
MIKE GONZALES 1934-39

THE PLAYERS:

CARMEN HILL
pitcher 1930

**FRED
FRANKHOUSE**
pitcher 1930

EARL SMITH
catcher 1930

**CLARENCE
MITCHELL**
pitcher 1930

HOMER PEEL
outfielder 1930

DOC FARRELL
shortstop 1930

**AL
GRABOWSKI**
pitcher 1930

BILL HALLAHAN
pitcher 1930-36

**HERMAN
"HI" BELL**
pitcher
1930

St. Louis Cardinals (continued)

HAROLD HAID
pitcher 1930

GEORGE FISHER
outfielder 1930

CHICK HAFEY
outfielder 1930-31

FLINT RHEM
pitcher
1930-32, 1934, 1936

JIM BOTTOMLEY
first baseman
1930-32

**GEORGE
PUCCINELLI**
outfielder
1930, 1932

ANDY HIGH
infielder
1930-31

TONY KAUFMANN
pitcher
1930-31, 1935

PEPPER MARTIN
outfield, third base
1930-39

SPARKY ADAMS
infielder 1930-33

FRANK FRISCH
infielder 1930-37
(manager 1933-38)

GEORGE WATKINS
outfielder 1930-33

JIM LINDSEY
pitcher
1930-33, 1934

BURLEIGH GRIMES
pitcher
1930-31, 1933-34

St. Louis Cardinals (continued)

CHARLIE GELBERT
infielder
1930-32, 1935-36

DIZZY DEAN
pitcher 1930-37

GUS MANCUSO
catcher 1930-32

RAY BLADES
outfielder
1930-32

SYL JOHNSON
pitcher 1930-33

GABBY STREET
catcher 1931
(manager 1930-33)

JIMMY WILSON
catcher, outfielder
1930-33

TAYLOR DOUTHIT
outfielder 1930-31

WALLY ROETTGER
outfielder 1931

JAKE FLOWERS
infielder 1931-32

JESSE HAINES
pitcher 1930-37

ERNIE ORSATTI
outfield, first base
1930-35

JOE BENES
infielder
1931

RAY CUNNINGHAM
infielder
1931-32

BILL SHERDEL
pitcher
1930, 1932

JAMES "RIP" COLLINS
first baseman
1931-36

OLIVER "JOEL" HUNT
outfielder
1931-32

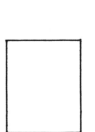

ED DELKER
infielder
1931-32

St. Louis Cardinals (continued)

MIKE GONZALES
catcher 1931-32
(manager 1938)

ALLYN
STOUT
pitcher
1931-33

JOE MEDWICK
outfielder
1932-39

TEX
CARLETON
pitcher
1932-34

BENNIE FREY
pitcher 1932

BUD TEACHOUT
pitcher 1932

BILL DeLANCEY
catcher
1932, 1934-35

PAUL
DERRINGER
pitcher
1931-33

DICK
TERWILLIGER
pitcher 1932

HARVEY HENDRICK
third baseman 1932

CHARLIE
WILSON
infielder
1932-33, 1935

ROSCOE
"WATTY" HOLM
outfielder
1932

RUBE BRESSLER
outfielder 1932

SKEETER WEBB
shortstop 1932

RAY STARR
pitcher
1932

RAY PEPPER
outfielder
1932-33

JAMES WINFORD
pitcher 1932, 1934-37

ESTEL
CRABTREE
utility 1933

JIMMY REESE
(SOLOMON)
second baseman
1932

HOD FORD
infielder
1932

St. Louis Cardinals (continued)

LEO DUROCHER
shortstop 1933-37

JOE SPRINZ
catcher 1933

BOB O'FARRELL
catcher 1933, 1935

GENE MOORE
outfielder
1933-35

**CLIFFORD
"PAT" CRAWFORD**
infielder 1933-34

LEW RIGGS
infielder 1934

ETHAN ALLEN
outfielder 1933

ROGERS HORNSBY
second baseman 1933

BILL WALKER
pitcher 1933-36

FRAN HEALY
catcher 1934

CHICK FULLIS
outfielder
1934, 1936

SPUD DAVIS
catcher 1934-36

JACK ROTHROCK
outfielder 1934-35

GORDON SLADE
infielder 1933

**BILL
LEWIS**
catcher
1933

**BURGESS
WHITEHEAD**
infielder
1933-35

JIM MOONEY
pitcher 1933-34

**GEORGE
"KIDDO" DAVIS**
outfielder
1934

DICK WARD
pitcher 1935

DAZZY VANCE
pitcher 1933, 1934

BUSTER MILLS
outfielder 1934

RED WORTHINGTON
outfielder 1934

PAUL DEAN
pitcher
1934-39

SAM NARRON
catcher 1935

St. Louis Cardinals (continued)

PHIL COLLINS
pitcher 1935

TOM WINSETT
outfielder
1935

ED HEUSSER
pitcher
1935-36

MIKE RYBA
pitcher
1935-38

TERRY MOORE
outfielder 1935-39

ART GARIBALDI
infielder
1936

WALTER ALSTON
first baseman 1936

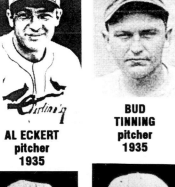

AL ECKERT
pitcher
1935

BUD TINNING
pitcher
1935

BILL McGEE
pitcher
1935-39

RAY HARRELL
pitcher
1935, 1937-38

BRUCE OGRODOWSKI
catcher 1936-37

COTTON PIPPEN
pitcher 1936

ROY PARMELEE
pitcher 1936

LES MUNNS
pitcher 1936

LOU SCOFFIC
outfielder
1936

NELSON POTTER
pitcher
1936

HEINIE SCHUBLE
third baseman
1936

BILL COX
pitcher 1936

LYLE JUDY
second baseman
1935

LYNN KING
outfielder
1935-36, 1939

NORBERT KLEINKE
pitcher 1935, 1937

St. Louis Cardinals (continued)

GEORGE EARNSHAW
pitcher 1936

JOHNNY VERGEZ
third baseman 1936

FRED ANKENMAN
shortstop 1936

EDWIN "PEPPER" MORGAN
outfielder 1936

STUART MARTIN
second baseman 1936-39

SI JOHNSON
pitcher 1936-38

DON GUTTERIDGE
third baseman 1936-39

DON PADGETT
utility 1937-39

JIMMY BROWN
infielder 1937-39

ABE WHITE
pitcher 1937

JOHNNIE CHAMBERS
pitcher 1937

DICK SIEBERT
first baseman 1937-38

FRENCHY BORDAGARAY
utility 1937-38

HOWIE KRIST
pitcher 1937-38

MICKEY OWEN
catcher 1937-39

JOHNNY MIZE
first baseman 1936-39

RANDY MOORE
utility 1937

JOHN BLAKE
pitcher 1937

BOB WEILAND
pitcher 1937-39

LON WARNEKE
pitcher 1937-39

NATE ANDREWS
pitcher 1937, 1939

St. Louis Cardinals (continued)

HERB BREMER
catcher 1937-39

TOM SUNKEL
pitcher
1937, 1939

JIM BUCHER
second baseman
1938

ROY HENSHAW
pitcher 1938

ENOS SLAUGHTER
outfielder
1938-39

MAX LANIER
pitcher 1938-39

MORT COOPER
pitcher 1938-39

JOE ORENGO
shortstop 1939

PREACHER ROE
pitcher 1938

HAROLD EPPS
outfielder 1938

GUY BUSH
pitcher
1938

MAX MACON
pitcher 1938

TUCK STAINBACK
outfielder 1938

FRANK CRESPI
shortstop 1938-39

CURT DAVIS
pitcher
1938-39

LYNN MYERS
infielder
1938-39

CLYDE SHOUN
pitcher 1938-39

JOE STRIPP
third baseman
1938

St. Louis Cardinals (continued)

LYN LARY
infielder
1939

**HERMAN
FRANKS**
catcher
1939

JOHNNY HOPP
first baseman
1939

BOB BOWMAN
pitcher 1939

BUSTER ADAMS
outfielder 1939

EDDIE LAKE
shortstop
1939

JOHN ECHOLS
second baseman
1939

BOB REPASS
second baseman
1939

UNIFORMS:

Washington Nationals/Senators

FRONT OFFICE:

CLARK GRIFFITH
President 1930-39

WM. RICHARDSON
VP/Treasurer 1930-39

EDWARD EYNON, Jr.
Secretary 1930-39
Traveling Secy. 1935-39

FIELD MANAGERS:

WALTER JOHNSON
1930-32

JOE CRONIN
1933-34

BUCKY HARRIS
1935-39

COACHES:

PATSY GHARRITY 1930-32
AL SCHACHT 1930-34
NICK ALTROCK 1930-39
SPENCER ABBOTT 1935
JOHN KERR 1935
EARL McNEELY 1936-37
CLYDE MILAN 1938-39

THE PLAYERS:

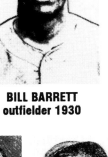

**EMILE
"RED" BARNES**
outfielder
1930

BILL BARRETT
outfielder 1930

**GEORGE
LOEPP**
outfielder
1930

**CARLOS
MOORE**
pitcher
1930

**PATSY
GHARRITY**
first baseman
1930

ELMER BOSS
first baseman
1930

SAM RICE
outfielder
1930-33

**GARLAND
BRAXTON**
pitcher
1930

HARRY CHILD
pitcher 1930

BEN TATE
catcher 1930

**ALVIN
CROWDER**
pitcher
1930-34

Washington Nationals/Senators (continued)

OSSIE BLUEGE
infielder 1930-39

ART SHIRES
first baseman
1930

JIM McLEOD
infielder
1930, 1932

**CARL
FISCHER**
pitcher
1930-32, 1937

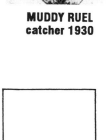

MUDDY RUEL
catcher 1930

JACKIE HAYES
second baseman
1930-31

GOOSE GOSLIN
outfielder
1930, 1933, 1938

JAKE POWELL
outfielder
1930, 1934-36

JOE CRONIN
shortstop, infielder
1930-34
(manager 1933-34)

AD LISKA
pitcher 1930-31

JOE JUDGE
first baseman
1930-32

MYLES THOMAS
pitcher 1930

LLOYD BROWN
pitcher 1930-32

DAVE HARRIS
outfielder
1930-34

RAY TREADAWAY
third baseman
1930

BUMP HADLEY
pitcher
1930-31, 1935

HEINIE MANUSH
outfielder 1930-35

BUDDY MYER
second baseman
1930-39

**"SAD SAM"
JONES**
pitcher
1930-31

PINKY HARGRAVE
catcher 1930-31

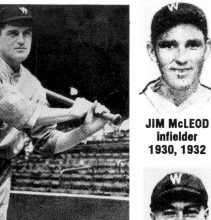

Washington Nationals/Senators (continued)

JOE KUHEL
first baseman
1930-37

FRED "FIRPO"
MARBERRY
pitcher
1930-32, 1936

BOB BURKE
pitcher 1930-35

HARRY RICE
outfielder
1931

CLIFF
BOLTON
catcher
1931, 1933-36

NICK ALTROCK
pinch-hitter
1931, 1933

MOE BERG
catcher
1932-34

CARL REYNOLDS
outfielder 1932, 1936

ROY SPENCER
catcher 1930-32

SAM WEST
outfielder
1930-32, 1938-39

WILLIAM
ANDRUS
third baseman
1931

BABE PHELPS
catcher 1931

JOHN GILL
outfielder
1931, 1934

DAN MUSSER
third baseman
1932

BOB
FRIEDRICH
pitcher
1932

ED EDELEN
pitcher 1932

MONTE WEAVER
pitcher 1931-38

WALT
TAUSCHER
pitcher
1931

BUCK JORDAN
first baseman 1931

WALT MASTERS
pitcher 1931

FRANK
RAGLAND
pitcher
1932

DICK
COFFMAN
pitcher
1932

WES
KINGDON
infielder
1932

Washington Nationals/Senators (continued)

BILL McAFEE
pitcher 1932-33

BUD THOMAS
pitcher
1932-33, 1939

**EDWARD
"BABE" LINKE**
pitcher
1933-37

FRED SCHULTE
outfielder 1933-35

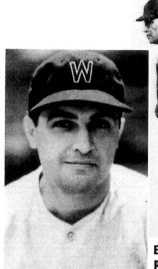

EARL WHITEHILL
pitcher 1933-36

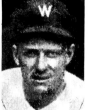

**HOWARD
MAPLE**
catcher
1932

**ALPHONSE
"TOMMY" THOMAS**
pitcher 1932-35

ED CHAPMAN
pitcher 1933

JACK RUSSELL
pitcher 1933-36

LUKE SEWELL
catcher, utility
1933-34

CECIL TRAVIS
utility 1933-39

**WALTER
STEWART**
pitcher
1933-35

JOHN KERR
infielder
1932-34

**JOHN
CAMPBELL**
pitcher
1933

BOB BOKEN
infielder
1933-34

RAY PRIM
pitcher
1933-34

ALEX McCOLL
pitcher 1933-34

**ORVILLE
ARMBRUST**
pitcher 1934

**ALLEN
BENSON**
pitcher
1934

BOB KLINE
pitcher 1934

Washington Nationals/Senators (continued)

ED
PHILLIPS
catcher
1934

JOHN
MILLIGAN
pitcher
1934

FRED
SINGTON
outfielder
1934-37

JOHNNY
STONE
outfielder
1934-38

LYN LARY
shortstop
1935

JOHN
REDMOND
catcher
1935

GUS DUGAS
outfielder
1934

PETE SUSKO
first baseman
1934

RED KRESS
utility 1934-36

PHILIP
HENSIEK
pitcher
1935

JAMES
HOLBROOK
catcher
1935

ELMER
KLUMPP
catcher
1934

REESE DIGGS
pitcher 1934

SYD COHEN
pitcher
1934, 1936-37

ALAN
STRANGE
shortstop
1935

AL McLEAN
pitcher 1935

JOHN
"RED" MARION
outfielder
1935

BILL BEAN
pitcher 1935

JIM HAYES
pitcher 1935

ORLIN
"BUCK" ROGERS
pitcher 1935

LEON PETTIT
pitcher 1935

HENRY
COPPOLA
pitcher
1935-36

Washington Nationals/Senators (continued)

BUCK NEWSOM
pitcher 1935-37

CHICK STARR
catcher 1935-36

ROBERTO ESTALELLA
third base, outfield
1935-36, 1939

BILL DIETRICH
pitcher 1936

WALTER MILLIES
catcher
1936-37

PETE APPLETON (JABLONOWSKI)
pitcher 1936-39

JIM DESHONG
pitcher 1936-39

JOHN MIHALIC
infielder
1935-37

DICK LANAHAN
pitcher
1935, 1937

DEE MILES
outfielder
1935-36

ALEX SABO
catcher 1936-37

RAY PHEBUS
pitcher 1936-38

MIKE GUERRA
catcher 1937

HERB CROMPTON
catcher
1937

BUDDY LEWIS
third baseman
1935-39

JOE BOKINA
pitcher 1936

JOE CASCARELLA
pitcher 1936-37

KENDALL CHASE
pitcher
1936-39

JESSE HILL
outfielder
1936-37

BEN CHAPMAN
outfielder 1936-37

SHANTY HOGAN
catcher 1936-37

JOHNNY RIDDLE
catcher
1937

MILT GRAY
catcher 1937

Washington Nationals/Senators (continued)

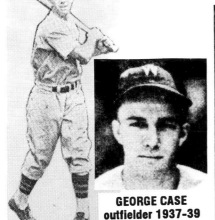

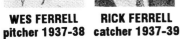
GEORGE CASE
outfielder 1937-39

NEWT JACOBS
pitcher 1937, 1939

AL SIMMONS
outfielder
1937-38

MEL ALMADA
outfielder
1937-38

CHIEF HOGSETT
pitcher 1938

ZEKE BONURA
first baseman 1938

TAFT WRIGHT
outfielder 1938-39

WES FERRELL
pitcher 1937-38

RICK FERRELL
catcher 1937-39

JIMMY
BLOODWORTH
second baseman
1937, 1939

JOSEPH
KOHLMAN
pitcher
1937-38

RENE
MONTEAGUDO
pitcher 1938

TONY GIULIANI
catcher 1938-39

MICKEY
LIVINGSTON
catcher 1938

JEROME LYNN
second baseman
1937

ARNOLD
ANDERSON
pitcher
1937

JIMMY
WASDELL
first baseman
1937-39

JOE
KRAKAUSKAS
pitcher
1937-39

HARRY
KELLEY
pitcher
1938-39

DUTCH LEONARD
pitcher 1938-39

Washington Nationals/Senators (continued)

WALT MASTERSON pitcher 1939

EARLY WYNN pitcher 1939

ELMER GEDEON outfielder 1939

BOB PRICHARD first baseman 1939

ALEX CARRASQUEL pitcher 1939

UNIFORMS:

MICKEY VERNON first baseman 1939

JOE HAYNES pitcher 1939

AL EVANS catcher 1939

JOHN WELAJ outfielder 1939

MORRIS ADERHOLT second baseman 1939

CHARLIE GELBERT infielder 1939

BOB LOANE outfielder 1939

JAKE EARLY catcher 1939

ED LEIP second baseman 1939

LOUIS THUMAN pitcher 1939

JAMES QUICK shortstop 1939

WILLIAM HOLLAND pitcher 1939

ALEX PITKO outfielder 1939

THE SEASONS

1930

Cubs pitcher Hal Carlson died unexpectedly in 1930.

Phils owner William Baker passed away in December 1930.

"Dapper" Dan Howley was the Reds' new field boss for 1930.

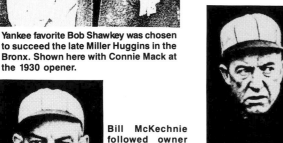

Yankee favorite Bob Shawkey was chosen to succeed the late Miller Huggins in the Bronx. Shown here with Connie Mack at the 1930 opener.

Bill McKechnie followed owner Fuchs as Braves pilot.

1930 was to be the final season for the great Grover Alexander.

Player/Coach Eddie Collins broke Cobb's record for longevity, pinch-hitting in his 25th season.

Ruth and Gehrig combined for 90 HRs and 327 RBIs in 1930 but the New Yorkers failed to wrest the AL flag from Mack's Athletics.

Lefty O'Doul and Chuck Klein come racing home at Philadelphia's Baker Bowl after Brooklyn catcher Al Lopez makes an errant throw.

The new decade began with a season of lightning and thunder—not from the weather, but from the bats of major league hitters. The most awesome display of hitting in this century made the news every day in 1930. Batting averages soared as did pitchers' ERAs throughout the big leagues. To illustrate this phenomenon, no less than nine of the sixteen ML clubs had a TEAM batting average over .300, led by McGraw's Giants with .319. And Washington's mound staff, with a 3.96 mark, was the only one with an ERA under 4.00. Phillies pitchers, already handicapped by the small dimensions of Baker Bowl, had the highest team ERA, an astronomical 6.71. The bombardment was so excessive that a "deadening" of the baseball was mandated for the following year in an effort to restore a more normal balance between pitching and hitting. The only two hurlers able to ward off the daily assault with any consistency were Lefty Grove (28-5, 2.54 ERA) and Dazzy Vance (17-15, 2.61 ERA). Bill Terry's .401 average (the last National Leaguer to reach this figure to date) topped the long list of major leaguers over .300. Rotund Hack Wilson had an epic season of run production with 56 home runs (still an NL record) and the staggering total of 190 RBIs (still a major league record). Clearly, to hit an even .300 in this remarkable year was by no means a creditable accomplishment.

The New York Yankees, still a formidable aggregation, were suddenly relegated to the status of also-rans in 1929-30, as Connie Mack's Athletics surged to the top of the AL heap with back-to-back 100+ seasons. Mack became the major league's winningest manager with his eighth pennant in 1930. The sudden death of Yankee Manager Miller Huggins in late 1929 left the Bronx club demoralized and new pilot Bob Shawkey was unable to elevate the team higher than third, 10 games behind Walter Johnson's surprising Washington club. The Chicago Cubs, under Joe McCarthy, also stumbled back into second place in 1930, following a convincing NL championship. At season's end McCarthy was out, replaced by Rogers Hornsby. The Yankees quickly signed "Marse Joe" and filled the role of the late Huggins with another equally legendary field boss for 1931 and beyond. First-year Manager Gabby Streets' St. Louis Cardinals finished up a somewhat "roller coaster" pennant race on top of the Cubs, Giants, and Brooklyn. The key to their success was the acquisition of pitcher Burleigh Grimes from the Braves early in the year. Grimes contributed 13 victories with a remarkable (for 1930, anyway) 3.02 ERA. Of course, a Cardinal team BA of .314 and a league-leading 1004 runs scored also had something to do with their winning games. Pat Malone won 20 games for the runner-up Cubs to pace their staff. Top winner in the American League was Lefty Grove, with a sparkling 28-5 record to go along with Earnshaw's 22 wins in pacing the champion Athletics. Al Simmons led the Mackmen's offense with his league-leading .381 average and 165 RBIs. Ruth and Gehrig had their usual power-laden years with 49 & 41 homers and 153 & 174 runs driven in. Wes Ferrell, Lefty Stewart, and Ted Lyons were the only other 20-game winners in the AL. Red Sox hurlers Milt Gaston and Jack Russell both lost 20 games, but Gaston deserved a better fate with a respectable (for 1930, that is) 3.92 ERA. Their Boston teammates decided not to join the offensive bandwagon that season and hit a more normal .264.

Besides Street and Shawkey, the other new ML pilots were Bill Killefer (Browns), Donie Bush (White Sox), Heinie Wagner (Red Sox), Dan Howley (Reds), and "Deacon" Bill McKechnie (Braves). Among the promising rookies in 1930 were Wally Berger, Al Lopez, Gus Suhr, Ben Chapman, and Lefty Gomez. Some of baseball's greats made their last appearances as players in 1930—namely, Hank Gowdy, George Sisler, Grover Alexander, and Eddie Collins (his 25th big league season). Other individual achievements that stood out included the ending of Cleveland third baseman Joe Sewell's consecutive game streak at 1102 and Lou Gehrig's eight RBIs in two different games. Carl Reynolds of the White Sox had three homers plus two singles in a July 2 game, giving him 14 total bases, only two shy of the record. Another important baseball event in 1930 took place in the minor leagues when the first permanent lighting system was installed at the Des Moines, Iowa, ballpark. The idea caught on quickly and was soon duplicated in many other cities throughout the minors.

The St. Louis Cardinals made a game fight in the 1930 Fall Classic with Bill Hallahan and Jess Haines handcuffing the hard-hitting A's in games 3 & 4. But Earnshaw and Grove proved even more stingy as the Macks captured their second straight World Series in six games. President Herbert Hoover attended the series opener in Philadelphia, as he had also done in the 1929 finale. Al Simmons led the Philadelphia assault with a pair of home runs and a .364 batting average. Shortstop Charley Gelbert, who hit a meager .304 (10 points under their .314 team BA) during the season, was the only Cardinal regular to surpass .300 in the series—a testimonial to the clutch hurling of the Athletics staff after such a bountiful year for hitters. This Cardinal club would be heard from again, as the nucleus of the famed "Gas House Gang" (namely, Pepper Martin and Dizzy Dean) had only briefly been seen in action that season.

The Giants' great first sacker "Memphis Bill" Terry finished the 1930 season with a .401 BA, the last NL player to reach that lofty percentage.

Jimmy Foxx crosses the plate on his dramatic 9th inning blast in game 5 of the 1930 World Series.

The first permanent lighting system was erected at Des Moines' ballpark in early 1930.

The Brooklyn Robins made a strong bid for the NL flag, led by (L to R): Glenn Wright, Del Bisonette, Wally Gilbert, and Babe Herman.

Al Simmons is greeted by the batboy after his home run in the final game of the Fall Classic.

Hack Wilson led the slugging barrage in 1930 with 56 HRs, 190 RBIs.

Cubs pilot Joe McCarthy was fired at season's end for failing to repeat as NL champs. He was quickly snapped up by the Yankee organization to replace Bob Shawkey.

The Yanks' Ben Chapman was a top rookie prospect in 1930.

Cleveland's Joe Sewell's consecutive game streak ended at 1102 in May.

White Sox outfielder Carl Reynolds hit a record-tying three HRs in three successive innings plus two straight singles for five hits in early July.

Winning hurler George Earnshaw is mobbed after the final game victory over the Cardinals in the '30 Series.

1931

The awesome batting feats of 1930 forced league officials to once again alter the interior windings of baseballs in an effort to "deaden" the sphere. The strategy seemed to bear fruit as team batting averages plummeted back to more normal sub-.300 levels as did team ERA numbers. Another important ruling over the winter of 1930-31 that helped bring the averages down was the revocation of the sacrifice fly rule. Spring training had barely begun when the first of a number of legendary baseball figures expired. In late March, former president and founder of the American League Ban Johnson died, as did current AL President Ernest Barnard. Longtime league Secretary Will Harridge was immediately appointed to succeed Barnard. A month later Garry Herrmann, former Cincinnati owner and chairman of baseball's National Commission from 1903 to 1920, passed on. In October the "Old Roman," Charles Comisky, president and founder of the Chicago White Sox, succumbed after a long struggle with diabetes and other maladies. J. Louis Comiskey succeeded his father as club president. Other notable deaths in 1931 were former Cubs President Charles Murphy, Pirates Treasurer Sam Dreyfuss, and Jimmy McAleer, one-time Browns manager and Red Sox executive. L. C. Ruch was the Phillies' new president, succeeding William Baker, who died in late 1930. The only new field managers for 1931 were Shano Collins with Boston (AL), Joe McCarthy with the Yanks, and Rogers Hornsby, who had replaced McCarthy as Cubs pilot at the end of 1930.

The Great Depression cut ever deeper into the profits of major league baseball in 1931 as overall attendance dropped 15%. The absence of a real pennant race in both leagues didn't help matters as 1930 champions St. Louis and Philadelphia repeated with comfortable margins between them and their closest pursuers. The Cardinals, in fact, became the first NL team to win over 100 games since 1913. The Athletics seemed more invincible than ever, racking up 107 victories. But the 1931 season was full of interesting moments and notable achievements. Philadelphia's Lefty Grove had a "career" season, virtually unbeatable with a 31-4 won-loss record and a minute 2.05 ERA. Along the way, he posted a 16-game winning streak. Lou Gehrig continued his streak with his 1000th consecutive game in August and set a new AL mark with 184 runs batted in. He also tied the mighty Ruth with the major league-leading home run total of 46. The Bambino also had another productive year in the RBI department with 163. The Yankee club set a new team record of 1067 runs scored and began what was to be a record total of consecutive games without being shut out. Earl Webb of the Red Sox set another new record with 67 doubles, as did Lloyd Waner with 681 at-bats. On July 12, the Cubs and Cardinals set a new single-game record of 23 two-base hits, a figure somewhat "tainted" by ground rules in effect for that contest. The only no-hit games of 1931 were tossed by Wes Ferrell on April 29 and Bob Burke on August 8. A pair of baseball's "ancients" defied conventional wisdom by participating in pinch-hitting roles—Cardinals Manager Gabby Street at age 49 and Washington Coach Nick Altrock at age 55. Cincinnati tied its own NL season record with 194 twin-killings.

After the awesome hitters' year of 1930, the baseballs of both leagues were "deadened."

Three "giants" of 20th-century ML baseball died during 1931: (L to R) Ban Johnson, Charles Comiskey, and Garry Herrmann.

Will Harridge was named to succeed the late Ernest Barnard as AL President.

In 1931 game action at Detroit, the Tigers' Johnny Stone slides safely into second. White Sox infielders Jeffries and Cissell and Umpire Hildebrand are the other participants.

Cubs player/manager Rogers Hornsby scores on a home run vs. the Giants at the Polo Grounds.

The great Lefty Grove ran up 16 straight victories en route to a magnificent 31-4 season in 1931 and an MVP Award for his efforts.

St. Louis' Frankie Frisch sparked the Red Birds to the '31 championship and was rewarded with the first modern-era MVP honors in the NL.

Although THE SPORTING NEWS had previously conducted its own "unofficial" vote in prior seasons for the Most Valuable Player Awards, the baseball writers initiated the now annual tradition for the 1931 season. Grove, with his spectacular season, was the AL selection despite Gehrig's productive year. The NL Award went to Frankie Frisch for his all-around contribution to the Cardinals' great success. Al Simmons continued his awesome assault on AL pitching with a lofty .391 batting average, which topped the majors. Chick Hafey led the senior circuit with .350. Sophomore Yankee outfielder Ben Chapman led the majors with 61 stolen bases, the highest total since the heyday of Ty Cobb. Some promising newcomers in 1931 included Billy Jurges, Hal Schumacher, Rip Collins, Paul Derringer, Ernie Lombardi, and Van Lingle Mungo in the NL; Red Rolfe, Gee Walker, and Marvin Owen in the AL. The Browns' Sam Gray and the White Sox's Pat Caraway shared the dubious distinction of each losing 24 games, made even less forgiving with horrendous ERAs posted by both hurlers.

The disappointing absence of spirited pennant races was somewhat atoned for in the 1931 World Series, which went the full seven games for the first time since 1926. Once again, President Hoover attended the opener,

either because he was a "closet" Philadelphia fan or more likely because he was already stumping for the upcoming presidential election. Lefty Grove carried the momentum of his great season in the series and won two of the Athletics' three victories. Earnshaw captured the other Mack victory with a masterful two-hit shutout. The Cards' "Wild Bill" Hallahan and Burleigh Grimes were also equal to the task and contained the hard-hitting Philadelphians in games 2, 3, 5, and 7. But the real story behind the St. Louis triumph was the sensational clutch hitting and daring baserunning of rookie outfielder John "Pepper" Martin, the "wild horse of the Osage." Martin hit .500 (12 for 24), the only Cardinal regular to hit over .300, with 19 total bases and five stolen bases to ignite the Redbird offense. Down 4-0 after eight innings against Burleigh Grimes in the final game, the Mackmen made a stirring 9th inning effort to get it all back by scoring twice on Roger Cramer's clutch single. But Hallahan came in to relieve Burleigh and slammed the door to give the National League its first world championship in five years. It was to be the last World Series appearance for Connie Mack, as he began to siphon off his magnificent athletes one by one, replacing them with cold cash and mediocre journeymen over the next several seasons.

The Tribe's Wes Ferrell tossed a no-hitter in late April.

Joe McCarthy began his legendary career as field boss of the Yankees.

Lou Gehrig extended his streak to 1000 games and established a new AL record with 184 RBIs.

The Phils' Chuck Klein topped the senior circuit with 31 HRs, 121 RBIs.

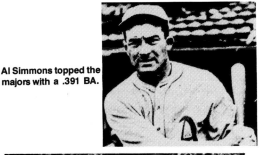
Al Simmons topped the majors with a .391 BA.

Chick Hafey was the NL's top batsman at .350.

Bob Burke authored a no-hit game for Washington in August.

Pepper Martin (left) and Dizzy Dean would become the main characters of the Cardinals' famed "Gas House Gang." St. Louis won NL pennants in '30, '31, and '34.

The sensation of the '31 Series, Pepper Martin, scores again for the Cards in their conquest of the mighty Mackmen.

1932

HIT MOVIES OF 1932

ARROWSMITH
BAD GIRL
THE CHAMP
GRAND HOTEL
SHANGHAI EXPRESS
DR. JEKYLL AND MR. HYDE
THE GUARDSMAN
FIVE STAR FINAL
ONE HOUR WITH YOU
THE SMILING LIEUTENANT

Cleveland's mammoth Municipal Stadium opened for baseball on June 30th in a game vs. the Athletics.

The great John McGraw (left) resigned after 30 years as Giants manager. His talented protege, first baseman Bill Terry (right), was his replacement.

Perennial dynasties by the champion Cardinals and Athletics proved too expensive to maintain when dwindling gate receipts coupled with the high salaries demanded by star players forced both clubs to sell off some of their expensive talent for cash. St. Louis shipped series pitching star Burleigh Grimes to the Cubs and batting champion Chick Hafey to Cincinnati. Before the year was over, Mack began his great "fire sale" of the thirties when Al Simmons, Mule Haas, and Jimmy Dykes were sold to the Chicago White Sox. Even having a winning club on the field, it would seem, was not the salvation for the financial plight that faced all teams during the doldrums of the Great Depression. Two more club owners passed on in 1932—Barney Dreyfuss of Pittsburgh and William Wrigley of the Chicago Cubs. Several new faces in the managerial ranks made their debut in 1932—Lew Fonseca with the White Sox, George Gibson with the Pirates, and Max Carey at Brooklyn. Marty McManus relieved Shano Collins at Boston in June, but was unable to lift the Bosox out of the AL basement. The legendary John McGraw jolted the baseball world by resigning as the Giants' pilot in June because of failing health, not helped by the team's unaccustomed second-division status at the time. First baseman Bill Terry was picked to succeed McGraw and finished out the decade as manager. Another shocking managerial switch occurred in August when the irascible Rogers Hornsby was replaced by popular Cubs first baseman Charley Grimm, even as the Cubs were in second place and very much in the thick of the pennant race. Cleveland observed a major milestone in club history in June by inaugurating the only new big league stadium of the decade, the giant "horseshoe" on Lake Erie, Municipal Stadium.

The 1932 season was packed with remarkable individual achievements and moments of high drama. On June 3, Lou Gehrig became the first ML player to hit four home runs in a single game in this century. On July 4, the ordinarily reticent Yankee catcher Bill Dickey "cold-cocked" Washington's Carl Reynolds and drew a huge fine and suspension from AL President Will Harridge. Umpire George Moriarity was "ambushed" by White Sox players under the stands in a mysterious melee that also resulted in fines and reprimands for all involved. The Chicago Cubs, an exciting contender that summer that was drawing exceptional crowds for key games, were confronted with a public relations crisis with respect to their uniquely generous "ladies day" policies. They found themselves swarmed with hordes of non-paying female guests, which cost them dearly in gate receipts, and had to do some fancy maneuvering to avoid fan riots in accommodating the ladies. The Athletics' Roger Cramer had a career day on June 20, going six for six in a nine-inning game. On August 5, Detroit's pitching ace Tommy Bridges retired the first 26 Washington batters. Then, with Detroit leading 13-0, pinch hitter Dave Harris singled to spoil the perfect outing. Washington Manager Walter Johnson was "roasted" for his seemingly heartless decision to pinch hit in that situation, but Bridges was philosophical to the end and bore no grudge toward the Senators' pilot. In a curious incident that impacted the pennant race, Cubs shortstop Billy Jurges was shot in the hand by a lady fan and veteran Mark Koenig was acquired to fill in during the balance of the campaign. The arrival of Koenig and his remarkable contribution became part of a controversial verbal exchange during the post-season series with New York. Jimmy Foxx made a dramatic run to match Babe Ruth's season record of 60 home runs but fell two short, hitting his 58th in the season's final game. Alvin Crowder's major league-leading 26 wins helped Washington surge to a surprising third-place finish. He finished the year with 15 straight, one shy of tying the record.

Charley Grimm replaced Hornsby as Cubs pilot late in the 1932 season.

Infielder Mark Koenig joined the Cubs in mid-season and helped spark them to a pennant.

Washington's Alvin Crowder hurled 15 straight wins and finished with 26, tops in the majors.

The A's Roger Cramer went 6 for 6 in a June contest.

Tommy Bridges came within one out of a perfect game vs. Washington.

In the 1932 opener at Comiskey Park, the Browns' Fred Schulte flies out to center in a loss to the White Sox.

The New York Yankees once again scored over 1000 runs and, continuing their record streak of avoiding shutouts all season long, ran away from the pack with relative ease, ending Connie Mack's domination of the AL. Lefty Gomez had another fine season with 24 victories despite a 4.21 ERA. It looked like the Yankees of old, with Ruth and Gehrig once again providing the fireworks. Red Ruffing chipped in with 18 wins and 190 Ks, tops in the AL. Dale Alexander, who split the season between Detroit and Boston, was the batting champ with a .367 mark. And Lefty Grove had his usual stellar season with 25 victories and a league best 2.84 ERA. In the senior circuit, the race was more interesting as the Cubs managed to emerge the final victors with only 90 wins. Lon Warneke led the staff with 22 wins and a 2.37 ERA. Surprising Pittsburgh, despite their absence of the long ball and average pitching, held the top spot in July and finished only four games in arrears. Brooklyn finally reinstated their identity as "Dodgers," after a decade or more as "Robins," and made a spirited run at the end, finishing third under their new pilot, Max Carey. Rotund Hack Wilson and Lefty O'Doul gave the Brooklyns some batting punch to fuel their late-season drive. Even the usually lowly Phillies, with an MVP year from Chuck Klein and a career year from Don Hurst, were still in the hunt in the late stage of the campaign.

The Fall Classic between Yanks and Cubs proved to be no contest as the New Yorkers thundered past the Chicagoans in four straight games. The series was marked by an unusually vociferous exchange of name-calling and bench-jockeying, mainly between Ruth and members of the Cubs over the Chicagoans' denial of championship shares to Mark Koenig, who hit .353 as an emergency replacement for Jurges, and to departed Manager Rogers Hornsby. The gregarious Babe rose to the occasion in heroic fashion by following a barrage of taunting from the Cubs bench in game 3 at Wrigley Field. The Babe delivered his legendary "called shot" home run, which silenced his tormentors and symbolized their inevitable fate. Gehrig added his own exclamation point with another towering blast following Ruth's drive. It was a humiliation that Cub fans had to live with for many more years. For the Yankees, it looked like they still had the manpower to resume their AL dominance for the coming seasons.

Lou Gehrig staged a home run "clinic" on June 3 with four for the day.

The Cards' Joe Medwick was a rookie "find" in '32.

The Pirates show-cased another promising freshman in short-stop Arky Vaughan.

Gov. Roosevelt, campaigning for the White House job, greets rival Series managers Grimm and McCarthy at Wrigley Field in October 1932. FDR's son Jimmy is on the right.

Brooklyn's Lefty O'Doul was the NL's top batsman for 1932.

Dale Alexander split the '32 season between Detroit and Boston, but led the AL with a .367 BA.

The great Bambino congratulates Jimmy Foxx on his MVP season, which included a run at the Babe's HR mark, which fell two short at 58.

Lefty Grove accepts his MVP trophy for a great 1931 season.

The most controversial home run in World Series history—Babe Ruth connects off the Cubs' Charlie Root. Did he call it or didn't he?

1933

The 1933 season gave baseball some refreshing new scenarios to keep up general interest in the game. The World Series featured two clubs who hadn't won for nearly a decade. A novel contest in mid-season that pitted the greatest players for each league against each other was staged for the first time and a popular tradition was born. A rare "double triple" was accomplished with two Philadelphia stars capturing baseball's coveted "triple crown." Some new club ownerships surfaced in several cities, the most newsworthy being the purchase of the lowly Boston Red Sox by millionaire Tom Yawkey. Yawkey was determined to rescue the Bosox from their treadmill to oblivion by completely renovating Fenway Park and reaching into his deep pockets to procure players of star caliber to help resurrect the franchise. Other new club presidents who assumed command with less fanfare were Gerald Nugent of the Phillies and Stephen McKeever at Brooklyn. Some new field managers also debuted in 1933. Star shortstop Joe Cronin took over the Washington club, replacing the popular Walter Johnson. Johnson replaced Roger Peckinpaugh at Cleveland shortly into the '33 season. After consecutive seasons in the NL basement under dapper Dan Howley, the Reds hired former White Sox pilot Donie Bush to lead them hopefully upward in the standings. In St. Louis, Rogers Hornsby replaced Browns pilot Killefer and Gabby Street surrendered the reins of the Red Birds to infielder Frankie Frisch. The grim reaper once again took its toll of baseball notables in 1933. Old-time stars Tim Keefe and Kid Gleason died early in the year. Then two more club executives, owner Phil Ball of the Browns and President William Veeck of the Cubs, passed away in October. Tragedy struck the Phillies club when infielder Mickey Finn died in early July.

Some general developments made important news in 1933. The Pennsylvania legislature finally gave the Pittsburgh and Philadelphia clubs a break by rescinding the antiquated "blue laws," which prohibited Sunday baseball in the state. It was good news for these clubs, eager to exploit new avenues to increase lagging attendance. The repeal of Prohibition also helped the baseball operations in most cities, not only with increased concessions revenues but hopefully winning back a sizable number of fans who had stayed away during the "dry" years. The minor leagues, partly due to the growing phenomenon of night games, also had better news as there were no more league failures for the first time in several years. Another factor which certainly helped the minors was the growing trend by big league clubs to develop farm systems and new working agreements after their proven success by the Cardinals' organization.

The Phillies' Chuck Klein had a "career" year in 1933, capturing a triple crown.

Jimmy Foxx repeated as the AL's MVP, also capturing a triple crown to make it a clean sweep for Philadelphia.

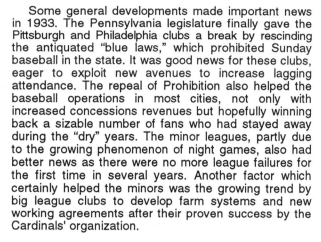

Cubs President William Veeck died in 1933.

Gerald Nugent was the new boss of the Phillies' organization.

Wealthy Tom Yawkey took control of the Red Sox fortunes.

The woeful Browns engaged an old St. Louis favorite, Rogers Hornsby (right), to try to incite the team to more winning ways in 1933. Shown here with veteran coach Charley O'Leary.

Walter Johnson was let go as Senators pilot, but took the same job with Cleveland for 1933.

The Phillies' Mickey Finn met an untimely death in mid-summer.

Paul Derringer set a decade low in 1933 with 27 losses.

Long-time Browns owner Philip Ball passed away at season's end.

Tigers owner Frank Navin (left) inspects the new left field screen being erected at Navin Field, with chief scout Wish Egan.

Arch Ward, Sports Editor of the CHICAGO TRIBUNE, got the blessings and cooperation of baseball bigwigs in arranging a special exhibition game at Comiskey Park which would feature the top stars of each league on opposing teams. Players were selected by a national newspaper poll. John McGraw was persuaded to manage the National Leaguers and Connie Mack led the Americans. The visiting NL players were outfitted in special uniforms for the occasion while the AL opted for their everyday home suits. The game drew sizable national media coverage and also attracted a capacity crowd to view the spectacle. Babe Ruth's two-run homer was the difference in a 4-2 AL victory and plans were made immediately for an encore in a NL park the following year. Meanwhile, in the pennant races, Joe Cronin's Senators got some steady offense combined with some fine pitching by Crowder, Whitehill, and Lefty Stewart to pull away from the Yankees and capture their first flag since the mid-twenties. The second-place Yanks were finally shut out (by Lefty Grove on August 3) to end their streak of 308 games. The race was closer in the senior circuit as Bill Terry's Giants got a phenomenal year from Carl Hubbell (23 wins, 10 shutouts, 1.66 ERA) to lead the New Yorkers to their 13th NL pennant after a disappointing sixth-place finish in 1932.

Twin triple-crown seasons by the Phils' Chuck Klein and the Atheletics' Jimmy Foxx topped individual achievements for 1933. Foxx's great year earned his league's MVP Award, but Klein's statistics were overshadowed by Hubbell's spectacular pitching in the NL MVP voting. Dizzy Dean came into his own with 20 wins and a league-leading 199 strikeouts, which included a new single-game high of 17 on July 30. Veteran Heinie Manush led the Washington attack with a .336 season which featured a 33-game hitting streak. Paul Derringer lost a total of 27 games, 25 with the last-place Reds, but his 3.23 ERA was evidence that he simply pitched all year without adequate or timely support. The Browns' Sam West enjoyed a 6-for-6 day versus the White Sox on April 13.

In the post-season classic, the pitching of Carl Hubbell (0.00 ERA) and Hal Schumacher proved too formidable for Washington as the Giants captured their first post-McGraw world championship in five games. Earl Whitehill's five-hit shutout in game 3 was the only taste of glory for the Griffs. Mel Ott and Kiddo Davis were hitting stars for New York, with Ott's 10th-inning homer deciding the issue in the final game at Griffith Stadium. In another flurry of post-season player shifts, the Senators traded Goose Goslin to Detroit for Johnny Stone. Along with Goslin, Detroit purchased catcher Mickey Cochrane from the Athletics—two moves that would profoundly change the fortunes of the Tiger club for the better. Other blockbuster transactions that took place in the post-season included Yawkey's purchase of Lefty Grove, Rube Walberg, and Max Bishop from the Macks and the surprise acquisition of triple-crown winner Klein by the Cubs from the beleaguered Phillies.

Dizzy Dean "arrived" as a top-flight NL hurler in 1933, winning 20 and striking out a record 17 in one game.

Star shortstop/manager Joe Cronin celebrates the AL pennant clincher with joyous owner Clark Griffith.

A huge crowd filled the Polo Grounds at the 1933 World Series opener.

The American League's finest pose for an all-star portrait at the inaugural midsummer classic in Chicago's Comiskey Park.

Cards outfielder George Watkins takes a Lon Warneke pitch in the ribs at the NL 1933 opener at Wrigley Field.

The Giants' perennial "meal ticket," Carl Hubbell, pitched the New Yorkers to the NL flag and earned the MVP Award for his great season.

Rival pilots for the 1933 post-season classic, Bill Terry (left) and Joe Cronin greet each other at the opening game.

"Prince Hal" Schumacher teamed with Hubbell to seal the Giants' world championship.

The great Mel Ott crosses the plate after his series-winning HR in the 10th inning of the final game at Washington.

1934

League Presidents Harridge and Heydler confer with Reach and Spalding execs on standardizing baseball construction in early 1934.

John McGraw, the New York Giants' legendary pilot, died in early 1934.

For the mighty Sultan of Swat, 1934 was to be his last year with the Yankees.

Brooklyn's Wilbert Robinson also passed on in late 1934.

Two American League clubs with wealthier ownership, Detroit and Boston, gambled over the winter with some daring acquisitions of superstar players. For one (Detroit) it worked wonders, but for the other (Boston) it failed to transform the franchise into a contender. Tom Yawkey was determined to rescue the Red Sox from their endless second-division status and he further demonstrated his commitment by totally renovating and expanding Fenway Park for 1934 at an enormous cost. Both leagues agreed in January to standardize the baseball to assure its uniformity of construction and erase any arguments about differences of play in two circuits—at least with respect to the performance of the ball itself. William Walker was named Cubs president to succeed Veeck and another millionaire owner surfaced in February with the purchase of the Cincinnati franchise by Powell Crosley, Jr. The New York area, and indeed the baseball world, was saddened by the deaths of immortals John McGraw in February, then Wilbert Robinson in August. A host of new field managers made their debut in 1934, most notably the fiery backstop Mickey Cochrane in Tigertown. Other new faces in major league dugouts were the Phillies' Jimmy Wilson, the Reds' Bob O'Farrell (then replaced by Chuck Dressen in mid-season), Brooklyn's Casey Stengel, and the Red Sox's new man Bucky Harris. After another dismal start by the White Sox, Lew Fonseca gave way to Jimmy Dykes. George Gibson resigned as Pirates boss after 51 games and local favorite Pie Traynor took the reins. Before the season started, veteran pitching stars Eppa Rixey and Red Faber announced their retirement. And 1934 was to be the final year for Burleigh Grimes, Hack Wilson, and the great Babe Ruth (as a Yankee). It would also be the last year for National League President John Heydler.

In the American League flag chase, defending champion Washington's pitching corps failed miserably to repeat their strong success of '33. Ace Alvin Crowder struggled to a 4-10 record, then was shipped to Detroit, where he seemed to rediscover himself and helped the Tigers down the stretch. The Yankees got another productive year out of Gehrig (a major league-leading 49 HRs, 165 RBI), but the aging Babe finally slowed down to a mere 22 homers. Gomez (26 wins) and Ruffing (19) helped the New Yorkers win 94 games, but the Tigers caught fire and pulled away at the end with 101 victories. With "Black Mike" Cochrane leading the charge, the Bengal bashers found the winning formula with a team batting average of .300. Young "Schoolboy" Rowe was the pitching sensation of the junior circuit with 16 straight wins en route to a 24-win season. Tommy Bridges followed closely behind him with 22 victories. The Red Sox's new blood proved a disappointment as premier hurler Grove had his only poor season in the decade with an 8-8 record and an incredulous 6.52 ERA. In the senior circuit, a lively pennant race boiled down to defending champ New York and the resurgent St. Louis Cardinals, the famed "Gas House Gang." In the season finale that Brooklyn fans relished with glee, Stengel's sixth-place Dodgers twice defeated the hated Giants to hand over the flag to St. Louis. The Dean brothers were the talk of baseball that year, with Diz amassing 30 victories and brother Paul contributing 19 more, including a no-hitter on September 21. Scrappy shortstop Leo Durocher hit only .260, but proved to be a key sparkplug for the "Gas House" machine. The MVP Awards went to Dean for his spectacular pitching and to Cochrane for his inspiring leadership behind the plate. Lou Gehrig's triple-crown winning numbers would have easily handed him MVP honors had the Yankees finished on top. Mel Ott had another fine season leading the NL with his 35 homers and 135 RBIs. Paul Waner was the NL bat champ at .362. The second annual All-Star game at New York's Polo Grounds went to the AL 9-7. The hometown's pitching hero, Carl Hubbell, thrilled the audience by fanning five consecutive AL sluggers. At season's end, the great Ruth was handed his unconditional release.

Wealthy Powell Crosley was new owner of the Reds.

Casey Stengel was the Dodgers' new manager.

Popular Pie Traynor replaced George Gibson as Bucs pilot in June.

Carl Hubbell is presented with his '33 MVP Award at the 1934 All-Star contest at the Polo Grounds.

The World Series for 1934 was a natural, matching up the two most exciting teams and the best available rosters of "marquis" players. The Dean brothers, Pepper Martin, Leo Durocher, Frankie Frisch, et al. vs. the "Schoolboy," "Black Mike," and the "G-men." The Motor City was especially delirious with the surprising transformation of "also-rans" into legitimate winners for the first time in 25 years. The Series lived up to its promise, going the full seven games and, excepting the results of game 7, it was a toss-up. Rowe, Bridges, and the submariner Eldon Auker gave the Detroits a victory apiece, but the Dean brothers proved unbeatable with two victories each. Hank Greenberg and Charley Gehringer led the Tiger hitters in their losing cause. Pepper Martin, Rip Collins, and Joe Medwick each had 11 hits to pace the Cardinal offense. After a seesaw battle in the first six games, the seventh game at Detroit's Navin Field brought disaster for the hometown fans. Behind Dizzy Dean, the Redbirds quickly piled up a huge lead in the early innings and Dean proved untouchable, shutting down the Tiger bats 11-0. One of the most celebrated incidents in Series history occurred that day when Joe Medwick collided with Tigers' third baseman Marv Owen in the 6th inning. Frustrated Detroit fans, already down 9-0, took offense at Medwick's tactics and bombarded him with fruits, vegetables, bottles, et cetera when he took his left field position. Commissioner Landis finally interceded and removed Medwick from the game for his own safety. Tiger fans would have to wait another year to claim the big prize.

The Yanks' Lefty Gomez won pitching's version of the "triple crown" in the AL.

Paul Waner hit .362 to lead his league.

The hottest pitchers in each league, Dean and Rowe, were showcased in the post-season classic.

Besides his pitching virtuosity, Dizzy Dean also hit and ran the bases in leading the Cardinals to victory over Detroit in the Series. Here shown scoring the winning run in an early game at Detroit.

Lou Gehrig had yet another productive year in '34, capturing the "triple crown."

The other Dean brother, Paul, won 19, including a no-hit gem.

Catcher/Mgr. Cochrane's inspiring leadership led Detroit to a pennant and, for himself, MVP honors.

The "infamous" collision at third, with Medwick sliding in hard in game 7, won by St. Louis 11-0.

Judge Landis is explaining his decision to remove Medwick (center) from game 7 to Manager Frisch. It was already 9-0 in the Cards' favor.

1935

The National League had a new president in 1935 as Ford Frick replaced the retiring John Heydler. Judge Emil Fuchs, owner of the Boston Braves, gave Babe Ruth one last opportunity to thrill the fans by signing the Babe to his final player contract. Ruth's "last hurrah" was brief, as he called it quits early in the season. But he had one final Ruthian performance, slamming out three homers in a game at Pittsburgh's Forbes Field. The Reds' wealthy, energetic new owner, Powell Crosley, renamed the home park Crosley Field. He also hired a creative new VP/general manager in Larry MacPhail and together they made plans to install a permanent lighting system—a first for major league baseball. History was made on May 24 as the Reds and Phillies squared off for the first time under the new floodlights. In the American League, Boston's Tom Yawkey continued his free-spending acquisitions by hiring away Washington's star player/manager Joe Cronin to fill the same capacity at Fenway. In what was tantamount to a managerial swap, Bucky Harris returned to his former job as Clark Griffith's field boss. The only other managerial change was at Cleveland in mid-season when Walter Johnson surrendered the Tribe job to former Indian catching great Steve O'Neill. The "Big Train" remained a beloved hero in DC and was given a day in his honor by Washington fans. Cleveland's gigantic new stadium was the site of the third All-Star classic, won by the AL 4-1 before 70,000 fans.

The Detroit Tigers, after a slow start, got it going in the latter stages of the season and passed by New York, surprising Cleveland to capture their second consecutive pennant. Solid pitching by the starting four of Bridges, Rowe, Auker, and Crowder and a big year for slugging first baseman Hank Greenberg (.328, 36 HR, 170 RBI) were the keys in their drive to the top. Tiger outfielder Pete Fox also contributed with a 29-game hitting streak. Joe Cronin's Red Sox once again failed to elevate themselves into contention, even with fine seasons from Lefty Grove and Wes Ferrell—proving that only two such solid hurlers are not necessarily enough to win pennants. The National League race proved more exciting as the Chicago Cubs fulfilled their "every third year" destiny by overtaking the Cardinals and Giants with an amazing 21-game winning streak in September. Pitching depth by Cub starters Warneke, French, Lee, Root, and Henshaw and an MVP year for catcher Gabby Hartnett helped to sustain their final surge to the top. McKechnie's forlorn Braves established a decade low with a staggering 115 losses and decided to disguise themselves behind a new identity for 1936.

Ford Frick was the new NL prexy.

New Bosox pilot Joe Cronin (right) is greeted by Joe McCarthy at the '35 opener.

Veteran Ump Hank O'Day died in 1935.

A's exec Tom Shibe also passed away in '35.

Babe Ruth, shown with Braves slugger Wally Berger, signed for one last year in Boston, where it all began.

The Phils' Lou Chiozza helped make history with the ML's first hit under the arcs on May 24 at Cincinnati.

Washington's all-time favorite, Walter Johnson, was honored at Griffith Stadium just before he was let go as Tribe pilot.

One-time Indians backstop Steve O'Neill replaced Johnson as Cleveland manager.

The White Sox' Vern Kennedy blanked the Indians with nary a hit in late August.

The 1935 season had its share of outstanding player achievements as well as oddities and misfortunes. The batting champions in both leagues were Pittsburgh's Arky Vaughan (.385) and Washington's Buddy Myer (.349). Dizzy Dean followed his 30-win year with 28 in '35 while brother Paul once again chalked up 19. Vern Kennedy of the White Sox tossed the first no-hit gem in the AL since 1931, blanking Cleveland on August 31. Cardinals veteran Jesse Haines reached a club milestone with his 200th career win. The incomparable Dazzy Vance finished his great career in 1935 with the club he had his finest seasons with—Brooklyn. The Pirates' Gus Suhr continued his modest "iron man" streak by appearing in his 628th straight game (about 1000 behind Gehrig). Among the oddities were the following: the Cards' Rip Collins played an entire nine-inning game at first without a putout, and even more curious was a Cincinnati doubleheader in which third baseman Billy Sullivan played the full 18 innings without a fielding chance. In a tragic note, Dodger outfielder Len Koenecke, after being released by Manager Casey Stengel in September, became distraught and went berserk on a chartered flight over Canada. When the pilot attempted to subdue him with a fire extinguisher, Koenecke was killed by the blow.

Tigers owner Frank Navin, despite his sober countenance and tight-fisted reputation, was obsessed with a lifetime goal of bringing a world championship to Detroit. In 1935 his dream came true and a month later he was dead of a heart attack. Despite the loss of RBI leader and league MVP Hank Greenberg from an injury in game 2, the Bengals got some clutch pitching from Bridges, Rowe, and Crowder and prevailed over the Cubs in six games. In the final game at Navin Field, the Tiger heroes were Bridges, Cochrane, and Goslin. Curve-ball ace Tommy retired the side after Stan Hack opened the Cubs' ninth with a booming triple. Then in the bottom of the ninth, Mickey Cochrane raced over with the winning run on Goose Goslin's hit. It was the proudest moment in the history of the franchise as the city of Detroit went delirious over their new champions. For the "snake-bitten" Cubs, it was another chapter in their seemingly endless futility in World Series play.

Hank Greenberg was AL MVP for the winning Tigers, but an injury forced him out of the Series.

League MVP Gabby Hartnett contributed to the Cubs' late surge for the NL pennant.

Brooklyn's Len Koenecke was killed in a scuffle on an airplane.

Washington's Buddy Myer led AL batsmen at .349.

The Braves' Ben Cantwell symbolized the team's futility with 25 losses.

Chicago's starting four of (L to R): Larry French, Lon Warneke, Bill Lee, and Charley Root were an important ingredient in the Cubs' 1935 winning formula.

The decade's top slugger, Jimmy Foxx, scores on a home run in the '35 All-Star contest at Cleveland's Municipal Stadium.

Arky Vaughan gave Pittsburgh its second straight batting title with a lofty .385 mark in '35.

The '35 Series opener at Navin Field saw the Chicagos draw first blood, 3-0.

Cochrane scores the run in the 9th inning of game 6 that gave the Tigers their first world championship.

Goose Goslin (center) delivered the big hit that drove in Cochrane (left) with the clincher. Winning pitcher Tommy Bridges (right) regales with his fellow Tiger heroes in the locker room.

1936

BABE RUTH   TY COBB   CHRISTY MATHEWSON

HONUS WAGNER   WALTER JOHNSON

The five charter members selected for the game's official Hall of Fame

Death took Giants owner Charles Stoneham in early 1936. His son Horace succeeded him.

NYC's Mayor La Guardia (right) ushers in the '36 Giants season. New owner Horace Stoneham is on the left.

In 1936, the Baseball Writers officially inaugurated the game's Hall of Fame by selecting the first five nominees—Ruth, Cobb, Wagner, Johnson, and Mathewson. Giants owner Charles Stoneham died in January and was succeeded by his son, Horace. In another spectacular spending spree, Boston's Tom Yawkey shelled out $300,000 to the Macks for Jimmy Foxx, Roger Cramer, Eric McNair, and John Marcum. Boston's NL entry officially renamed themselves Bees for 1936. Braves Field was now referred to as National League Park (or the "beehive") to help bury the old nickname. Detroit's new owner, Walter Briggs, for reasons unknown, disrupted his solid outfield corps of Fox, White, Goslin, and Gee Walker by purchasing another established star, Al Simmons, from Chicago. Construction began on the massive enlargement of Navin Field to accommodate more anticipated championships, but the post-1935 years only produced a series of disappointments and just plain bad luck. Early in 1936, MVP Hank Greenberg broke his wrist and was through for the year. Then, the once fiery Cochrane was felled with a crippling nervous breakdown that sidelined him for the season and demoralized the club further. They finished a distant second and were unable to seriously threaten the Yankee juggernaut for the balance of the decade. A pair of sensational rookies made the headlines in 1936. A seventeen-year-old farm boy from Iowa, Bobby Feller, astonished everyone with his blazing fastball and numerous strikeouts. He fanned 15 St. Louis Browns in his first major league start and later tied Dizzy Dean's game record of 17. The young outfielding sensation of the Pacific Coast League, Joe DiMaggio, made a sparkling Yankee debut with a .323 average plus 29 home runs and 125 runs batted in. The Cubs gave up on their seemingly impotent slugger Chuck Klein and traded him back to the Phillies.

The National League race once again was a dogfight between Chicago, St. Louis, and New York. This time, the Giants turned the tables on the Cubs by winning 15 straight in August to propel them into the top spot. Carl Hubbell and Mel Ott enjoyed especially productive seasons to lead the way. "King Carl" racked up 26 victories with a stingy 2.31 ERA and wound up his MVP year with 16 straight wins. Ott hit .328 and topped the NL with 33 homers plus 135 RBIs, second only to Joe Medwick's 138. Paul Waner gave Pittsburgh a second consecutive batting championship, hitting .373. The Pirates, once again lacking the long ball and saddled with only average pitching, finished a respectable fourth, eight games out. Brooklyn's fire-balling but erratic Van Lingle Mungo fanned 238 batters, the highest total thus far in the decade. The senior circuit finally tasted victory in the All-Star contest at Braves Field (oops! National League Park) on July 7. Dizzy Dean, Curt Davis, Carl Hubbell, and Lon Warneke held the AL sluggers in check for a 4-3 victory. Bees (Braves) management badly mismanaged ticket sales for the game and only 25,000 ended up watching the contest.

The Yankees' rookie sensation Joe DiMaggio is given the award for being the outstanding PCL player for 1935 by comedian Joe E. Brown.

Another 1936 rookie who got rave reviews was Cleveland's Bob Feller.

Despite the Bengals' failure to win another flag, Tommy Bridges had another fine year on the mound.

Brooklyn's Van Lingle Mungo replaced Dizzy Dean as the NL's strikeout king with 238 Ks.

Paul Waner was tops in the NL with a .373 BA.

The American League season became Yankee business as usual as McCarthy's legions piled up 102 victories, leaving champion Detroit 19-1/2 games in arrears. It looked like the Bronx Bombers of old as they pounded out 182 home runs, scored over 1000 runs, and hit .300 as a team. Lou Gehrig once again led the assault with 49 circuit blasts and 152 RBIs. Rookie DiMaggio and catcher Bill Dickey also made major contributions with their bats. The high-priced "ringers" on Yawkey's Boston club once again failed to deliver even an improvement in their standing, finishing under .500 with a 74-80 record. Jimmy Dykes' White Sox showed some signs of life, finishing third, thanks partly to the pitching of Vern Kennedy (21-9) and a career year at the plate for shortstop Luke Appling, who led the majors with a .388 BA. Cleveland's Hal Trosky also had a career season with 42 homers and a league-leading 162 RBIs.

The World Series of 1936 was the first all-New York classic since the early twenties. Carl Hubbell and Hal Schumacher managed to muzzle the Yankee artillery for two victories, but in the end the awesome run-production of the McCarthy machine proved invincible. Two of the Yankee victories were by scores of 18-4 and 13-5. Tony Lazzeri highlighted the game 2 slaughter with a rare Series grand slam. The Yankee lineup hit .302 for the Series, led by the unlikely tandem of Jake Powell (.455) and Red Rolfe (.400). Giants shortstop Dick Bartell was the top hitter in a losing cause with eight hits and a .381 average. By the final game at Yankee Stadium, New York fans must have already conceded the final outcome, as only 50,000 turned out to watch the lights go out for Bill Terry's Giants. A new era of Yankee dominance was well underway.

Tony Lazzeri is about to deliver a grand slam in game 2 of the 1936 World Series at the Polo Grounds.

Detroit Manager Mickey Cochrane spent much of 1936 recovering from a series of mysterious maladies.

Lou Gehrig's productive '36 season (49 HRs, 152 RBIs) earned him MVP honors.

"King Carl" Hubbell won 16 straight en route to an MVP year and 26 wins.

Joe McCarthy (left), subbing for ill Mickey Cochrane, meets his NL counterpart Charley Grimm at the '36 All-Star game in Boston, won by the NL, 4-3.

Across the Harlem River, a full house of Yankee faithful jammed the outfield bleachers in the "House that Ruth Built."

The Tribe's Hal Trosky led the majors with 162 RBIs.

White Sox shortstop Luke Appling had his finest year, hitting .388, tops in the majors.

Starting pitchers Hubbell (left) and Ruffing shake hands before opening the '36 Classic with a 6-1 Giant victory.

Hal Schumacher (left) and Jo-Jo Moore were the heroes of the only other Giant victory in game 5.

Jake Powell (left) and Red Rolfe led the Yankee assault in their six-game series conquest of their cross-town rivals.

1937

NAP LAJOIE   **TRIS SPEAKER**   **CY YOUNG**

Three more immortals were enshrined in Cooperstown's planned Hall of Fame.

Chicago's bespectacled Bill Dietrich (third from left) authored a 1937 no-hitter. Here he poses with previous no-hit hurlers (L to R): Wes Ferrell (1931), Ted Lyons (1926), and Vern Kennedy (1935).

Three more names were added to the Hall of Fame roster with the selection of Nap Lajoie, Tris Speaker, and Cy Young. Connie Mack, the chief decision-maker for years in the Athletics' operation, was officially named president of the club. The St. Louis Browns, long suffering with losing teams and pitiful attendance, named a new president for 1937, Donald Barnes. As part of a revitalization program for the franchise, a new team crest was chosen and displayed on the team's shirt sleeves for 1937. Unfortunately, new faces in the front office and cosmetic additions to the uniform do not win games, as the lackluster Brownies lost 108 games and in mid-season replaced the short-tempered pilot Rogers Hornsby with St. Louis favorite Sunny Jim Bottomley. Another franchise that tried to change its luck with a new uniform scheme (green trimmings, no less) and a new field boss (battling Burleigh Grimes) was the Brooklyn club. They likewise continued to flounder in 1937, finishing sixth with 91 losses. Cincinnati also plummeted even deeper under Chuck Dressen and replaced him with coach Bobby Wallace at season's end. Another major league owner died in July—John Shibe of the Athletics. Death claimed some baseball names from the game's early days with the passing of Ned Hanlon and George Wright. More tragic were the untimely deaths of more contemporary big leaguers in November—Ed Walsh, Jr., son of the former White Sox pitching great, from a lingering heart ailment and Reds pitcher Benny Frey, who took his own life.

Some surprise deals in 1937 sent Lon Warneke from the Cubs to the Cardinals in exchange for first baseman Rip Collins, and the Ferrell battery went from the Red Sox to Washington for Buck Newsom and Ben Chapman. The Detroit club again failed to regain its 1935 winning formula, finishing second, far behind the Yankees in a strange year of good news/bad news. The good news for the Motor City included a league-leading attendance figure of over one million, seemingly justifying the costly park expansion going on at the time. Two Tiger sluggers also had some impressive numbers in 1937—Hank Greenberg drove in an AL near-record total of 183 runs and rookie catcher Rudy York topped Ruth's single-month home run record by hitting 18 round trippers in August. And, in a doubleheader against St. Louis, the Tigers scored a record total of 37 runs. But the bad news was devastating to the club's pennant hopes: after seemingly recovering from his ailments of '36, catcher/manager Cochrane was beaned by Yankee hurler Bump Hadley and even hovered between life and death after the accident. He survived, but the accident ended his great playing career and ultimately his brief but glorious reign as field boss. Another fatal blow to the Tiger club was the abrupt ineffectiveness of ace pitcher Schoolboy Rowe.

Donald Barnes (left) confers with AL chief Will Harridge (center) and former St. Louis Browns President Louis Von Weise after the club was sold to Barnes' group.

A's prexy John Shibe died in July, giving Connie Mack full control of the club.

Death claimed Ump Cy Pfirman in 1937.

Cincy hurler Benny Frey was a victim of suicide.

Bad luck continued to haunt the Tigers' Mike Cochrane, nearly fatally beaned by Yankee pitcher Bump Hadley (inset).

Joe Medwick and Charley Gehringer had their finest years and were logical MVP selections for 1937. "Ducky" captured a rare triple crown and the "mechanical man" took the AL batting title with a lofty .371. Lefty Gomez won a pitcher's version of the triple crown, leading the AL in wins (21), strikeouts (194), and ERA (2.33). Carl Hubbell carried his late '36 win streak into '37 and extended it to 24, ending up with 22 season victories. Cleveland's Johnny Allen won his first 15 decisions, only to lose his 16th, 1-0, at Detroit on the last day of the season. The "new" Boston Bees produced a rare tandem of "veteran" rookie hurlers, Lou Fette and Jim Turner, both 20-game winners for a second-division club. Young White Sox pitcher Monty Stratton finally lived up to expectations with a 15-5 WL record. Gus Suhr's longevity streak came to an end at 822 when his mother's death forced him out of the lineup. Charley Gehringer's three hits in the '37 All-Star contest at Washington led the AL to another victory 8-3, and raised Charley's career All-Star BA to .529. In the third inning of that game, an Earl Averill line drive broke Dizzy Dean's toe, an injury that ultimately shortened Dean's great career.

Bill Terry, who had retired as a player after '36, led his Giants to a second straight flag in a tight race with Chicago. Cliff Melton joined Hubbell as a 20-game winner to anchor the pitching rotation. Mel Ott produced 31 round trippers to tie Medwick for the lead in that department. But the potent offense of the Yankee bats produced a pair of 8-1 victories over the two Giant aces to open the series. King Carl salvaged a 7-3 win in game 4, but McCarthy's men cruised to another world championship behind Gomez, Ruffing, and Pearson. Tony Lazzeri led the Bronx hit parade with an even .400. Jo-Jo Moore and Hank Leiber batted .391 and .364 in a losing effort. For the new version of the Yank's "Murderers' Row," dispatching the National League's best was becoming a routine post-season formality.

A tough 1-0 loss by the Indians' Johnny Allen denied him a perfect 16-0 record.

The "Mechanical Man," Detroit's Charley Gehringer, hit a career high .371 and was the AL's MVP.

Slugger Hank Greenberg had his biggest RBI year with a near-record 183.

Gus Suhr's modest "iron man" streak ended at 822 games.

Tony Lazzeri was the Yanks' top hitter in the Fall Classic.

Lefty Gomez posted league-leading pitching stats in 1937.

Sophomore Joe DiMaggio led the majors with 46 home runs in '37.

Diz Dean's broken foot incurred at the 1937 All-Star contest put him out of action and ultimately shortened his pitching career.

Lou Gehrig's home run helped the AL to an 8-3 All-Star triumph at Washington's Griffith Stadium.

The lowly Boston Bees did manage to produce a rare tandem of 20-game winners—Jim Turner (L), Lou Fette (R).

Joe Medwick, the NL's MVP, recorded a rare "triple crown" in 1937.

Tiger catcher Rudy York hit a record 18 HRs in August.

A frustrated Bill Terry can scarcely watch the Yankee machine dispose of his Giants in five games.

Yankee owner Jake Ruppert joins the locker room celebration after the 1937 World Series triumph at the Polo Grounds.

1938

Phillies owner Gerry Nugent (seated on left) signs an agreement with Mack's Athletics for joint tenancy of Shibe Park, spelling the final demise of Baker Bowl in 1938.

A familiar figure in an unfamiliar role, Babe Ruth (far left) joins an on-field argument in his new job as a Brooklyn coach in 1938.

The mighty Babe was back in baseball in 1938, but not in the manager's role he had coveted. The Brooklyn Dodgers, aware of his tremendous box-office charisma, hired Ruth as a coach, but in truth his purpose was simply to participate in batting practice and deliver his famous long ball to the pre-game shows. The Dodger organization injected new vitality in the front office by luring Business Manager Larry MacPhail from Cincinnati. MacPhail wasted no time in re-energizing the franchise and taking some bold new initiatives.The unorthodox green-trimmed uniforms of 1937 were scrapped in favor of a more traditional style, but with script royal blue lettering on the front. Spunky shortstop Leo Durocher was obtained from St. Louis to incite the Bums to loftier goals. Ebbets Field was slated to become the second major league park with night baseball and before the year was out, the Dodgers would take the lead in discarding the nonsensical pact with the other NYC clubs that "blacked out" radio broadcasting. The Philadelphia Phillies ended an era by finally abandoning their ancient home, Baker Bowl, and signed an agreement to share Shibe Park with the Athletics. In Detroit, the Motor City fans anxiously awaited the inauguration of their expansive new version of Navin Field, which would henceforth be known as Briggs Stadium. The Chicago Cubs, after losing out by an eyelash in 1937, went all out to reclaim NL honors by purchasing Dizzy Dean from St. Louis for the unheard of price of $185,000. They did achieve that goal, but Dean's contribution turned out to be minimal. The New York Yankees' young phenom, Joe DiMaggio, proved to be an unusually shrewd businessman as he held out for $25,000—a tactic he would repeat in future years. The wandering superstar Al Simmons found himself in Washington for the 1938 season.

More managerial shifts were also the order of business in 1938. Deacon Bill McKechnie left the Bees to take charge in Cincinnati and Casey Stengel took the Boston job. Ossie Vett replaced Steve O'Neill at Cleveland and Gabby Street was the Browns' new field boss. Into the season, the now floundering Tigers fired the popular Mickey Cochrane and coach Del Baker took the reins. Walter O. Briggs was by now weathering a firestorm of fan backlash which had begun with the earlier trade of popular heroes Gee Walker and Marvin Owen to Chicago for Vern Kennedy, Tony Piet, and Dixie Walker. In a rather peculiar maneuver for a potential contender, Cubs Manager Charlie Grimm gave way to the popular catcher Gabby Hartnett in July and retreated to the radio booth. The Cubs, with higher expectations of immediate success, were admittedly stumbling at the time but in the end all was well as Hartnett led them to the top. With the famed "Gas House Gang" wallowing in the second division and playing under .500, Frankie Frisch was history and coach Mike Gonzales finished out their disappointing season as field boss.

Dizzy Dean (center) became a Chicago Cub as the 1938 season opened. Phil Wrigley shelled out $185,000 for the Red Birds' one-time star pitcher.

Casey Stengel replaced Deacon Bill McKechnie as boss of the Boston Bees.

Fiery Frankie Frisch, shown here arguing with Umpire Ernest Quigley, was relieved of his Cardinal manager's job in late '38.

New Cleveland pilot Ossie Vitt is welcomed to the league by Mickey Cochrane on opening day.

Promising White Sox pitcher Monty Stratton's career was ended by a tragic hunting accident in late 1938.

Some exciting highlights thrilled the fans across the major leagues in 1938. Cincinnati's Johnny Vander Meer did the undoable by hurling consecutive no-hit games, the second one before Brooklyn's very first night-game crowd. Bob Feller topped off a 17-win season by fanning 18 Tigers in his final outing, establishing a new major league record. Rapid Robert also became the second AL pitcher in the decade to surpass 200 Ks for a season. The Yanks' Monte Pearson no-hit Cleveland on August 27, 13-0. Boston's Pinky Higgins had 12 consecutive hits, another record. And Hank Greenberg made a strong bid at the Babe's cherished season record of 60 home runs, finishing two short at 58.

The Pittsburgh Pirates finally found a home run threat in outfielder Johnny Rizzo (23) and actually held the top spot for much of the summer. But the fates were against them in a crucial series with the surging Cubs at Wrigley Field in late September. Catcher/Manager Gabby Hartnett electrified the hometown fans with a game-winning home run in the twilight that all but eliminated Pittsburgh from the chase. Big Bill Lee was the workhorse down the stretch for the winning Cubbies with 22 victories, including nine shutouts. Cincinnati finally emerged from mediocrity under new manager McKechnie with 82 victories, paced by pitcher Paul Derringer (21-14) and an MVP season from catcher Ernie Lombardi (.342, 19 HR, 95 RBI). The Boston Red Sox also finally got some mileage from their high-priced help by finishing second to the Yankee juggernaut, aided by the blossoming of their home-grown second baseman, Bobby Doerr. The Yankees also were further blessed with their own home-grown second sacker, Joe Gordon, who proved a capable replacement for the departed Lazzeri.

The World Series was an encore of 1932 and the jubilant Cubs had delusions of atoning for their '32 destruction. But unfortunately, it was more or less "deja vu" all over again as the Chicagoans were once again hopelessly overmatched by the Bronx Bombers. Led by catcher Dickey and newcomer Gordon, the New Yorkers made it mercifully brief with a one-sided four-game sweep. For the almighty Yankees, it seemed to get easier every year to assert their supremacy over the baseball world. 1938 ended with a tragic note in the off-season when promising young White Sox pitcher Monty Stratton lost his leg in a hunting accident.

The Reds' Johnny Vander Meer (center, with new Mgr. McKechnie and catcher Lombardi) made history in 1938 with consecutive no-hitters.

Lou Gehrig's incredible streak reached 2000 in '38.

The Red Sox finally began to emerge as a contender in 1938. Their infield of (L to R): Doerr, Cronin, Higgins, and Foxx was arguably baseball's best.

Hank Greenberg made a stirring bid to match the Babe's mark of 60, but fell two short at 58.

Young pitching sensation Bobby Feller established a new strikeout record with 18 in one game.

Bill Lee was the champion Cubs top moundsman with 22 victories.

Red Ruffing emerged as the mainstay of the 1938 Yankee pitching corps.

Gabby Hartnett's finest moment—a game-clinching HR in the twilight in a crucial contest in late September at Wrigley Field.

Rival managers Hartnett and McCarthy pose at Wrigley Field before yet another Yankee World Series victory.

1939

Newly named Brooklyn Manager Leo Durocher welcomes new player Dixie Walker. Both were destined to play key roles in the resurgence of the Dodger franchise.

The final year of the decade was an uplifting one for baseball if not for the world, at the precipice of global war. Despite the Yankees' total dominance, which was eroding the delicate balance of parity, overall attendance was holding at a higher level than the middle years of the decade and seemed to be on the verge of an upward trend with the ending of the Great Depression. All was in readiness for the upcoming Centennial celebration and the official opening of the Hall of Fame in Cooperstown. Three more immortals were added to the list of inductees—George Sisler, Eddie Collins, and Willie Keeler. In January, longtime owner of the Yankee franchise Col. Ruppert was dead and Ed Barrow was the new chief executive of the world champions. J. Louis Comiskey also died in 1939 and the White Sox franchise fell into the laps of the remaining family members of the Comiskey estate. Larry MacPhail took full control of the Brooklyn operation with his appointment as president in May. With the naming of Leo Durocher as field manager, the Dodgers' fortunes were destined to turn upward. The new "Dodger mania" was catching on, as over one million fans paid their way into Ebbets Field in 1939. Night baseball was now firmly established as three more big league parks installed lighting systems for 1939—Shibe Park, Comiskey Park, and Cleveland's Municipal Stadium. And radio broadcasting in the Big Apple was restored with all three New York City-based clubs hiring play-by-play announcers. Even the astounding new technology of television got into the act with the first experimental telecast of a Dodger game. Besides Durocher, three new faces in the managerial ranks were Fred Haney (Browns), Ray Blades (Cardinals), and Doc Prothro (Phillies). Former Cards' pilot Frankie Frisch signed on in Boston as a play-by-play radio broadcaster.

Some impressive new home run records were established in June. First, the Giants hit five in one inning against the Reds. Then, the Yanks hit eight in the first game of a doubleheader vs. the A's, then added five more in the nightcap for a total of 13 for the day. But the biggest news story for baseball in 1939 centered around the already epic career of the "Iron Horse," Lou Gehrig. Lou's incredible consecutive game streak reached 2,130 when the Yankees were in Detroit in May. Gehrig's performance was painfully below his standards and showed no sign of improvement, so he voluntarily benched himself for "the good of the team." The discovery of his rare fatal affliction soon followed and Lou announced that 1939 would be his last year as a player. His moving tribute at Yankee Stadium later that summer has since become an unforgettable chapter in baseball lore. Another poignant story took place in Chicago when the White Sox staged a benefit game for their former pitching prospect Monty Stratton, now an amputee and an honorary coach for the Pale Hose. A new rookie sensation burst upon the major league stage with the arrival of lanky Ted Williams. The "Splendid Splinter" hit .327 with 31 homers (one completely out of Detroit's Briggs Stadium) and a major league-leading 145 runs driven in. In New York, the great Joe DiMaggio enjoyed his best year yet with a .381 BA that gave him the batting championship as well as the league's MVP Award. Cleveland's Bobby Feller also hit his Hall of Fame stride with a 24-9 season and 246 strikeouts. But the top pitching performance of 1939 belonged to Cincinnati's Bucky Walters. Bucky won pitching's "triple crown" and his 27 victories led the Reds to their first pennant in 20 years, an output that easily made him the NL's Most Valuable Player. Washington unveiled a swift new base-stealing threat in George Case. Besides Ted Williams, the 1939 rookie crop was a dandy with names like Charlie Keller, Early Wynn, Mickey Vernon, Bob Elliott, Jack Kramer, Harold Newhouser, Barney McCosky, Paul "Dizzy" Trout, and Fred Hutchinson. Yankee Stadium hosted the 1939 All-Star contest, won by the Americans 3-1 and featuring a home run by hometown hero DiMaggio.

1939's outstanding rookie was Red Sox outfielder Ted Williams.

Veteran Jimmy Foxx was 1939's top home run man with 35 for the runner-up Bosox.

Frank McCormick drove in 128 runs in the Reds' first pennant season since 1919.

Washington's George Case became the AL's new base-stealing leader with 51—the most since Ben Chapman's 61 in 1931.

Yankees' owner Jake Ruppert (left) died in January and Ed Barrow (right) became head man in the Bronx.

The New York Yankees continued their invincible pace with another convincing domination of the American League. The steady hitting of DiMaggio, Rolfe, and Keller produced another near-1000 runs (967) and 106 wins, 17 more than distant runner-up Boston. Meanwhile, over in the senior circuit, crafty Manager Bill McKechnie put the Reds on top in May and never looked back. Frank McCormick's league-leading 128 RBIs led the attack, but the pitching tandem of Walters and Paul Derringer was the real key to the Reds' success. They won 52 games between them and both finished with ERAs under 3.00. Derringer lost a tight pitching duel 2-1 to Red Ruffing in the World Series opener at Yankee Stadium. After that, the New Yorkers cruised to three straight relatively easy victories to sweep the Reds and retain their world championship laurels for the fourth straight year, the first time that had been accomplished in the long history of the game. And so the decade of the thirties ended with the unchallenged supremacy of Joe McCarthy's version of the fabled Bronx Bombers. The future of major league baseball looked considerably rosier than ten years earlier, and it entered the second century of the game with renewed optimism.

Yankee Stadium was the scene of 1939's most touching moment—a special tribute to the fallen "Iron Horse," Lou Gehrig.

Joe DiMaggio served notice that 1939 was to be his most productive year yet by homering in the opener at Washington.

Detroit made an important acquisition in obtaining solid outfielder Earl Averill from Cleveland.

The Cards' Johnny Mize led the NL in BA (.349) and HRs (28) for 1939.

Cincinnati's Crosley Field enjoyed record crowds in nailing down the 1939 NL championship.

The pitching of Bucky Walters during the 1939 Reds pennant chase was the stuff of legends, leading the NL in victories, strikeouts, and ERA.

Walters' pitching mate was veteran Paul Derringer, who chipped in with 25 wins.

The Reds' celebration after clinching the NL flag proved to be short-lived.

The Yankees had even more reason to celebrate as they cruised to a World Series victory in four straight games. Along the way, they celebrated shortstop Frank Crosetti's birthday.

HALL OF FAMERS 1930-39

The following members of baseball's Hall of Fame were active in some capacity with major league baseball (or Negro Leagues) at some time in the decade of the 1930s.

Grover Alexander
Walter Alston
Luke Appling
Earl Averill
Dave Bancroft
Ed Barrow
Cool Papa Bell
Chief Bender
Jim Bottomley
Lou Boudreau
Roger Bresnahan
Max Carey
Oscar Charleston
Mickey Cochrane
Eddie Collins
Earle Combs
Charles Comiskey
Tom Connolly
Joe Cronin
Kiki Cuyler
Ray Dandridge
Dizzy Dean
Bill Dickey
Martin Dihigo
Joe DiMaggio
Bobby Doerr
Hugh Duffy
Billy Evans
Johnny Evers
Red Faber
Bob Feller
Rick Ferrell
Jimmy Foxx
Ford Frick
Frankie Frisch
Lou Gehrig

Charley Gehringer
Josh Gibson
Warren Giles
Lefty Gomez
Goose Goslin
Hank Greenberg
Clark Griffith
Burleigh Grimes
Lefty Grove
Chick Hafey
Jesse Haines
Will Harridge
Bucky Harris
Gabby Hartnett
Harry Heilmann
Billy Herman
Rogers Hornsby
Waite Hoyt
Cal Hubbard
Carl Hubbell
Travis Jackson
Judy Johnson
Walter Johnson
George Kelly
Chuck Klein
Bill Klem
K. M. Landis
Tony Lazzeri
Buck Leonard
Fred Lindstrom
Pop Lloyd
Ernie Lombardi
Al Lopez
Ted Lyons
Connie Mack
Larry MacPhail

Heinie Manush
Rabbit Maranville
Joe McCarthy
Bill McGowan
John McGraw
Bill McKechnie
Joe Medwick
Johnny Mize
Hal Newhouser
Mel Ott
Satchel Paige
Herb Pennock
Sam Rice
Branch Rickey
Eppa Rixey
Wilbert Robinson
Edd Roush
Red Ruffing
Babe Ruth
Ray Schalk
Joe Sewell
Al Simmons
George Sisler
Enos Slaughter
Casey Stengel
Bill Terry
Pie Traynor
Dazzy Vance
Arky Vaughan
Bill Veeck
Honus Wagner
Bobby Wallace
Lloyd Waner
Paul Waner
George Weiss
Ted Williams

Hack Wilson
Early Wynn
Tom Yawkey

BASEBALL WRITERS (SPINK AWARD)

Warren Brown
John Carmichael
Gordon Cobbledick
Dan Daniel
John Drebinger
Frank Graham
Tommy Holmes
James Isaminger
Harold Kaese
John Kieran
Fred Lieb
Tom Meany
Sid Mercer
Edgar Munzel
Shirley Povich
Grantland Rice
Damon Runyon
H. G. Salsinger
J. G. T. Spink
J. Roy Stockton

BROADCASTERS (FRICK AWARD)

Mel Allen
Red Barber
Bob Elson
Russ Hodges
Byrum Saam

INDEX